222 BASIC
Computer Programs
for Home, School & Office

Universal BASIC books by Don Roberts

222 BASIC Computer Programs for Home, School & Office
Universal BASIC Computer Program Writing Workbook

222 BASIC
Computer Programs
for Home, School & Office

by Don Roberts

ARCsoft Publishers
WOODSBORO, MARYLAND

FIRST EDITION
TENTH PRINTING

Post Office Box 132, Woodsboro, Maryland 21798 USA

Printed in the United States of America

ISBN 0-86668-039-X

Preface

Microcomputers are everywhere! They are the most popular electronic tool today. Their lightweight desktop, lap or pocket designs, and powerful BASIC language programming capabilities, place them at the forefront of the new wave of high technology sweeping homes, offices, laboratories, schools.

Not toys at all, these powerful, miniature decision makers are highly useful in a business workspace, learning arena, scientific environment, as well as for practical jobs around the home.

The number of jobs to which a microcomputer can be put is limited only by the scope of the imagination. In this program-packed book we have attempted to create 222 new, specific, practical, serviceable, hard-working sets of applications software in BASIC for your use.

The programs in this book are written for newcomers and beginners, as well as for advanced users of microcomputers who might be searching for new and different ways to make their machines do real work. Our intention has been to provide a giant library of easy-to-type ready-to-run or nearly-ready BASIC programs so your computer can perform useful tasks. You type them in and your computer does the rest.

— Don Roberts

Table of Contents

Gee Whiz!

For The Family

Home Finance Programs

Learning Programs

Business Matters

Math Helper Programs

Random Numbers

Introduction

With the immense popularity of microcomputers has come a great need for practical, useful software to make these machines do real work. The computers are very fast and have large memories. They are powerful, flexible and versatile. But what can they do?

The aim of this book is to provide 222 complete easy-to-type, nearly-ready-to-run (many ready to run) sets of program listings for you to use in making your own microcomputer—desktop, lap, briefcase, pocket—work for you.

Once you've purchased a computer and know how to turn it on, you need down-to-earth workable programs to run the computer. In this book, we provide program ideas and appropriate complete easy-to-type sets of program listings for you to use in your own computer, to make it work for you.

The 222 BASIC programs in this library are considered *not machine specific.* That is, they are designed to run on any computer which is set up for programming in the BASIC language. Some of these programs may run in your computer exactly as you find them in this book. More likely, you will make minor modifications to some program lines.

In writing a *universal* non-machine specific book, the

most universal forms of BASIC are used. However, each hardware manufacturer offers his equipment with a slightly different version of BASIC. Please check your computer's instruction manual for the list of BASIC words in its vocabulary.

See how each BASIC word is used in your computer. Compare that usage with the use of similar words in this book. Note any differences and make appropriate changes to any program as you type it into your computer.

These programs have a timeless quality to them and will be as useful tomorrow as today. It is hoped they provide an exciting learning invitation to the new and beginning programmer, and refreshing exercise for more advanced computer owners.

The book has been divided into several sections to make future reference easier:

Fun & Games includes game programs and programs designed to make computer games easier to write and use.

Text On Text has programs which are useful when using the computer to handle words and symbols.

Number Crunching is a section of programs designed to turn your computer into a powerful math machine.

Gee Whiz includes programs you will use to WOW your friends, neighbors, relatives.

Learning Programs contains educational materials, useful for students and teachers. Learn geography, chemistry, astronomy, science, history, and more.

Family Programs are personal improvement software for use in and around the home.

Business Matters includes programs for use in the small-business office, professional office, and other workspace environment.

Money, Financial & Banking is a section devoted to personal money management.

Graphs has various easy-to-use video displays.

Random Numbers shows different ways to obtain pseudorandom numbers and things to do with those numbers.

Odds & Ends is just that.

Naturally, these sections are not rigid dividing lines. You probably will find programs in the business or learning sections which are useful in your home. Or you may take one of the home programs to work or school. Try them all. They're great fun to run. And they are especially designed to be short so you won't have to spend hours typing them into your computer.

Making them RUN

These programs will run on any computer which can be programmed in the BASIC language. However, it is likely you will need to modify some or all of the lines of a program to make it work with the version of BASIC in your computer. Each hardware manufacturer makes his own BASIC slightly different from all other manufacturers.

Graphics commands, especially, will differ from computer system to computer system.

Multiple-statement lines, using the colon (:) symbol, can be quite different in various hardware brand names. Many computers don't even permit multiple statements on one BASIC program line. If you find that your computer will not accept two BASIC statements on one line, change the one line into two or more, each with its own individual line number.

Such things as line numbering, spacing between words or symbols, logical tests, multiplication symbols, print **statements, precision math, and other instructions and results may be different.**

Refer to your owner's manual to compare your computer's version of BASIC to that found in this book.

We assume you have read the owner's manual and instructional pamphlets which came with your computer and any accessories you may have. You know how to hook the computer to your TV or other accessories you have. You know how to type programs into the computer. If you don't know these beginning steps, please review the instructions in the owner's manual.

Computers used to test the programs in this book include IBM, IBM PCjr, Texas Instruments TI-99/4A, TIMEX 1000, Sinclair ZX-81, TRS-80 Color Computer, Commodore 64, VIC 20, APPLE II, APPLE IIe, Atari 400, Atari 800, TRS-80 Model 4, TRS-80 Model 16, TRS-80 pockets, PC-1, PC-2, PC-3, PC-4, and Sharp pockets. Each program in this book was tested on one of the above computers.

Since the programs in this book have been written and

tested on a wide variety of systems, you will find differences in random number generation, ASCII character-string numbers, screen PRINT locations, optional LET use, CLS and other screen-clearing methods, spacing between BASIC commands and variables, TIME$ and DATE$, and other BASIC vocabulary and formats.

Different computers use RND, RAN, RAND, and other BASIC words to generate a random number. And not all allow resetting the generator's seed through words like RANDOMIZE or RAND. Check the BASIC language in your computer to see which word generates a random number and which resets the random number generator seed. You may need to modify games and other random-number-using programs in this book.

As a general rule, microcomputers use the ASCII numbers 65 to 90 to represent the upper-case alphabet letters A to Z. But not all computers do. And the other ASCII keyboard numbers may vary. See your owner's manual for the ASCII character set used in your computer. You may need to make changes in programs using CHR$ and other BASIC words.

How do you print a particular letter or number at one specific spot on the face of your video monitor or TV screen? Some computers use PRINT AT. Others require PRINT @. Others use even different methods of locating a spot on the video display. Check your owner's manual for the proper BASIC words used to locate displays on the screen.

Most computers allow the use of the BASIC word LET to be optional. You probably can include it where it is shown in this book. But, you may have to add it where it is not shown.

How do you erase all of your video display at one time. The most common BASIC command to accomplish this is CLS but your computer may use PRINT CHR$(147) or CALL CLEAR or some other BASIC phrase. Check it out before using a program.

Must you include a space after a BASIC command word, before a variable or whatever follows that BASIC command? Some computers require it; some don't. Some even put the space in for you so you can forget worrying about it. Look in your BASIC manual to see how your computer handles this matter.

Does your computer have a built-in real-time clock and calendar? These often are read in a BASIC program using the words TIME or TIME$ and DATE or DATE$. If you don't have these features, see our *60-Second Timer* program for an example of a timing loop you can write.

Can your computer read a key directly from one stroke on the keyboard, without the need for you to press ENTER or RETURN? This ability usually comes with the BASIC word INKEY$ but might be some other word, such as CALL KEY. Better look in your computer's BASIC manual for the proper words before starting.

These are the major areas of potential difference in the programs in this book. Please familiarize yourself with the BASIC language, as used in your own computer, before attempting to use the programs in this book. We have made these programs straightforward and simple to use. They should be easy to modify for use in your computer.

Standalone vs. subroutine

The programs in this book may be used as portions of larger lists of instructions to your computer. They can be written in as GOTO or GOSUB objects. To do so, make appropriate changes to the first line (usually numbered 10 in this book) and to the last line of each program.

If you create a subroutine, remember that every GOSUB must have a RETURN. RETURN must be the last line of every subroutine.

If you work one of these programs into a larger set of instructions, be especially careful of your memory (variable) names or labels. They must agree with, and fit into, those you are using in the main program. Also, be careful of line numbers. No two programs can occupy the exact same set of line numbers.

By the way, if you want to load more than one of these programs into your computer at the same time, be sure to use different sets of line numbers for different programs. For example, only one line can be numbered 10. There cannot be two lines numbered 10 in the computer at the same time.

We use the words ENTER and RETURN interchangeably. Programmers today generally mix the use of the two words, to mean the same thing.

As your knowledge of BASIC and how it makes your

computer work grows, you will be able to build on these elementary programs to create ever-more-complex schemes for practical applications.

Try them all. They are great fun to run. And they are especially designed to be short so you won't have to spend hours typing any one program into your computer.

Endless running

Many of the programs in this book will continue to run until you command them off manually via the BREAK key. You may stop any run, at any time, by pressing BREAK.

REMarks

As you read through the programs in this book, you will notice very few REM, or remarks, statements. The author's training in writing BASIC-language computer programs included an emphasis on brevity and saving memory space. A sharp editing pencil was in order—and still is!

REMarks and explanations in software are out. Honing, fine tuning and waste trimming are in. Use of coding form program-writing worksheets is encouraged. Such worksheets can be found in the publication, *Computer Program Writing Workbook,* available from ARCsoft Publishers. Your objective always should be to make the most efficient use of available memory.

Here's another important note to remember: even though they may be headed toward the same goal, no two programmers will write the exact same list of BASIC instructions, or program lines, from scratch. As you load these programs into your computer, one at a time, you'll make modifications to suit your personal needs and interests if you want to. For instance, the exact wording of PRINT statements can be changed. Or two or more programs can be combined into one grand scheme. Your applications may vary.

These programs are useful in themselves. They also make good starting points for further development as you learn more and more about how to program your own computer. Read these programs. Type them into your computer. Watch them run. Analyze how the lines in the listings cause the computer to step through a sequence of operations to reach a final goal. You'll see how programs are organized, how they work. You can use these fun and practical programs and then, later, modify them to do more or different work. Expand them to suit your needs as your interests grow.

Learning programming

These programs are written to be typed into your computer just as you find them here—with no extra programming needed. We assume you know how to turn on your computer and how to go about typing in a program.

Many of the programs and most of the programming advice in this book will be of interest to old hands, as well as newcomers, since we are presenting new twists and more powerful exercises aimed at making your computer do more work, more quickly.

Amidst the refreshing programs in this book, you will find countless ideas for using your computer. Each piece of software is intended to make you a more versatile programmer and make your programming chores lighter.

This is not a replacement for the owner's manual which came with your computer. You need to read it thoroughly, then use this book as a supplement.

Use this book to stimulate your thinking about how to approach various software problems and projects. Use it to get good ideas for new and different approaches to all of your programming goals. As you grow and develop as a program author, modify these programs to make your computer do even more.

Happy programming!

Chinese Zodiac

The most-famous oriental zodiac calendar is divided into twelve-year groups, each year having a different animal sign. The sign under which a person is born is believed to determine the circumstances of his life and the kind of person he is.

The animals are rat, ox, tiger, rabbit, dragon, snake, horse, sheep, monkey, cock, dog and boar.

Run this program. When asked by the computer, type in the year of your birth. The computer will find which animal sign corresponds to your birth year and present you with information concerning your own circumstances.

The computer names the animal, describes your personality traits, tells which other animal signs are compatible with your own, and tells which animal signs are your opposite.

This game goes on endlessly until you press the BREAK key to stop the run.

Program Listing

```
10 PRINT CHR$(147):REM SCREEN CLEAR
20 INPUT"YEAR OF BIRTH";Y$
30 X$=RIGHT$(Y$,2)
40 N=VAL(X$)
50 IF (N/12)=INT(N/12) THEN 200
60 IF ((N-1)/12)=INT((N-1)/12) THEN 250
70 IF ((N-2)/12)=INT((N-2)/12) THEN 300
80 IF ((N-3)/12)=INT((N-3)/12) THEN 350
90 IF ((N-4)/12)=INT((N-4)/12) THEN 400
100 IF ((N-5)/12)=INT((N-5)/12) THEN 450
110 IF ((N-6)/12)=INT((N-6)/12) THEN 500
120 IF ((N-7)/12)=INT((N-7)/12) THEN 550
130 IF ((N-8)/12)=INT((N-8)/12) THEN 600
140 IF ((N-9)/12)=INT((N-9)/12) THEN 650
150 IF ((N-10)/12)=INT((N-10)/12) THEN 700
160 IF ((N-11)/12)=INT((N-11)/12) THEN 750
170 GOTO 10
200 PRINT:PRINT Y$;" SIGN: RAT"
210 PRINT:PRINT"YOU ARE:"
215 PRINT"AMBITIOUS, SINCERE"
220 PRINT:PRINT"COMPATIBLE WITH:"
```

```
225 PRINT"DRAGON, MONKEY"
230 PRINT:PRINT"OPPOSITE OF:"
235 PRINT"HORSE"
240 GOTO 800
250 PRINT:PRINT Y$;" SIGN: OX"
260 PRINT:PRINT"YOU ARE:"
265 PRINT"LEADER, BRIGHT, CHEERY"
270 PRINT:PRINT"COMPATIBLE WITH:"
275 PRINT"SNAKE, COCK"
280 PRINT:PRINT"OPPOSITE OF:"
285 PRINT"SHEEP"
290 GOTO 800
300 PRINT:PRINT Y$;" SIGN: TIGER"
310 PRINT:PRINT"YOU ARE:"
315 PRINT"SENSITIVE, COURAGEOUS"
320 PRINT:PRINT"COMPATIBLE WITH:"
325 PRINT"HORSE, DOG"
330 PRINT:PRINT"OPPOSITE OF:"
335 PRINT"MONKEY"
340 GOTO 800
350 PRINT:PRINT Y$;" SIGN: RABBIT"
360 PRINT:PRINT"YOU ARE:"
365 PRINT"TALENTED, AFFECTIONATE"
370 PRINT:PRINT"COMPATIBLE WITH:"
375 PRINT"SHEEP, BOAR"
380 PRINT:PRINT"OPPOSITE OF:"
385 PRINT"COCK"
390 GOTO 800
400 PRINT:PRINT Y$;" SIGN: DRAGON"
410 PRINT:PRINT"YOU ARE:"
415 PRINT"ROBUST, PASSIONATE"
420 PRINT:PRINT"COMPATIBLE WITH:"
425 PRINT"MONKEY, RAT"
430 PRINT:PRINT"OPPOSITE OF:"
435 PRINT"DOG"
440 GOTO 800
450 PRINT:PRINT Y$;" SIGN: SNAKE"
460 PRINT:PRINT"YOU ARE:"
465 PRINT"WISE, INTENSE"
470 PRINT:PRINT"COMPATIBLE WITH:"
475 PRINT"OX, COCK"
480 PRINT:PRINT"OPPOSITE OF:"
```

```
485 PRINT"BOAR"
490 GOTO 800
500 PRINT:PRINT Y$;" SIGN: HORSE"
510 PRINT:PRINT"YOU ARE:"
515 PRINT"ATTRACTIVE, POPULAR"
520 PRINT:PRINT"COMPATIBLE WITH:"
525 PRINT"TIGER, DOG"
530 PRINT:PRINT"OPPOSITE OF:"
535 PRINT"RAT"
540 GOTO 800
550 PRINT:PRINT Y$;" SIGN: SHEEP"
560 PRINT:PRINT"YOU ARE:"
565 PRINT"STYLISH, PRIVATE"
570 PRINT:PRINT"COMPATIBLE WITH:"
575 PRINT"BOAR, RABBIT"
580 PRINT:PRINT"OPPOSITE OF:"
585 PRINT"OX"
590 GOTO 800
600 PRINT:PRINT Y$;" SIGN: MONKEY"
610 PRINT:PRINT"YOU ARE:"
615 PRINT"PERSUASIVE,INTELLIGENT"
620 PRINT:PRINT"COMPATIBLE WITH:"
625 PRINT"DRAGON, RAT"
630 PRINT:PRINT"OPPOSITE OF:"
635 PRINT"TIGER"
640 GOTO 800
650 PRINT:PRINT Y$;" SIGN: COCK"
660 PRINT:PRINT"YOU ARE:"
665 PRINT"PIONEERING,"
666 PRINT"SEEKING TRUTH"
670 PRINT:PRINT"COMPATIBLE WITH:"
675 PRINT"SNAKE, OX"
680 PRINT:PRINT"OPPOSITE OF:"
685 PRINT"RABBIT"
690 GOTO 800
700 PRINT:PRINT Y$;" SIGN: DOG"
710 PRINT:PRINT"YOU ARE:"
715 PRINT"GENEROUS, LOYAL"
720 PRINT:PRINT"COMPATIBLE WITH:"
725 PRINT"HORSE, TIGER"
730 PRINT:PRINT"OPPOSITE OF:"
735 PRINT"DRAGON"
```

```
740 GOTO 800
750 PRINT:PRINT Y$;" SIGN: BOAR"
760 PRINT:PRINT"YOU ARE:"
765 PRINT"GALLANT, NOBLE"
770 PRINT:PRINT"COMPATIBLE WITH:"
775 PRINT"RABBIT, SHEEP"
780 PRINT:PRINT"OPPOSITE OF:"
785 PRINT"SNAKE"
800 PRINT
810 PRINT"TO DO MORE,"
820 INPUT"PRESS RETURN";K$
830 GOTO 10
```

Secret Letter

Guess-the-number games can be great fun but they're old-hat in the world of personal computers. So we've come up with something that captures that old fun and adds a more challenging, more exciting play. This is the guess-the-secret-letter game.

The computer ponders a moment, then thinks of a letter. It knows that secret letter but it doesn't let you know. Your job is to figure it out.

It starts by displaying the full alphabet of 26 letters on its screen. You make a guess by pressing a letter key. No need to press ENTER.

The computer responds with a CORRECT or WRONG message. If wrong, it displays the entire alphabet again but this time *without* the letter or letters you have chosen previously. By the way, the tricky part is in having the computer come back and display the entire alphabet without the chosen letter or letters. This is accomplished in the subroutine in lines 700 to 810.

You will note there is a processing delay of 5 or 6 seconds so the computer sends out a wait message.

The computer uses its random-number generator to select the mystery letter. This is done by selecting an ASCII number from 65 to 90, in the subroutine at lines 500 to 520. Number 65 corresponds to the letter A and 90 to letter Z.

In playing the game, you make your selection by pressing a letter key, anywhere from A through Z. No need to press ENTER.

The computer keeps track of your number of attempts and tells you, after each try, how many incorrect guesses you have made. If you make a correct guess, the computer will tell you how many tries it took to get it right.

It provides an interesting afternoon's diversion, consuming many hours of fun. The game plays continuously until you press the BREAK key.

Program Listing

```
10  CLS:CLEAR
20  DIM N(26),V(26)
30  GOSUB 500
40  GOTO 160
50  GOSUB 700
60  GOSUB 600
70  PRINT"GUESS THE LETTER"
80  GOSUB 600
90  PRINT:PRINT B$:PRINT
100 LET G$=INKEY$
110 IF G$="" THEN 100
120 CLS:LET T=T+1
130 LET N(T)=ASC(G$)
140 IF ASC(G$)=P THEN 300
150 PRINT:PRINT"WRONG ";T;" TIMES"
160 PRINT:PRINT"PLEASE STANDBY"
170 PRINT"PROCESSING WILL TAKE 6 SECONDS"
180 GOTO 50
300 PRINT"CORRECT"
310 PRINT CHR$(P);" IS THE LETTER"
320 PRINT
400 PRINT"YOU GOT IT IN ";T;" TRIES"
410 PRINT
420 CLEAR:GOTO 20
430 END
500 FOR W=1 TO VAL(RIGHT$(TIME$,2))
    :P=INT(91*RND(1)):NEXT W
510 IF P<65 THEN 500
520 RETURN
600 FOR Q=1 TO 16
```

```
610 PRINT "*";
620 NEXT Q
630 PRINT
640 RETURN
700 LET B$=""
710 FOR Q=1 TO 26
720 IF N(Q)=0 THEN V(Q)=Q+64
730 FOR Z=1 TO 26
740 IF V(Q)=N(Z) THEN V(Q)=0
750 NEXT Z
760 LET B$=B$+CHR$(V(Q))
770 NEXT Q
780 PRINT
790 PRINT"THANK YOU FOR WAITING"
800 PRINT
810 RETURN
```

Shell Game

Hey, Man! Here's a great new game which can only be played on a powerful computer such as yours.

The dark squares on the display screen are cups. Under one is a letter P, representing a pea. But which cup covers the pea? You guess by pressing the appropriate number key, either 1, 2 or 3. No need to press ENTER. The computer shuffles its cups after each guess.

Upon first starting this program, the computer will display a menu asking you to select an option. Press R to read the rules. Press P to play the game. Press Q to quit or end the game. You can return to the main menu at any time by pressing the ESCape key.

The number of right and wrong guesses is shown on the screen. See how much you can win in 10 minutes of play. Then see how much your friends can win in the same length of time. Or you can compete by number of games played. Or play solitaire by yourself. The object is to locate the pea! It may or may not move after each guess, depending upon the secret decision of the computer. Go for it!

Program Listing

```
10 CLS:CLEAR
```

```
20 RV$=CHR$(27)+"p":NV$=CHR$(27)+"q"
100 PRINT @ 55,RV$;"SHELL GAME";NV$
110 LINE(89,7)-(149,15),1,B
120 LINE(87,5)-(151,17),1,B
130 PRINT @ 130,"TO PLAY";SPACE$(5)
    ;"PRESS P"
140 PRINT @ 170,"FOR RULES";SPACE$(3)
    ;"PRESS R"
145 PRINT @ 210,"TO QUIT";SPACE$(5)
    ;"PRESS Q"
150 K$=INKEY$
160 IF K$="" THEN 150
170 IF K$="P" THEN 200
180 IF K$="R" THEN 1100
185 IF K$="Q" THEN 1300
190 GOTO 150
200 PRINT @ 130,SPACE$(19):PRINT @ 170
    ,SPACE$(19):PRINT @ 210,SPACE$(19)
210 PRINT @ 130,"1":PRINT @ 140,"2"
    :PRINT @ 150,"3"
220 GOSUB 900
300 K$=INKEY$
310 IF K$="" THEN 300
315 IF ASC(K$)=27 THEN 10
320 IF VAL(K$)<1 OR VAL(K$)>4 THEN 300
330 GOSUB 1000
340 GOSUB 500
350 ON X GOSUB 800,700,600
360 FOR T=1 TO 500:NEXT T
400 IF VAL(K$)=X THEN R=R+1:GOTO 420
410 W=W+1
420 PRINT @ 40,R;"RIGHT"
430 PRINT @ 71,W;"WRONG"
440 GOTO 220
500 FOR Q=1 TO VAL(RIGHT$(TIME$,2))
    :X=INT(4*RND(1)):NEXT Q
510 IF X<1 THEN 500
520 RETURN
600 LINE(55,37)-(69,50),1,BF
610 LINE(115,37)-(129,50),1,BF
620 LINE(175,37)-(189,50),1,B
630 PRINT @ 230,"P"
```

```
640 RETURN
700 LINE(55,37)-(69,50),1,BF
710 LINE(115,37)-(129,50),1,B
720 LINE(175,37)-(189,50),1,BF
730 PRINT @ 220,"P"
740 RETURN
800 LINE(55,37)-(69,50),1,B
810 LINE(115,37)-(129,50),1,BF
820 LINE(175,37)-(189,50),1,BF
830 PRINT @ 210,"P"
840 RETURN
900 LINE(55,37)-(69,50),1,BF
910 LINE(115,37)-(129,50),1,BF
920 LINE(175,37)-(189,50),1,BF
930 RETURN
1000 LINE(55,37)-(69,50),2,BF
1010 LINE(115,37)-(129,50),2,BF
1020 LINE(175,37)-(189,50),2,BF
1030 RETURN
1100 CLS
1110 PRINT @ 56,RV$;"RULES";NV$
1120 LINE(95,7)-(125,15),1,B
1130 LINE(93,5)-(127,17),1,B
1140 PRINT:PRINT"A 'PEA' IS UNDER ONE
     CUP? WHICH: NUMBER 1, 2 OR 3? THE
     COMPUTER  SHUFFLES CUPS"
1150 PRINT"AFTER EACH GUESS. TO GUESS,
     PRESS NUMBER OF CUP.";SPACE$(9)
     ;"(NOW PRESS ANY KEY)"
1160 IF INKEY$="" THEN 1160
1170 PRINT @ 120,SPACE$(156)
1180 PRINT @120,"COMPUTER SHOWS NUMBER
     OF RIGHT GUESSES & WRONG GUESSES. ";
1190 PRINT"TO END THE GAME ANYTIME,
     PRESS ESCape KEY.";SPACE$(3);"(NOW
     PRESS ANY  KEY)"
1200 IF INKEY$="" THEN 1200
1210 CLS:GOTO 100
1300 CLS
1310 PRINT @ 55,RV$;"END OF GAME";NV$
1320 LINE(89,7)-(155,15),1,B
```

```
1330 LINE(87,5)-(157,17),1,B
1340 END
```

Backward Writer

Type in a message of up to 85 characters in response to the computer's request. The computer will turn your message around and print it backwards on the display

The 85 characters includes letters, numbers, symbols and spaces. You may use any combination. For a test, try it with the 26 letters of the alphabet as we have done in our SAMPLE RUN below. Type Z to A in backwards order. You will be amazed at the speed with which your computer turns it around!

Program Listing

```
10  CLS:CLEAR
20  INPUT"TYPE A MESSAGE OF UP TO 85
    CHARACTERS ";A$
30  IF A$="" THEN 20
40  L=LEN(A$)
50  FOR J=L TO 1 STEP -1
60  B$=B$+MID$(A$,J,1)
70  NEXT J
80  CLS
90  PRINT B$
100 IF INKEY$="" THEN 100
110 GOTO 10
```

Sample Run

```
TYPE A MESSAGE OF UP TO 85 CHARACTERS ?
ABCDEFGHIJKLMNOPQRSTUVWXYZ

ZYXWVUTSRQPONMLKJIHGFEDCBA
```

High Ball

No excitement at the office water cooler? Bored in study hall? Nothing to do on a rainy Saturday at home?

Here's a fast game of Highball in which the highest-scoring player wins.

The game is built for five players. You type in the first name, or initials or other identifying label, for each of the five players. The computer draws straws and randomly assigns numbers to each player. It sorts to find which player has the *highest* number and declares that player the winner.

The number of players is controlled by the FOR/NEXT loop in lines 105 to 180. Change the number 5 at the end of line 105 to change the number of players.

This is an ideal bit of speedy entertainment. The game runs endlessly until you press BREAK to stop it.

Program Listing

```
10 CLS:CLEAR:RV$=CHR$(27)+"p":NV$=CHR$
   (27)+"q"
20 DIM P$(5),S(5)
30 PRINT @ 56,RV$;"HIGH BALL";NV$
40 LINE(95,7)-(149,15),1,B
50 LINE(93,5)-(151,17),1,B
100 PRINT @ 122,"TYPE IN FIRST NAMES OF
    FIVE PLAYERS"
105 FOR L=1 TO 5
110 PRINT @ 203,"PLAYER NUMBER ";L;
115 INPUT P$(L)
120 PRINT @ 219,SPACE$(20)
130 IF LEN(P$(L))>12 THEN PRINT @ 243,
    "NAME TOO LONG, TRY AGAIN":GOTO 110
140 PRINT @ 243,SPACE$(30)
150 FOR Q=1 TO VAL(RIGHT$(TIME$,2))
    :S(L)=INT(100*RND(1)):NEXT Q
160 IF L=1 THEN H=S(L)
170 IF S(L)>H THEN H=S(L)
180 NEXT L
190 CLS:PRINT
200 FOR L=1 TO 5
210 IF S(L)=H THEN PRINT S(L),P$(L)
    ;"<------WINNER"
220 IF S(L)<>H THEN PRINT S(L),P$(L)
230 NEXT L
240 PRINT"PRESS ANY KEY TO PLAY AGAIN"
```

```
250 IF INKEY$="" THEN 250
270 GOTO 10
```

Remarkable Person

This is a fun program to impress your friends with the speed and "intelligence" of your computer. It is a great demonstrator of computer graphics as shown on the computer's display. Note the reverse box!

Press any key on the keyboard to do a new name. Press BREAK to end the run.

Program Listing

```
10 CLS:CLEAR
30 INPUT"WHAT IS YOUR FIRST NAME";FN$
40 INPUT"WHAT IS YOUR LAST NAME ";LN$
50 IF FN$="" OR LN$="" THEN 10
60 CLS
70 LF=LEN(FN$):LS=LEN(LN$)
80 BF=(21-LF-LS)/2
90 BS=BF
100 IF INT((LF+LS)/2)<>(LF+LS)/2 THEN
    BS=BS-1
110 IF 21-LF-LS<1 THEN PRINT "NAME TOO
   LONG",,"GIVE ME A SHORTER ONE"
   :GOTO 30
120 BF$=SPACE$(BF)
130 BS$=SPACE$(BS)
140 RV$=CHR$(27)+"p":NV$=CHR$(27)+"q"
150 LINE(59,15)-(185,40),1,B
160 LINE(57,13)-(187,42),1,B
170 PRINT @ 90,RV$;BF$;FN$;" ";LN$;BS$;NV$
180 PRINT @ 130,RV$"         IS         "
    ;NV$
190 PRINT @ 170,RV$;" A REMARKABLE PERSON
    ";NV$
200 IF INKEY$="" THEN 200
210 GOTO 10
```

Computer Guesses Your Secret Number

Wow! Everybody has heard of the high/low game in which a computer selects a secret number and you try to guess it. But, what if *you* think up the secret number and the computer tries to guess it?

When you run this program, think of a secret number from one to 63. The computer will ask some easy questions and then guess your secret number every time!

To ask its questions, the computer displays sets of various numbers. It does this six times. Each time you tell it nothing more than whether or not your secret number is in the set of numbers shown on the display. You tell it this simply by pressing Y for yes or N for no.

After its sixth query, it will correctly tell you what the mystery number was. Naturally, you can't change the mystery number after the start of the game and you must tell the computer truthful answers to each of the six questions.

At the start of a RUN, the computer will ask for your name. You give it and then read an opening explanation bill-board on the display screen. Then press ENTER to start. At completion of a game, press ENTER to play a new game. The program runs on endlessly until you stop it by pressing the BREAK key.

Program Listing

```
10 CLS:CLEAR
20 INPUT"WHAT IS YOUR NAME";N$
30 PRINT"OKAY,";N$;", THINK OF A NUMBER"
40 PRINT"FROM 1 TO 63"
45 INPUT"PRESS ENTER TO START";Q$
50 CLS
55 S=0
60 FOR J=1 TO 6
70 T=1
75 PRINT;
80 FOR K=1 TO 32
90 READ A
```

```
100 IF A<10 THEN PRINT A;"  ";:GOTO 120
110 PRINT A;" ";
120 IF K=8*T THEN PRINT;:T=T+1
130 NEXT K
140 PRINT N$;", ";
150 INPUT"IS YOUR NUMBER HERE";R$
160 IF LEFT$(R$,1)="Y" THEN S=S+2^(J-1)
170 IF LEFT$(R$,1)<>"Y" AND LEFT$(R$,1)
    <>"N" THEN 150
175 CLS
180 R$=" "
190 NEXT J
200 PRINT @ 90,"YOUR NUMBER IS";S
210 PRINT @ 164," ";: INPUT"TO PLAY
    AGAIN, PRESS ENTER";P$
220 RESTORE
230 GOTO 10
300 DATA 1,3,5,7,9,11,13,15,17,19,21,23
    ,25,27,29,31,33,35,37
310 DATA 39,41,43,45,47,49,51,53,55,57
    ,59,61,63
320 DATA 2,3,6,7,10,11,14,15,18,19,22
    ,23,26,27,30,31,34,35,38
330 DATA 39,42,43,46,47,50,51,54,55,58
    ,59,62,63
340 DATA 4,5,6,7,12,13,14,15,20,21,22
    ,23,28,29,30,31,36,37,38
350 DATA 39,44,45,46,47,52,53,54,55,60
    ,61,62,63
360 DATA 8,9,10,11,12,13,14,15,24,25,26
    ,27,28,29,30,31,40,41,42,43,44,45
    ,46,47,56,57,58,59,60,61,62,63
370 DATA 16,17,18,19,20,21,22,23,24,25
    ,26,27,28,29,30,31,48,49
380 DATA 50,51,52,53,54,55,56,57,58,59
    ,60,61,62,63
390 DATA 32,33,34,35,36,37,38,39,40,41
    ,42,43,44,45,46,47,48,49
400 DATA 50,51,52,53,54,55,56,57,58,59
    ,60,61,62,63
```

Guess The Letter

We always did say what list of programs would be complete without our old friend, the Hi-Lo Game. Well, it would be less than interesting to do a simple old Hi-Lo so let's try something a bit more challenging.

This is a guess-the-letter game. The computer will display the full alphabet and asks that you guess a secret letter being held by the computer.

The computer reports WRONG or CORRECT in reply to your guess. If WRONG it then displays several letters, including the mystery letter. It allows you six tries to get the right letter.

The program offers BEEP sound cues. You enter the letter Y or the letter N in answer to the question of whether or not you want to play another game. The computer reports your number of tries as a score.

Program Listing

```
 10 CLEAR:DIM A$(Ø)*26:DIM LT$(Ø)*26
 20 A$(Ø)="ABCDEFGHIJKLMNOPQRSTUVWXYZ"
 30 GOSUB 500
 40 WAIT 150
 50 PRINT A$(Ø)
 60 BEEP 1,10:PAUSE "GUESS THE LETTER"
 70 G$=INKEY$
 80 IF G$="" THEN GOTO 70
 90 T=T+1
100 IF ASC (G$)=P THEN GOTO 300
200 W=W+1:M=6-T
210 IF M=Ø THEN GOTO 350
220 BEEP 1,10:PAUSE "WRONG"
230 FOR L=(C-M) TO (C+M)
240 IF L<1 THEN GOTO 270
250 IF L>26 THEN GOTO 270
260 LT$(Ø)=LT$(Ø)+CHR$ (L+64)
270 NEXT L
280 WAIT 200
290 PRINT LT$(Ø):LT$(Ø)="":GOTO 60
300 BEEP 3,10:PAUSE "CORRECT!"
```

```
310 PAUSE CHR$ P;" IS THE LETTER"
320 PAUSE "YOU GOT IT IN ";T;" TRIES"
330 GOTO 400
350 BEEP 2,10:PAUSE "YOU LOSE"
360 PAUSE "YOU TOOK ";T;" TRIES"
400 BEEP 1,10
410 PAUSE "AGAIN:YES(Y) OR NO(N) ?"
420 CH$=INKEY$
430 IF CH$="" THEN GOTO 420
440 IF CH$="Y" THEN CLEAR:GOTO 10
450 IF CH$="N" THEN GOTO 470
460 GOTO 420
470 PRINT "THANK YOU FOR PLAYING"
480 END
500 RANDOM
510 P=RND 90
520 IF P<65 THEN GOTO 510
530 C=P-64
540 RETURN
```

Coasters

Coasters is a mixture of chance and common sense. It can be a gambling object when played with others, yet it is great fun when played alone. Two persons usually play but in this computer version, you play alone against the computer.

To play this game in a bar, you need nine coasters. Or identical squares of paper. The nine coasters are numbered 1 to 9 on one side and then turned over, numbered side down. The coasters are thoroughly shuffled and then lined up in a row.

The player chooses a coaster and turns it over. The first coaster chosen can be any one of the nine in any position. The number on the coaster is read.

From this point on, the number on the coaster determines which coaster next will be selected. Suppose on the first turn-over, the fourth coaster from the right was chosen and it revealed the number 3. On his next move, the player must take the third coaster in from *either* end of the row.

When the player makes his second move, his third move will be determined by the number on the second coaster. The number corresponds to the count of coasters in from *either* end of the row. And so on.

The player continues until no further moves are possible. The numbers on the coasters which remain are added up to give the player his score. The object is to obtain the lowest score. Ideally, you want to eliminate all of the coasters so you will have a score of zero.

Many players can take turns. The person with the lowest score at the end of a round of all players is the winner of that round. The winner of the most rounds is the winner for the day.

To play the game on your computer, start the program RUN. The computer will display the game name, COASTERS. While this display is going on, the computer is shuffling the nine coasters into random order.

Next, the computer will display nine solid coasters with their numbers hidden behind, out of sight. To make your play, press the number key of your choice, 1 through 9, on the keyboard. No need to press ENTER. The number you press will be for the position in the row of nine coasters.

The first number you select is your only totally-free choice. From then on, you must use the latest number from the last-revealed coaster to determine the position of your next move. The new move can be from either the right end or the left end of the row of nine coasters.

For instance, suppose the last coaster you revealed had the number 8. You may turn over coaster position 2 or position 8, so long as the one you wish hasn't been turned over already. If it has, you must select the other. If it also

has, then the game ends since you can't move any more. Add the remaining numbers to get your score by pressing the letter S on the keyboard. No need to press ENTER.

Pressing S reveals your score. Your lowest score of the day is your best game. If more than one person is playing, lowest score wins.

After reading the score, press any keyboard key to start a new game.

Program Listing

```
10 CLEAR :RANDOM:WAIT Ø:DIM N(9)
20 PRINT "********COASTERS********"
30 FOR L=1 TO 9
40 N(L)=RND 9
50 IF L=1 THEN 90
60 FOR LL=1 TO L-1
70 IF N(LL)=N(L) THEN 40
80 NEXT LL
90 NEXT L
100 BEEP 1,1:T=45:CLS
200 FOR C=Ø TO 46 STEP 6
210 GCURSOR C
220 GPRINT 127;127;127;127;127
230 NEXT C
300 K$=INKEY$
310 IF K$=""THEN 300
320 IF K$="1"THEN 450
330 IF K$="2"THEN 500
340 IF K$="3"THEN 550
350 IF K$="4"THEN 600
360 IF K$="5"THEN 650
370 IF K$="6"THEN 700
380 IF K$="7"THEN 750
390 IF K$="8"THEN 800
400 IF K$="9"THEN 850
410 IF K$="S"THEN 1000
420 IF K$=""THEN 300
450 CURSOR Ø
460 K=VAL K$
470 GOSUB 900
480 T=T-N(K)
490 GOTO 300
500 GCURSOR 6
```

```
510 K=VAL K$
520 GOSUB 900
530 T=T-N(K)
540 GOTO 300
550 GCURSOR 12
560 K=VAL K$
570 GOSUB 900
580 T=T-N(K)
590 GOTO 300
600 GCURSOR 18
610 K=VAL K$
620 GOSUB 900
630 T=T-N(K)
640 GOTO 300
650 GCURSOR 24
660 K=VAL K$
670 GOSUB 900
680 T=T-N(K)
690 GOTO 300
700 GCURSOR 30
710 K=VAL K$
720 GOSUB 900
730 T=T-N(K)
740 GOTO 300
750 GCURSOR 36
760 K=VAL K$
770 GOSUB 900
780 T=T-N(K)
790 GOTO 300
800 GCURSOR 42
810 K=VAL K$
820 GOSUB 900
830 T=T-N(K)
840 GOTO 300
850 GCURSOR 48
860 K=VAL K$
870 GOSUB 900
880 T=T-N(K)
890 GOTO 300
900 IF N(K)=1THEN GPRINT Ø;66;127;64;Ø
910 IF N(K)=2THEN GPRINT 66;97;81;73;70
```

```
920 IF N(K)=3THEN GPRINT 65;73;77;75;49
930 IF N(K)=4THEN GPRINT 24;20;18;127;16
940 IF N(K)=5THEN GPRINT 39;69;69;69;57
950 IF N(K)=6THEN GPRINT 60;74;73;73;48
960 IF N(K)=7THEN GPRINT 1;1;121;5;3
970 IF N(K)=8THEN GPRINT 54;73;73;73;54
980 IF N(K)=9THEN GPRINT 6;73;73;41;30
990 RETURN
1000 PRINT "SCORE: ";T
1010 IF INKEY$ =""THEN 1010
1020 GOTO 10
```

Blues

This is a quiz game. Each answer in this quiz is a word, name or familiar phrase containing the word blue.

It's lots of fun and, after you have all of ours memorized, you easily can substitute other "blues" for the 19 we have here.

Be sure to observe quote marks, commas, spellings and spaces in DATA lines.

To change the quantity of blues, add DATA lines and change the number 19 in the FOR/NEXT loop in line 290. Also change the number 19 in the line 420 PRINT statement.

The program totals correct and incorrect answers and reports the numbers of rights and wrongs after you have been tested on all 19 blues.

The length of times of displays of the various messages can be changed by altering the numbers in the WAIT statements in lines 200, 240, 300, 350 and 400. The BASIC word RESTORE must be in the program as we have it in line 520.

After the end of a game, press any key to start over. This is an interesting trivia game which can be educational!

Program Listing

```
10 DATA "PANTS","BLUE JEANS"
20 DATA "BUILDING PLAN","BLUEPRINT"
```

```
 30 DATA "BANJO MUSIC","BLUEGRASS"
 40 DATA "LOYAL","TRUE BLUE"
 50 DATA "COP SHOW","HILL STREET BLUES"
 60 DATA "STOCKS","BLUE CHIPS"
 70 DATA "BROOKE SHIELDS","BLUE LAGOON"
 80 DATA "FATS DOMINO","BLUEBERRY HILL"
 90 DATA "STRAUSS","BLUE DANUBE"
100 DATA "LABORER","BLUE COLLAR"
110 DATA "SURPRISE","OUT OF THE BLUE"
120 DATA "PITCHER","VIDA BLUE"
130 DATA "RARELY","ONCE IN A BLUE MOON"
140 DATA "ELVIS","BLUE SUEDE SHOES"
150 DATA "KILLER","BLUEBEARD"
160 DATA "RHYME","LITTLE BOY BLUE"
170 DATA "TALK","BLUE STREAK"
180 DATA "INSURANCE","BLUE CROSS"
190 DATA "SONGS","BLUES"
200 CLEAR :WAIT Ø
210 FOR L=25 TO Ø STEP -1
220 CURSOR L:PRINT"*";
230 NEXT L
240 WAIT 120
250 CURSOR 11
260 PRINT "BLUES"
270 CURSOR 3
280 PRINT "IDENTIFY THESE BLUES"
290 FOR L=1 TO 19
300 WAIT Ø
310 READ A$,B$
320 PRINT A$;" ";
330 INPUT C$
340 CLS
350 WAIT 60
360 IF C$=B$THEN LET R=R+1:PRINT "CORRECT"
    :GOTO 380
370 W=W+1:PRINT "WRONG"
380 PRINT A$;": ";B$
390 NEXT L
400 WAIT 120
410 PRINT "YOU HAD ";R;" RIGHT"
420 PRINT "AND ";W;" WRONG IN 19 TRIES"
500 PRINT "TO GO AGAIN, PRESS ANY KEY"
```

```
510 IF INKEY$ =""THEN 510
520 RESTORE
530 GOTO 200
```

Coin Toss

Flip a coin! Here's the heads or tails of it. As written it uses RUN to start a RUN immediately upon turning on the computer. Turn on the computer and it automatically starts the run, presenting the results of a toss: either heads or tails. It allows you to carry your computer around to settle arguments. Press any key for a new coin toss.

Program Listing

```
20 IF RND (2)<2 THEN PAUSE "HEADS"
   :GOTO 40
30 PAUSE "TAILS"
40 IF INKEY$ ="" THEN GOTO 40
50 CLS :GOTO 20
```

Horoscope

This fun program will entertain your family and friends for hours. It makes a great party game, too.

The player, or user, talks with the computer, giving his name, month of birth and date of birth. The computer then tells the player his sign of the zodiac and what it means. The computer describes the player's personality and predicts the player's future.

If you find the program a bit long to type in, shorten it by using the sign-of-the-zodiac response only. For instance, between lines 700 and 790 you could delete 710 and 750 or 720 to 750. That would make the program shorter and easier to type in, but without most of the exciting description.

Program Listing

```
10 CALL CLEAR
20 INPUT "WHAT'S YOUR NAME?":N$
30 CALL CLEAR
```

```
40 PRINT "HI, ";N$;", NICE TO MEET YOU"
50 PRINT
60 INPUT "IN WHAT MONTH WERE YOU BORN?":M$
70 PRINT M$;" IS A NICE MONTH"
80 PRINT "WHAT DATE IN ";M$
90 INPUT D
100 CALL CLEAR
200 IF M$="DECEMBER" THEN 700
210 IF M$="JANUARY" THEN 800
220 IF M$="FEBRUARY" THEN 900
230 IF M$="MARCH" THEN 1000
240 IF M$="APRIL" THEN 1100
250 IF M$="MAY" THEN 1200
260 IF M$="JUNE" THEN 1300
270 IF M$="JULY" THEN 1400
280 IF M$="AUGUST" THEN 1500
290 IF M$="SEPTEMBER" THEN 1600
300 IF M$="OCTOBER" THEN 1700
310 IF M$="NOVEMBER" THEN 1800
320 GOTO 60
500 PRINT
510 PRINT
520 INPUT "TO DO ANOTHER, PRESS ENTER":KY$
530 GOTO 10
700 IF D<22 THEN 1810
710 PRINT "SO, ";N$;" YOU'RE A CAPRICORN"
720 PRINT "CAPRICORN IS THE GOAT"
730 PRINT
740 PRINT "YOU ARE TOUGH HEAD-TO-HEAD."
750 PRINT "YOU MISTRUST PEOPLE BUT"
760 PRINT "YOU LIKE SMALL CHILDREN."
770 PRINT
780 PRINT "YOU WILL TAKE A TRIP!"
790 GOTO 500
800 IF D<20 THEN 710
810 PRINT "SO, ";N$;" YOU ARE AN AQUARIUS"
820 PRINT "AQUARIUS IS THE WATER BEARER"
830 PRINT "YOU ARE A LIQUID PERSON,"
840 PRINT "YOU DO SNEAKY THINGS BUT"
850 PRINT "PEOPLE SECRETLY ADMIRE YOU."
860 PRINT "YOU SOON WILL FIND A REWARD!"
870 GOTO 500
```

```
900 IF D<19 THEN 810
910 PRINT "SO, ";N$;", YOU ARE A PISCES"
920 PRINT "PISCES IS THE FISH"
930 PRINT "YOU OFTEN FEEL WEAK BUT"
940 PRINT "PEOPLE THINK YOU OTHERWISE."
950 PRINT
960 PRINT "A STRANGER SOON"
970 PRINT "WILL AFFECT YOUR LIFE!"
980 GOTO 500
1000 IF D<21 THEN 910
1010 PRINT "SO, ";N$;", YOU ARE AN ARIES"
1020 PRINT "(NOT THE CAR, STUPID!)"
1030 PRINT "ARIES IS THE RAM"
1040 PRINT
1050 PRINT "YOU SOMETIMES FEEL DEVILISH"
1060 PRINT "BUT OTHERS THINK OF YOU"
1070 PRINT "AS A SAINT."
1080 PRINT "AVOID MOUNTAINS AND CAVES!"
1090 GOTO 500
1100 IF D<20 THEN 1010
1110 PRINT "SO, ";N$;", YOU ARE TAURUS"
1120 PRINT "TAURUS IS THE BULL"
1130 PRINT
1140 PRINT "MOST OF THE TIME"
1150 PRINT "YOU ARE COMPLETELY HONEST"
1160 PRINT "BUT OTHERS THINK YOU ARE"
1170 PRINT "FULL OF BULL."
1180 PRINT "A NICE FRIEND WILL VISIT."
1190 GOTO 500
1200 IF D<21 THEN 1110
1210 PRINT "SO, ";N$;", YOU ARE GEMINI"
1220 PRINT "GEMINI IS 'THE TWINS'"
1230 PRINT
1240 PRINT "IT'S HARD FOR YOU TO DECIDE,"
1250 PRINT "YOU OFTEN SPLIT A DECISION."
1260 PRINT "YOU SEE TWO SIDES BUT"
1270 PRINT "FRIENDS FIND YOU DECISIVE."
1280 PRINT "AVOID NEWSPAPER REPORTERS!"
1290 GOTO 500
1300 IF D<21 THEN 1210
1310 PRINT "SO, ";N$;", YOU ARE A CANCER"
1320 PRINT "CANCER IS THE CRAB"
```

```
1330 PRINT
1340 PRINT "YOU LIKE TO VENT YOUR"
1350 PRINT "FEELINGS WHEN THINGS"
1360 PRINT "GO WRONG AND FRIENDS"
1370 PRINT "SOMETIMES EXCLUDE YOU."
1380 PRINT "JEWELS WILL BE IN YOUR PATH."
1390 GOTO 500
1400 IF D<23 THEN 1310
1410 PRINT "OKAY, ";N$;", YOU ARE LEO"
1420 PRINT "LEO IS THE LION"
1430 PRINT
1440 PRINT "YOUR ROAR IS WORSE"
1450 PRINT "THAN YOUR BITE."
1460 PRINT "YOUR FRIENDS THINK"
1470 PRINT "YOU ARE A PUSSYCAT."
1480 PRINT "FUR IS IN YOUR FUTURE."
1490 GOTO 500
1500 IF D<23 THEN 1410
1510 PRINT "SO, ";N$;", YOU ARE A VIRGO"
1520 PRINT "VIRGO IS THE VIRGIN."
1530 PRINT
1540 PRINT "CLEANLINESS IS YOUR VIRTUE."
1550 PRINT "CASUAL ASSOCIATES THINK"
1560 PRINT "YOU ARE TIGHT, BUT THOSE"
1570 PRINT "CLOSE TO YOU KNOW BETTER."
1580 PRINT "AVOID CARS, BARS AND STARS!"
1590 GOTO 500
1600 IF D<24 THEN 1510
1610 PRINT "OKAY, ";N$;", YOU ARE A LIBRA"
1620 PRINT "LIBRA IS 'THE BALANCE'"
1630 PRINT
1640 PRINT "EVERYTHING WORKS OUT FOR"
1650 PRINT "YOU IN THE END BUT PERILS"
1660 PRINT "ALONG THE WAY SOMETIMES"
1670 PRINT "SEEM TO GREAT."
1680 PRINT "YOU WILL FIND THE TRUTH!"
1690 GOTO 500
1700 IF D<24 THEN 1610
1710 PRINT "RIGHT ON, ";N$;" YOU ARE A
     SCORPIO."
1720 PRINT "SCORPIO IS THE SCORPION"
1730 PRINT
```

```
1740 PRINT "YOU ARE TRUSTWORTHY, LOYAL,"
1750 PRINT "HELPFUL, FRIENDLY,"
1760 PRINT "COURTEOUS, KIND, OBEDIENT,"
1770 PRINT "CHEERFUL, THRIFTY AND SEXY."
1780 PRINT "YOU WILL WIN!"
1790 GOTO 500
1800 IF D<22 THEN 1710
1810 PRINT "WELL, ";N$;", A SAGITTARIUS"
1820 PRINT "SAGITTARIUS IS THE ARCHER"
1830 PRINT
1840 PRINT "YOU FIRE FROM THE HIP"
1850 PRINT "BUT FRIENDS LIKE YOU ANYWAY"
1860 PRINT "HAPPINESS WILL BE YOURS"
1870 PRINT "BUT WATCH OUT FOR FALSENESS"
1880 GOTO 500
```

Poetrywriter™

Well, we said it could do *anything*! All you have to do is explain to your computer about adjectives, nouns, verbs and adverbs. Give it a nice little vocabulary. And off it goes, writing poetry.

The vocabulary is held as DATA in lines 20 to 200. The relationship of the words in each of those program lines is important if you want the computer to make sense with proper syntax.

Each DATA line has seven items (after the BASIC word DATA). The seventh "word" actually is a phrase as we use it but is treated as one unit. The seven items are separated by commas.

We use the first English word in the DATA line for transitions. The second and third English words are adjectives.

The fourth word is a plural noun. The fifth word is a verb. The sixth word is an adverb. And the seventh item is a colorful phrase. It could just as well be a single word.

The computer randomly selects one of each of the seven types of English words and puts them together to form sentences.

Random number generators are in lines 300, 400, 500, 600, 700, 800, and 900. Punctuation and print-out order is determined in lines 1000 to 1100.

The computer will write poems all day until you press its BREAK key.

Program Listing

```
10 CALL CLEAR
15 RANDOMIZE
20 DATA THE,BIG,BLUE,MARBLES,RUN,
   SMOOTHLY,IN THE SAND
30 DATA WHILE,JOLLY,GREEN,GIANTS,EAT,
   HEARTILY,ON THE HILL
40 DATA AND,FRIENDLY,OLD,BOYS,WEAR,
   WELL,AS THEY AGE
50 DATA OR,HARD,PLASTIC,BUTTONS,LAST,
   TOUGHLY,FOREVER
60 DATA WHEN,HAIRY,TINY,DOGS,PASS,
   RUGGEDLY,IN THE NIGHT
70 DATA FROM,WEALTHY,RED,BAGS,TALK,
   HAPPILY,FROM THE VALLEY
80 DATA FOR,LIVELY,MEAN,FOLKS,PLOW,
   NICELY,ABOVE THE CLOUDS
90 DATA THE,PRETTY,TIMELY,LOVERS,FLY,
   LOOSELY,IN THE GROUND
100 DATA MEANWHILE,SAD,YOUNG,CATS,GRIND,
    CONCRETELY,BEHIND THE BARN
110 DATA FROM,TIRED,POOR,DRINKERS,FLASH,
    BRIGHTLY,IN THE PAN
120 DATA ABOUT,TIGHT,BALD,WIVES,PLAY,
    NOISELY,BEYOND THE PALE
130 DATA THE,FOLDED,GLOWING,FARMERS,
    SHINE,MERRILY,TOWARD OUR LIVES
140 DATA AND,ROUGH,DARK,HENCHMEN,TRYST,
    SWEETLY,NEAR A TREE
150 DATA AS,TIMELY,ROUND,PRIESTS,FOLLOW,
    BLINDLY,DOWN THE TUBES
160 DATA WHILE,CRUNCHY,BULKY,STATUES,
    LIFT,WETLY,IN THE BOX
170 DATA AND,GOLDEN,SILVERY,BODIES,TURN,
    FREELY,IN THE WIND
180 DATA WHILE,NAKED,CARVED,FLOWERS,GLOW,
```

```
    SMARTLY,FROM A MOUNTAIN
190 DATA WHERE,SPARKLING,LOUD,MEN,FIGHT,
    WHOLEHEARTEDLY,TO THE DEATH
200 DATA AND,FRESH,NEW,ANCIENTS,HUMANIZE,
    BRAZENLY,FOR THE REST
300 GOSUB 1200
330 FOR L=1 TO R
340 READ V$
350 NEXT L
360 RESTORE
400 GOSUB 1200
430 FOR L=1 TO R-1
440 READ W$
450 NEXT L
460 RESTORE
500 GOSUB 1200
530 FOR L=1 TO R-2
540 READ X$
550 NEXT L
560 RESTORE
600 GOSUB 1200
630 FOR L=1 TO R-3
640 READ Y$
650 NEXT L
660 RESTORE
700 GOSUB 1200
730 FOR L=1 TO R-4
740 READ Z$
750 NEXT L
760 RESTORE
800 GOSUB 1200
830 FOR L=1 TO R-5
840 READ A$
850 NEXT L
860 RESTORE
900 GOSUB 1200
930 FOR L=1 TO R-6
940 READ B$
950 NEXT L
960 RESTORE
1000 D=D+1
1010 IF INT(D/2)=(D/2)THEN 1030
```

```
1020 PRINT A$;"  ";Z$;"  ";Y$
1025 GOTO 1040
1030 PRINT B$;"  ";A$;"  ";Z$;"  ";Y$
1040 IF INT(D/2)=(D/2)THEN 1060
1050 PRINT X$;"  ";W$;"  ";V$;","
1055 GOTO 1070
1060 PRINT X$;"  ";W$;"  ";V$;"."
1070 IF INT(D/2)=(D/2)THEN 1085
1080 GOTO 1090
1085 PRINT
1090 IF D<12 THEN 300
1100 D=0
1110 PRINT
1120 PRINT
1130 GOTO 300
1200 R=INT(133*RND)
1210 IF R<7 THEN 1200
1220 IF INT(R/7)<>(R/7)THEN 1200
1230 RETURN
```

Super Slot-0

Like any good slot machine, when you pull the handle it displays some objects. If you get no two alike, you lose. If you get two alike among the three objects, you win small. If all three are the same, you win big.

To simulate pulling the slot machine's lever arm, press the ENTER key on the keyboard.

One difference in our Slot-O game, the display is entirely at random. No one pushes a secret button under the table to make certain items pop up.

Get out your funny-money from that old Monopoly game, gather up your friends, and let's have some fun.

Program Listing

```
10 CALL CLEAR
20 GOSUB 500
30 PRINT
40 PRINT
50 PRINT
60 GOSUB 200
70 PRINT "***** ***** ***** *****"
```

```
80 PRINT "* ";A$;" * * ";B$;" * * "
   ;C$;" * * ";D$;" *"
90 PRINT "***** ***** ***** *****"
100 PRINT
105 PRINT
110 PRINT "TO PULL THE LEVER,"
120 INPUT "PRESS ENTER":KY$
130 GOTO 10
200 GOSUB 400
210 A$=CHR$(X)
220 GOSUB 400
230 B$=CHR$(X)
240 GOSUB 400
250 C$=CHR$(X)
260 GOSUB 400
270 D$=CHR$(X)
280 GOSUB 400
400 R=INT(5*RND)
410 IF R<1 THEN 400
420 IF R=1 THEN 800
430 IF R=2 THEN 900
440 IF R=3 THEN 1000
450 IF R=4 THEN 1100
460 RETURN
500 PRINT "**********************"
510 PRINT "* SUPER T.I. SLOT-O *"
520 PRINT "**********************"
530 RETURN
800 X=35
810 GOTO 460
900 X=36
910 GOTO 460
1000 X=37
1010 GOTO 460
1100 X=38
1110 GOTO 460
```

Draw Straws

Here's one of man's oldest decision makers. Several straws are broken off to the same length except for one extra-short straw. The length of all straws is concealed and each person draws a straw. The person drawing the shortest straw "wins." That is, he is selected by the luck of the draw.

Now, your computer can provide a fast and easy drawing where no straws are available. It does all the work for you by assigning electronic straws randomly to each person. Those straws are numbers. The shortest straw, or lowest number, "wins."

Program Listing

```
10 CALL CLEAR
20 B=0
30 C=0
40 D=0
50 L=0
60 X=0
70 GOSUB 500
80 PRINT
90 PRINT "DRAW STRAWS"
100 GOSUB 500
110 PRINT
120 PRINT
130 INPUT "PLAYER NO. 1:  ":B$
140 INPUT "PLAYER NO. 2:  ":C$
150 INPUT "PLAYER NO. 3:  ":D$
160 GOSUB 540
170 B=X
180 L=B
190 GOSUB 540
200 C=X
210 IF C<L THEN 230
220 GOTO 240
230 L=C
240 GOSUB 540
250 D=X
260 IF D<L THEN 280
270 GOTO 290
280 L=D
290 PRINT
300 PRINT
310 PRINT B$;":  ";B;
```

```
320 IF L=B THEN 350
330 PRINT
340 GOTO 360
350 PRINT " <<<<<"
360 PRINT C$;": ";C;
370 IF L=C THEN 400
380 PRINT
390 GOTO 410
400 PRINT " <<<<<"
410 PRINT D$;": ";D;
420 IF L=D THEN 450
430 PRINT
440 GOTO 460
450 PRINT " <<<<<"
460 PRINT
470 PRINT
480 INPUT "FOR MORE, PRESS ENTER":KY$
490 GOTO 10
500 FOR L=1 TO 11
510 PRINT "*";
520 NEXT L
530 RETURN
540 X=INT(100*RND)
550 RETURN
```

Funny similes

Give these newfangled gadgets an inch and they'll take a mile. In the case of the computer, give it some tacky retorts and it will spew out an endless string of dumb remarks.

The fun is in having the computer randomly select various words and combine them to make silly sayings.

The random number is used to match the words into similes.

Program Listing

```
10 RANDOMIZE
20 CALL CLEAR
30 DATA SHORT,TALL,FAT,LEAN,CLEAN
```

```
40 DATA DIRTY,GOOD,BAD,HAPPY,SAD
50 DATA GREEN,RED,YELLOW,BLUE,UGLY
60 DATA PRETTY,SHARP,DULL,TACKY,NATTY
70 DATA STRONG,WEAK,MEAN,NICE,DUMB
80 DATA GNOME,TREE,PIG,BOX,CLOCK
90 DATA TURKEY,GOLD,APPLE,DOG,ROOKIE
100 DATA BEET,BIRD,SKY,SIN,PEACH
110 DATA TACK,RAZOR,PIN,PLUG,BULL
120 DATA WORM,LION,LAMB,PUPPY,OX
130 PRINT "WHOM ARE WE DESCRIBING"
140 INPUT B$
150 PRINT
160 T=INT(26*RND)
170 IF T<1 THEN 160
180 IF T>25 THEN 160
190 FOR L=1 TO T
200 READ D$
210 NEXT L
220 RESTORE
230 T=INT(51*RND)
240 IF T<26 THEN 230
250 IF T>50 THEN 230
260 FOR L=1 TO T
270 READ E$
280 NEXT L
290 RESTORE
300 CALL SOUND(1,1000,19)
310 PRINT B$;" IS ";D$;" AS A ";E$
320 FOR L=1 TO 8
330 PRINT
340 NEXT L
350 INPUT "FOR ANOTHER, PRESS ENTER":KY$
360 GOTO 20
```

Traditional Dice Roll

Here's a simple, brief way to roll and display results for two dice.

Lines 100-110 get a random number between 1 and 6 and store it in A. Lines 200-210 get another random number from 1 to 6 and store it in B.

Lines 300-310 print the contents of A and B along with a suitable message.

Program Listing

```
10 RANDOMIZE
20 CALL CLEAR
100 A=INT(7*RND)
110 IF A<1 THEN 100
200 B=INT(7*RND)
210 IF B<1 THEN 200
300 PRINT "FIRST DICE:",A
310 PRINT "SECOND DICE:",B
400 FOR L=1 TO 10
410 PRINT
420 NEXT L
430 PRINT "TO ROLL DICE AGAIN,"
440 INPUT "PRESS ENTER ":KY$
450 GOTO 20
```

See Two Dice

This program rolls two dice and lets you see the results, as with real dice. This is especially useful in those games where it is important to see the value of each.

The subroutine in lines 100-140 generates the necessary pair of random numbers. Lines 60, 70 and 80 make the display you want.

Note that lines 60 and 80 each have nine asterisks. Line 140 is RETURN and must be the last line in the program.

After you type in and RUN the program, press ENTER on your computer 's keyboard to roll the dice.

Program Listing

```
10 RANDOMIZE
15 CALL CLEAR
20 PRINT "TO ROLL TWO DICE,"
30 INPUT "PRESS ENTER":KY$
40 PRINT
50 GOSUB 100
```

```
60 PRINT "*************"
70 PRINT "*  ";DL;"  *  ";DR;"  *"
80 PRINT "*************"
90 PRINT
95 GOTO 20
100 DL=INT(7*RND)
110 IF DL<1 THEN 100
120 DR=INT(7*RND)
130 IF DR<1 THEN 120
140 RETURN
```

See Four Dice

Two dice not enough for your game? Here's how to see four dice after a roll!

Naturally, this program works just like the other program except that the FOR/NEXT loop in lines 50-140 makes the computer roll and display four times rather than two times. If you need six, eight or ten dice on display, change the number two in line 50 to three, four or five.

Program Listing

```
 10 RANDOMIZE
 15 CALL CLEAR
 20 PRINT "TO ROLL TWO DICE,"
 30 INPUT "PRESS ENTER":KY$
 40 CALL CLEAR
 50 FOR L=1 TO 2
 60 DQ=INT(7*RND)
 70 IF DQ<1 THEN 60
 80 DR=INT(7*RND)
 90 IF DR<1 THEN 80
100 PRINT "*************"
110 PRINT "*  ";DQ;"  *  ";DR;"  *"
120 PRINT "*************"
130 PRINT
140 NEXT L
150 PRINT
160 PRINT
170 GOTO 20
```

Secret Message

Secret messages can be lots of fun! They often are composed of codes in which letters of the alphabet have been replaced by numbers.

In this easy-to-use program, the computer generates a list of pseudorandom numbers and assigns one number to each letter of the alphabet. You use the numbers, in lieu of letters, to write notes to your friends.

There is very little chance of the same number being assigned to two different letters because available numbers range from zero to 999.

When typing this program into your computer,be sure to separate the alphabet letters with commas in line 100.

By the way, note the nice two-column screen printing format! Line 250 does that.

Program Listing

```
10 RANDOMIZE
20 CALL CLEAR
100 DATA A,B,C,D,E,F,G,H,I,J,K,L,M
110 DATA N,O,P,Q,R,S,T,U,V,W,X,Y,Z
200 FOR N=1 TO 13
210 C=INT(1000*RND)
220 READ L$
230 D=INT(1000*RND)
240 READ J$
250 PRINT L$;"  ";C,J$;"  ";D
260 NEXT N
```

Original Hi/Lo Game

Here it is. Where everybody started in micro-computer programming back in the Seventies. The first game ever played was a high-low guess-the-number routine.

The computer selects a secret number. You try to guess it. The computer tells you whether or not you are too high, too low, or right on the number.

Here's how it works: the secret number can be zero to 1000. Line 100 generates a random number (the secret number) and stores it. Line 200 asks you to guess the number.

Lines 300-310 decide if you are right or wrong. Line 220 keeps track of the number of attempts.

Program Listing

```
10 RANDOMIZE
20 CALL CLEAR
30 T=0
100 R=INT(1001*RND)
200 INPUT "GUESS THE NUMBER ":B
210 PRINT
220 T=T+1
230 PRINT "THAT WAS TRY NUMBER ";T
300 IF B>R THEN 350
310 IF B<R THEN 330
320 GOTO 400
330 PRINT "TOO LOW"
340 GOTO 360
350 PRINT "TOO HIGH"
360 INPUT "GUESS AGAIN ":B
370 GOTO 210
400 CALL SOUND(99,440,1)
410 PRINT "YES, YOU GOT IT !"
420 PRINT R;" IS THE NUMBER"
430 PRINT "YOU GOT IT IN ";T;" TRIES"
440 PRINT
450 PRINT
460 PRINT
470 GOTO 30
```

Manual Box Mover

The computer can be made to take your message (of up to 34 characters and spaces) and center that message, and draw a box around it to highlight it.

Line 10 asks for a word or words of up to 34 total characters and spaces. Lines 30-80 draw a box around it. Line 100 positions it at the bottom of the video screen. Lines 110 to 130 display it, in its box.

At this point the computer waits for you to press any key (line 200). When you press a key on the keyboard, the program progresses to line 210. The entire message box is pushed *up* one line.

Each key press pushes the box up one more line. Imagination!

Program Listing

```
 10 HOME
 20 INPUT"MESSAGE TO BE BOXED ";M$
 30 LM=LEN(M$)
 40 LT=LM+4
 50 FOR L=1 TO LT
 60 AS$=AS$+"*"
 70 NEXT L
 80 P=(40-LT)/2
 90 HOME
100 FOR L=1 TO 20:PRINT:NEXT L
110 PRINT TAB(P) AS$
120 PRINT TAB(P) "* ";M$;" *"
200 GET KY$
210 CALL -912
220 GOTO 200
```

Backward Writer II

Type in any message of up to 26 characters in response to the computer's request. The computer will turn your message around and print it backwards on the display screen.

Program Listing

```
10 DIM X$(26)*26:DIM A$(Ø)*26
   :DIM Z$(Ø)* 26
20 INPUT "TYPE A MESSAGE",A$(Ø)
30 L=LEN A$(Ø)
40 FOR J=L+1 TO 1 STEP -1
50 Z$(Ø)=Z$(Ø)+MID$ (A$(Ø),J,1)
60 NEXT J
70 PRINT Z$(Ø)
80 CLEAR:GOTO 10
```

Secret Message: Backward Writer

Again type in any message of up to 26 characters (including spaces, of course). You may use any combination of letters, numbers, symbols and spaces up to a total of 26.

The computer will reverse it and display it. Try it with the alphabet. Type in Z to A in backwards order.

Program Listing

```
 10 CLEAR:DIM A$(Ø)*26:DIM B$(Ø)*26
 20 INPUT "TYPE 26-CHARACTER MESSAGE"
    ,A$(Ø)
 30 IF A$(Ø)="" THEN GOTO 20
 40 L=LEN (A$(Ø))
 50 FOR J=L TO 1 STEP -1
 60 B$(Ø)=B$(Ø)+MID$ (A$(Ø),J,1)
 70 NEXT J
 80 PAUSE B$(Ø)
 90 IF INKEY$="" THEN GOTO 90
100 GOTO 10
```

Print Character Set

If you have misplaced the character set, here's a way to see it all on paper. This program causes the computer to run through its list and print numbers, symbols, upper-case alphabet and lower-case alphabet.

Program Listing

```
10 CLS:CLEAR:DIM C$(Ø)*47:DIM D$(Ø)*47
20 FOR L=33 TO 80
30 C$(Ø)=C$(Ø)+CHR$ L
40 NEXT L
50 FOR L=81 TO 127
60 D$(Ø)=D$(Ø)+CHR$ L
70 NEXT L
80 LPRINT C$(Ø);D$(Ø)
```

Whodunit?

The lord of the manor has been found murdered. The butler, the gardener, the nanny all seem guilty. And a burglar was on the scene. Whodunit?

Program Listing

```
 10 LET A$="CAT BURGLAR"
 20 LET B$="GARDNER"
 30 LET C$="NANNY"
 40 LET D$="BUTLER"
 50 LET W=Ø
 60 LET R=Ø
 70 RAND
100 LET S=INT (5*RND)
110 IF S=1 THEN LET X$=A$
120 IF S=2 THEN LET X$=B$
130 IF S=3 THEN LET X$=C$
140 IF S=4 THEN LET X$=D$
150 IF S<1 OR S>4 THEN GOTO 100
200 PRINT "WHO KILLED THE DUKE?"
210 PRINT
220 PRINT "WAS IT THE",,A$,B$,C$,D$
230 PRINT
240 PRINT "WHODUNIT?"
250 INPUT P$
260 IF P$=X$ THEN GOTO 400
300 CLS
310 PRINT "NO, NOT THE ";P$
320 LET W=W+1
330 PRINT
340 GOTO 200
400 CLS
410 PRINT "HOORAY",,"THATS RIGHT"
420 PRINT P$;" DID IT"
430 LET R=R+1
440 PRINT
500 PRINT "YOUR SCORE IS"
510 PRINT R;" RIGHT ";W;" WRONG"
```

Klingon Killer

BLEEP. BLEEP. BLEEP. The warning alarm is screaming. A Klingon raider has been spotted. It is attacking. You swing your laser gun and fire. Will you kill him? Damage him? Miss him? If you miss, will he get you?

Program Listing

```
 10 LET V=Ø
 20 LET W=Ø
 30 RAND
 40 PRINT "***********************"
 50 PRINT "* RAIDERS ATTACKING *"
 60 PRINT "***********************"
 70 PRINT ,,"STANDBY TO FIRE LASERS"
 80 PRINT ,,"HOW MANY SHOTS WILL YOU FIRE?"
 90 INPUT Q
100 LET S=INT (6*RND)
110 IF S=1 THEN GOTO 200
120 IF S=2 THEN GOTO 300
130 IF S=3 THEN GOTO 400
140 IF S=4 THEN GOTO 500
150 IF S=5 THEN GOTO 600
160 GOTO 100
200 CLS
210 PRINT "YOU DAMAGED HIM"
220 PRINT
230 GOTO 70
300 CLS
310 PRINT "YOU MISSED"
320 GOTO 220
400 CLS
410 PRINT "YOU MISSED BUT"
420 PRINT "HE FIRED AT YOU"
430 PRINT
440 PRINT "HE MISSED"
450 GOTO 220
500 CLS
510 PRINT "YOU GOT HIM"
520 PRINT "HE IS DEAD IN SPACE"
```

```
530 LET W=W+1
540 GOTO 700
600 CLS
610 PRINT "OH NO"
620 PRINT "HE GOT YOU"
630 PRINT "EL ZAPPO"
640 PRINT "FINIS"
650 LET V=V+1
700 PRINT
710 PRINT
720 PRINT "SCORE:"
730 PRINT "KLINGONS ";V,"YOU ";W
740 PAUSE 240
750 CLS
760 GOTO 40
```

Memory Tester I

Now you can rate the holding power of your very own memory, all in the privacy of your own home or office. Simply say how much of a challenge you think you can withstand and such a test will be devised.

Think you know it all? Try this.

Program Listing

```
 10 PRINT "MEMORY TEST"
 20 PRINT "***********"
 30 LET W=Ø
 40 LET A$="ACT"
 50 LET B$="RADIO"
 60 LET C$="DOG"
 70 LET D$="LAMP"
 80 LET E$="BREAD"
 90 LET F$="LOG"
100 LET G$="POCKET"
110 LET H$="TABLE"
120 LET I$="COLOR"
130 LET J$="TRAIN"
140 LET K$="BOOK"
150 LET L$="FLOWER"
160 LET M$="DRAIN"
```

```
170 LET N$="SUPPER"
180 LET O$="PLAN"
190 LET P$="CAT"
200 LET Q$="EVENT"
210 LET R$="TOY"
220 LET S$="CLOCK"
230 LET T$="SHIP"
240 LET X=Ø
250 LET U$=A$
260 LET V$=B$
270 LET W$=C$
280 LET X$=D$
290 GOSUB 600
300 LET U$=E$
310 LET V$=F$
320 LET W$=G$
330 LET X$=H$
340 GOSUB 600
350 LET U$=I$
360 LET V$=J$
370 LET W$=K$
380 LET X$=L$
390 GOSUB 600
400 LET U$=M$
410 LET V$=N$
420 LET W$=O$
430 LET X$=P$
440 GOSUB 600
450 LET U$=Q$
460 LET V$=R$
470 LET W$=S$
480 LET X$=T$
490 GOSUB 600
500 CLS
510 PRINT "YOU GOT ";W;" RIGHT","IN "
    ;X;" TRIES"
520 PRINT "*************************"
530 STOP
600 PRINT U$,V$,W$,X$
610 PAUSE 120
620 CLS
```

```
700 PRINT "WHAT WERE THOSE WORDS?"
800 PRINT "FIRST WORD:",
810 GOSUB 1200
820 IF Y$=U$ THEN GOSUB 1300
830 IF Y$<>U$ THEN GOSUB 1400
840 IF Y$<>U$ THEN GOTO 800
900 PRINT "SECOND WORD:",
910 GOSUB 1200
920 IF Y$=V$ THEN GOSUB 1300
930 IF Y$<>V$ THEN GOSUB 1400
940 IF Y$<>V$ THEN GOTO 900
1000 PRINT "THIRD WORD:",
1010 GOSUB 1200
1020 IF Y$=W$ THEN GOSUB 1300
1030 IF Y$<>W$ THEN GOSUB 1400
1040 IF Y$<>W$ THEN GOTO 1000
1100 PRINT "FOURTH WORD:"
1110 GOSUB 1200
1120 IF Y$=X$ THEN GOSUB 1300
1130 IF Y$<>X$ THEN GOSUB 1400
1140 IF Y$<>X$ THEN GOTO 1100
1150 CLS
1160 PRINT "WATCH CLOSELY"
1170 PAUSE 120
1180 CLS
1190 RETURN
1200 INPUT Y$
1210 PRINT Y$
1220 LET X=X+1
1230 RETURN
1300 PRINT "CORRECT"
1310 PAUSE 180
1320 LET W=W+1
1330 CLS
1340 RETURN
1400 PRINT "WRONG",,"TRY AGAIN"
1410 RETURN
```

Memory Tester II

Suppose I pick a number out of the air. Say, 5. You can remember that, right? Or 73. Or 841. But, just how big a number can you see briefly and remember? This program throws ever-increasingly-larger random numbers at you and asks you to remember them. And it keeps score. What's your memory's upper limit?

Program Listing

```
 10 LET W=Ø
 15 LET R=Ø
 20 LET Z=1
 30 LET S=INT(100*RND)
 40 LET N=INT(S*Z)
 60 PRINT "REMEMBER ";N
 65 PAUSE 100
 70 CLS
 80 IF W=3 THEN PRINT "FORGET IT"
 85 IF W=3 THEN GOTO 145
 90 PRINT "WHAT WAS IT ?"
 95 INPUT S
100 IF S<>N THEN PRINT "WRONG"
105 IF S<>N THEN LET W=W+1
110 IF S<>N THEN GOTO 80
115 PRINT "RIGHT"
120 LET R=R+1
125 LET W=Ø
130 LET Z=11*Z
135 PRINT R;" RIGHT SO FAR"
140 GOTO 30
145 PRINT "YOU HAD ";R;" RIGHT"
150 PRINT "LETS START OVER"
155 GOTO 10
```

Smart Computer

This game is so quick you can work it in while your secretary is away sharpening her pencil. It's more or less the reverse of the old favorite High-Low Number bit. In this rendition, you come up with the secret three-digit number and the computer guesses it!

In old-fashioned High-Low, the computer could keep you guessing for hours. Here, the computer asks one little old question and...*bingo!* It has the correct answer in an instant.

The mystery number has to be a three-digit number with all digits the same.

Program Listing

```
10 CLS
20 PRINT "SELECT A THREE-DIGIT NUMBER"
30 PRINT "WITH ALL THREE DIGITS THE
   SAME"
40 PRINT
50 PRINT "ADD THE THREE DIGITS TOGETHER"
60 PRINT "WHAT IS THE SUM"
65 PRINT "OF THE THREE DIGITS ?"
70 INPUT N
75 CLS
80 LET Q=37*N
90 PRINT
100 PRINT "YOUR ORIGINAL NUMBER WAS ";Q
110 PRINT
120 PRINT
130 GOTO 20
```

Parameters

What! Another high-low numbers game? Yep. It's the all-time most favorite computer game.

Any rules? Sure. The computer picks a secret number. You try to guess it. The computer gives you too-high or too-low clues and keeps score.

Program Listing

```
10 RAND
20 LET T=Ø
30 LET R=INT (101*RND)
40 IF R<1 OR R>100 THEN GOTO 20
50 PRINT "GUESS MY SECRET NUMBER","(1
   TO 100)"
60 INPUT B
70 LET T=T+1
80 IF B>R THEN GOTO 200
```

```
 90 IF B<R THEN GOTO 300
100 PRINT
110 PRINT "YES",,R;" IS THE NUMBER"
120 PRINT "IT TOOK YOU ";T;" TRIES"
130 PAUSE 240
140 CLS
150 GOTO 20
200 CLS
210 PRINT B;" IS TOO HIGH"
220 PRINT "GUESS AGAIN"
230 GOTO 60
300 CLS
310 PRINT B;" IS TOO LOW"
320 GOTO 220
```

Wood Chuck Chuck

How much wood would a woodchuck chuck, if a woodchuck could chuck wood. How much wood could a woodchuck chuck, if a woodchuck would chuck wood? That's like asking how many angels can sit on the head of a pin. Or, more appropriately, how many trees in the forest.

But,wait. This little game takes that old ditty seriously. How much wood could Mr. Chuck throw around if he wanted to? Try it. If you're good enough, you'll end up in the Woodchuck Hall of Fame.

Program Listing

```
 10 PRINT "HOW MUCH WOOD",,"COULD A
    WOODCHUCK CHUCK"
 20 PRINT "IF A WOODCHUCK",,"COULD
    CHUCK WOOD?"
 30 PRINT "************************"
 40 PRINT "TOO MUCH"
 50 LET C=Ø
 55 LET E=Ø
 60 LET G=Ø
 70 PRINT "PRESS A KEY TO PLAY"
 80 IF INKEY$="" THEN GOTO 90
 90 GOSUB 1000
100 CLS
```

```
110 PRINT "HOW MANY LOGS",,"CAN THE
    WOODCHUCK CHUCK?"
120 INPUT B
130 LET C=C+1
140 IF B<>X THEN GOTO  400
150 LET G=G+1
160 PRINT "HOORAY",,"YOU GOT IT"
170 IF C=1 THEN PRINT "ON THE FIRST TRY"
180 IF C<>1 THEN PRINT "IN ";C;" TRIES"
190 PRINT
260  LET E=E+C
265 LET C=Ø
270 PRINT "WANT TO PLAY AGAIN?"
280 INPUT D$
290 IF D$="YES" THEN GOTO 90
300 GOTO 800
400 IF C=1 THEN GOTO 425
405 IF C=2 THEN GOTO 440
410 IF C=3 THEN GOTO 455
415 IF C=4 THEN GOTO 470
420 IF C>4 THEN GOTO 500
425 PRINT "YOUR FIRST TRY IS"
430 IF B<X THEN GOTO 480
435 GOTO 490
440 PRINT "YOUR SECOND GUESS IS"
445 IF B<X THEN GOTO 480
450 GOTO 490
455 PRINT "THIRD GUESS"
460 IF B<X THEN GOTO 480
465 GOTO 490
470 PRINT "FOURTH TRY",,"YOUR LAST CHANCE"
475 IF B<X THEN GOTO 600
477 GOTO 630
480 PRINT "TOO LITTLE"
485 GOTO 495
490 PRINT "TOO MUCH"
495 PRINT "TRY AGAIN"
497 GOTO 120
500 PRINT "SORRY",,"YOU ONLY GET 4
    CHANCES"
505 PRINT "THE WOODCHUCK COULD"
```

```
510 PRINT "CHUCK ";X;" LOGS"
520 PRINT "YOU LOSE",,"TOUGH LUCK"
530 PRINT
540 GOTO 260
600 PRINT "TOO LITTLE AGAIN"
610 GOTO 500
630 PRINT "STILL TOO HIGH"
640 GOTO 500
800 CLS
805 PRINT "YOU HAD ";G;" RIGHT"
810 PRINT "IN ";E;" TRIES"
815 LET H=INT (G/E)*1000)
820 PRINT
830 PRINT "YOU ARE BATTING ";H
900 STOP
1000 RAND
1010 LET X=INT (11*RND)
1020 IF X<1 OR X>10 THEN GOTO 1010
1030 RETURN
```

Murder In the Mansion

The wind howls around gnarled tree trunks and through heather across the moor. A dog barks in the distance. Inside the stately Victorian mansion, the upstairs maid weeps noisily into her handkerchief. The Baron has just been found dead in a pool of blood.

As Scotland Yard's chief inspector for the district, you've just been called in on the case. Besides the Pretty Maid, you find a motley cast of characters including the Stately Butler and the Old Nanny.

The case is perplexing. You're not sure how the old boy was done in, or even where he actually was killed. The identity of the killer is not immediately apparent.

The first major decision comes as you sort through the clues, trying to deduce where the Baron was killed. Satisfying that one, you search for the weapon. Once you know where and how he was murdered, the only remaining question is: Whodunit?

Program Listing

```
10 CLEAR
```

```
 20 LET A$="BUTLER"
 30 LET B$="MAID"
 40 LET C$="NANNY"
 60 PRINT "A WINTER EVE,"
 70 PRINT "A COUNTRY MANSION,"
 80 PRINT "THE BARON IS DEAD."
 90 PRINT "*******************"
100 PRINT "OUR CAST:"
110 PRINT "THE STATELY ";A$
120 PRINT "THE PRETTY ";B$
130 PRINT "THE OLD ";C$
150 LET E$="HAIRPIN"
160 LET F$="GUN"
170 LET G$="POKER"
190 LET I$="PANTRY"
200 LET J$="BEDROOM"
210 LET K$="LIBRARY"
230 RAND
240 LET M=INT (4*RND)
250 IF M<1 OR M>3 THEN GOTO 240
260 LET N=INT (4*RND)
270 IF N<1 OR N>3 THEN GOTO 260
280 LET R=INT (4*RND)
290 IF R<1 OR R>3 THEN GOTO 280
310 PRINT
330 PRINT "PRESS A KEY TO PLAY"
340 IF INKEY$="" THEN GOTO 340
350 CLS
360 PRINT "WHICH ROOM?"
370 PRINT I$,J$,K$
420 INPUT V$
430 IF M=1 THEN LET S$="PANTRY"
440 IF M=2 THEN LET S$="BEDROOM"
450 IF M=3 THEN LET S$="LIBRARY"
470 IF V$=S$ THEN GOTO 530
475 PRINT "CLUE:"
480 IF S$=I$ THEN PRINT "FOOD"
490 IF S$=J$ THEN PRINT "PILLOW"
500 IF S$=K$ THEN PRINT "BOOKS"
520 GOTO 360
530 CLS
540 PRINT "CORRECT. IN THE ";V$
```

```
550 PRINT "BUT WHICH WEAPON"
560 PRINT E$,F$,G$
610 INPUT W$
620 IF N=1 THEN LET T$="HAIRPIN"
630 IF N=2 THEN LET T$="GUN"
640 IF N=3 THEN LET T$="POKER"
660 IF W$=T$ THEN GOTO 720
665 PRINT "CLUE:"
670 IF T$=E$ THEN PRINT "COIFFURE"
680 IF T$=F$ THEN PRINT "BULLETS"
690 IF T$=G$ THEN PRINT "LOGS"
700 GOTO 550
720 CLS
730 PRINT "THE ";T$;" IS CORRECT"
740 PRINT "BUT WHODUNIT?"
750 PRINT A$,B$,C$
760 INPUT X$
770 IF R=1 THEN LET U$="BUTLER"
780 IF R=2 THEN LET U$="MAID"
790 IF R=3 THEN LET U$="NANNY"
810 IF X$=U$ THEN GOTO 865
820 IF U$=A$ THEN PRINT "HE SERVES"
830 IF U$=B$ THEN PRINT "SHE DUSTS"
840 IF U$=C$ THEN PRINT "LOVES KIDS"
860 GOTO 740
865 CLS
870 PRINT "YOU SOLVED THE CRIME"
880 PRINT "THE ";U$;" DID IT"
890 PRINT "IN THE ";S$;" WITH THE ";T$
```

Buried Treasure

The sun burns the beach sand as it glares across mirrored depths. An old salt, one leg gone below the knee, stumps down to the water's edge and glares back. A parrot chatters on his shoulder. The old man tosses a bottle into the ocean.

Hours later you awaken to find the tide moistening your toes and the bottle bumping against your leg. It's got paper inside.

Pulling the cork you find a map. A treasure map! The scrawl shows a quiet Cay with a peaceful finger of land extending into the sea. On the map is a giant X, marking the spot where the treasure is buried. Then, the only remaining question is: Where?

Program Listing

```
 10 PRINT "YOU SEARCH FOR"
 20 PRINT "*******************"
 30 PRINT "* BURIED TREASURE *"
 40 PRINT "*******************"
 50 PRINT
 60 PRINT "PRESS ANY KEY TO PLAY"
 65 LET W=Ø
 70 IF INKEY$="" THEN GOTO 70
 80 LET X=INT (7*RND)
 90 IF X<1 OR X>6 THEN GOTO 80
100 CLS
110 PRINT "*   *"
120 PRINT " * * "
130 PRINT "  *  "
140 PRINT " * * "
150 PRINT "*   *"
160 PRINT
170 PRINT "ON YOUR MAP, X MARKS THE SPOT"
180 PRINT
190 GOTO 950
200 PRINT "BUT WHERE IS IT?"
220 PRINT "IN THE GARDEN?"
225 INPUT D$
230 IF D$="YES" THEN GOTO 400
240 PRINT "SUNK IN THE POND?"
245 INPUT F$
250 IF F$="YES" THEN GOTO 500
260 PRINT "BESIDE THE TREE?"
265 INPUT H$
270 IF H$="YES" THEN GOTO 600
280 PRINT "BENEATH THE BOULDER?"
285 INPUT I$
290 IF I$="YES" THEN GOTO 700
300 PRINT "INSIDE THE CAVE?"
305 INPUT J$
```

```
310 IF J$="YES" THEN GOTO 800
320 PRINT "UNDER THE SHED?"
325 INPUT K$
330 IF K$ ="YES" THEN GOTO 900
340 GOTO 950
400 IF X=1 THEN GOTO 980
410 GOSUB 1000
420 GOTO 240
500 IF X=2 THEN GOTO 980
510 GOSUB 1000
520 GOTO 260
600 IF X=3 THEN GOTO 980
610 GOSUB 1000
620 GOTO 280
700 IF X=4 THEN GOTO 980
710 GOSUB 1000
720 GOTO 300
800 IF X=5 THEN GOTO 980
810 GOSUB 1000
820 GOTO 320
900 IF X=6 THEN GOTO 980
910 GO SUB 1000
920 GOTO 200
950 PRINT "IT HAS TO BE"
955 PRINT "IN THE GARDEN",,"SUNK IN THE
    POND","BESIDE THE TREE"
960 PRINT "BENEATH THE BOULDER","INSIDE
    THE CAVE",,"OR UNDER THE SHED"
965 PRINT
970 GOTO 200
980 PRINT "YOU FOUND THE CHEST","WITH
    $1 MILLION IN JEWELS"
985 PRINT
990 PRINT "YOU HAD ";W;" WRONG GUESSES"
995 PRINT "THATS GOOD"
999 STOP
1000 CLS
1010 PRINT "NO, NOT THERE",,"TRY AGAIN"
1020 LET W=W+1
1030 RETURN
```

Craps

The world's oldest game transformed into a futuristic setting: computer dice. The computer rolls the dice, notes your point, cheers your wins and commiserates after your losses.

Snake eyes. Lucky seven. The roll. The point. Just be sure not to crap out!

Program Listing

```
 10 RAND
 15 LET E=Ø
 20 LET D=Ø
 25 LET C=Ø
 30 PRINT "**********"
 40 PRINT "* CRAPS *"
 50 PRINT "**********"
 60 PRINT
 70 PRINT "TO ROLL DICE PRESS ANY KEY"
 80 IF INKEY$="" THEN GOTO 80
 90 GOSUB 600
100 LET C=C+1
110 CLS
120 PRINT "***** *****"
130 PRINT "* ";X;" * * ";Y;" *"
140 PRINT "***** *****"
150 LET Z=X+Y
160 IF C=1 THEN LET B=Z
170 IF C=1 THEN GOTO 190
180 IF Z=B THEN GOTO 400
190 IF Z=7 THEN GOTO 250
200 IF Z=2 THEN GOTO 300
210 PRINT "YOUR POINT IS ";B
220 GOTO 60
250 IF C=1 THEN PRINT "HOORAY",,"LUCKY
    SEVEN"
255 IF C=1 THEN PRINT "YOU WIN"
260 IF C=1 THEN LET D=D+1
265 IF C=1 THEN GOTO 500
270 PRINT "TOUGH LUCK",,"YOU CRAPPED OUT"
275 PRINT "YOU LOSE"
```

```
280 LET E=E+1
285 GOTO 500
300 PRINT "SORRY",,"SNAKE EYES"
310 GOTO 275
400 PRINT "POINT"
410 PRINT "YOU GOT ";B
420 PRINT "YOU WIN"
430 LET D=D+1
500 PRINT
510 PRINT "YOU ROLLED ";C;" TIMES"
520 PRINT
530 PRINT "WANT TO ROLL AGAIN?"
540 PRINT
550 INPUT F$
560 IF F$="YES" THEN GOTO 25
570 PRINT "OKAY"
580 PRINT "YOU WON ";D;" AND LOST ";E
590 STOP
600 LET X=INT (7*RND)
610 IF X<1 OR X>6 THEN GOTO 600
620 LET Y=INT (7*RND)
630 IF Y<1 OR Y>6 THEN GOTO 620
640 RETURN
```

Old West Shootout

You are Marshall Matt Dillon. Billy the Kid is in town. You can't avoid your duty: the kid must be arrested. It's high noon!

You must plug the gunfighter before he guns you down. But where is he hiding? He could be down in the corral or up on the hotel roof. He might have slipped into the stable or down behind the bar in the saloon. He could be inside the house or outside in the wagon. He might be behind the railroad station or in the doctor's office. And, worst of all, he may have brought a friend!

Follow the clues from your handy computer, fastest figurer in the West. Just don't stop any bullets.

Program Listing

```
10 CLEAR
```

```
 12 RAND
 13 LET P=Ø
 14 LET M=Ø
 15 LET Z=Ø
 16 LET O=Ø
 17 LET W=Ø
 20 LET A$="CORRAL"
 25 LET B$="HOTEL"
 30 LET C$="STABLE"
 35 LET D$="SALOON"
 40 LET E$="HOUSE"
 45 LET F$="WAGON"
 50 LET G$="STATION"
 55 LET H$="STORE"
 60 LET I$="OFFICE"
 85 PRINT "SHOOT THE GUNFIGHTER"
 90 PRINT "BEFORE HE SHOOTS YOU"
 95 PRINT
100 PRINT "HE MAY BE IN THE"
105 PRINT A$,B$,C$,D$,E$,F$,G$,H$,I$
110 PRINT
115 PRINT "WHERE?"
120 INPUT K$
130 PRINT "WHERE ARE YOU?",
135 INPUT L$
140 CLS
150 PRINT "YOU SHOOT"
155 PRINT "FROM THE ";L$
160 PRINT "INTO THE ";K$
165 PAUSE 120
170 GOSUB 1000
175 CLS
180 PRINT "BANG"
185 IF K$=Z$ THEN GOTO 300
190 IF L$=Z$ THEN GOTO 600
200 PRINT "YOU MISSED HIM"
205 LET P=P+1
210 LET W=W+1
215 LET Z=Z+1
220 IF W>2 THEN GOTO 700
230 LET V=S
```

```
245 PRINT "TRY AGAIN"
250 GOTO 95
300 CLS
305 PRINT "YOU GOT HIM",,"IN THE ";Z$
310 LET M=M+1
315 PRINT
320 PRINT
325 PRINT "OOPS, ANOTHER BAD GUY"
330 PRINT "WANNA FIGHT AGAIN?"
335 LET W=Ø
340 INPUT N$
345 CLS
355 IF N$="YES" THEN GOTO 85
357 PRINT "YOU MISSED ";P;" SHOTS"
360 PRINT "YOU WON ";M;" LOST ";O
370 STOP
600 PRINT "OOPS,",,"HE IS IN THE ";L$
605 PRINT "HE SHOT YOU"
610 LET O=O+1
615 GOTO 315
700 PRINT "HE GOT YOU",,"YOU ARE DEAD"
705 LET O=O+1
710 PRINT "HE WAS IN THE ";Z$
715 GOTO 315
1000 LET S=INT (10*RND)
1010 IF S=1 THEN LET Z$=A$
1020 IF S=2 THEN LET Z$=B$
1030 IF S=3 THEN LET Z$=C$
1040 IF S=4 THEN LET Z$=D$
1050 IF S=5 THEN LET Z$=E$
1060 IF S=6 THEN LET Z$=F$
1070 IF S=7 THEN LET Z$=G$
1080 IF S=8 THEN LET Z$=H$
1090 IF S=9 THEN LET Z$=I$
1100 IF S<1 OR S>9 THEN GOTO 1000
1110 RETURN
```

Scrambled Egg

Ttsae. *Let's see. Oh, I know. State?* Right. Try another. Nidlsa. *Good grief. That's too tough. Give me an easier one.* Okay. Fo. *Well, that's too easy.* What is it? *Of, of course. By the way, what is Nidlsa.* Island. *Oh!*

Try another.

Program Listing

```
 10 PRINT "******************"
 20 PRINT "* SCRAMBLED EGG *"
 30 PRINT "******************"
 40 CLEAR
 50 RAND
 60 PRINT
 70 LET W=Ø
 80 LET T=Ø
 90 LET C=Ø
100 PRINT "DO YOU WANT THE","HARD,
    HARDER, OR HARDEST WORDS?"
110 INPUT Y$
120 IF Y$="HARDEST" THEN GOTO 8000
130 IF Y$="HARDER" THEN GOTO 8500
140 IF Y$="HARD" THEN GOTO 9000
150 GOTO 110
200 CLS
210 PRINT "HERE IS THE ";Y$;" WORD"
220 GOSUB Z*500
230 PRINT
240 PRINT X$
250 PRINT
260 PRINT "WHAT IS THE WORD?",
270 INPUT Z$
275 LET T=T+1
280 PRINT Z$
290 IF Z$=L$ THEN GOTO 400
300 CLS
310 PRINT "WRONG",,"TRY AGAIN"
320 LET W=W+1
330 GOTO 230
400 CLS
410 PRINT "CORRECT"
420 LET C=C+1
430 PRINT
440 PRINT "WANT TO PLAY AGAIN?"
```

```
 450 INPUT Z$
 460 CLS
 465 IF Z$="YES" THEN GOTO 100
 470 IF Z$="NO" THEN GOTO 9500
 480 PRINT "ANSWER YES OR NO"
 490 GOTO 430
 500 LET L$="EGG"
 600 LET X$="GEG"
 700 RETURN
1000 LET L$="LOG"
1100 LET X$="GLO"
1200 RETURN
1500 LET L$="BEE"
1600 LET X$="EBE"
1700 RETURN
2000 LET L$="TRY"
2100 LET X$="RYT"
2200 RETURN
2500 LET L$="RADIO"
2600 LET X$="DIROA"
2700 RETURN
3000 LET L$="COURT"
3100 LET X$="RUCOT"
3200 RETURN
3500 LET L$="DREAM"
3600 LET X$="RAMED"
3700 RETURN
4000 LET L$="LIVER"
4100 LET X$="RIVEL"
4200 RETURN
4500 LET L$="COMPUTE"
4600 LET X$="PEMCUTO"
4700 RETURN
5000 LET L$="MANSION"
5100 LET X$="SOMNNAI"
5200 RETURN
5500 LET L$="VEHICLE"
5600 LET X$="ELCHIVE"
5700 RETURN
6000 LET L$="ILLEGAL"
6100 LET X$="GALELIL"
6200 RETURN
```

```
8000 LET Z=INT (13*RND)
8010 IF Z<9 OR Z>12 THEN GOTO 8000
8020 GOTO 200
8500 LET Z=INT (9*RND)
8510 IF Z<5 OR Z>8 THEN GOTO 8500
8520 GOTO 200
9000 LET Z=INT (5*RND)
9010 IF Z<1 OR Z>4 THEN GOTO 9000
9020 GOTO 200
9500 PRINT "OKAY"
9510 PRINT "******************"
9520 PRINT "YOU HAD ";C;" RIGHT"
9530 PRINT "AND";W;" WRONG"
9540 PRINT "IN ";T;" TRIES"
```

Lost Safari

Jim Buck, the famous safari guide, has been deep in the bush of darkest Africa, leading a party of big game hunters for days when word arrives at his London headquarters that he is lost. The telegram doesn't say what country on the African continent he is in. Nor does it tell what big game he is hunting. You'll have to apply your best deductive reasoning and come up with his prey and his location if you are to save his life and the lives of three men and two women on safari with Big Jim.

But the jungle is full of traps. Once you have discovered which animal he is hunting you'll know whether he is up-country or down-country or in the back country. But the jungle is full of traps. Having settled all that, it's still not clear whether you can fly in, in time to save the party from certain death at the hands of a tribe of giant pygmies. If only you can fly in in the right number of days, all will be saved. Hurry!

Program Listing

```
10 CLEAR
20 PRINT "LOST SAFARI"
30 PRINT "***********"
40 RAND
50 LET B$="RHINO"
```

```
 60 LET C$="GAZELLE"
 70 LET D$="HIPPO"
 80 LET E$="LION"
 90 LET F$="ZEBRA"
100 LET G$="TIGER"
110 LET H$="KENYA"
120 LET I$="CONGO"
130 LET J$=NIGERIA"
140 LET K$="SUDAN"
150 LET L$="TOGO"
160 LET M$="LESOTHO"
170 LET A1=INT(7*RND)
180 IF A1<1 OR A1>6 THEN GOTO 170
190 LET A2=INT(7*RND)
200 IF A2<1 OR A2>6 THEN GOTO 190
210 LET A3=INT(7*RND)
220 IF A3<1 OR A3>6 THEN GOTO 210
230 IF A1=1 THEN LET S$=B$
240 IF A1=2 THEN LET S$=C$
250 IF A1=3 THEN LET S$=D$
260 IF A1=4 THEN LET S$=E$
270 IF A1=5 THEN LET S$=F$
280 IF A1=6 THEN LET S$=G$
290 IF A2=1 THEN LET T$=H$
300 IF A2=2 THEN LET T$=I$
310 IF A2=3 THEN LET T$=J$
320 IF A2=4 THEN LET T$=K$
330 IF A2=5 THEN LET T$=L$
340 IF A2=6 THEN LET T$=M$
350 PRINT
360 PRINT "THE SAFARI IS LOST"
370 PRINT "SOMEWHERE IN"
380 PRINT
390 PRINT H$,I$,J$,K$,L$,M$
400 PRINT
430 PRINT "TO PLAY PRESS A KEY"
440 IF INKEY$="" THEN GOTO 440
450 CLS
460 PRINT "WHAT ARE THEY HUNTING?"
480 PRINT B$,C$,D$,E$,F$,G$
510 INPUT O$
```

```
530 IF O$=S$ THEN GOTO 580
540 GOSUB 1000
570 GOTO 480
580 GOSUB 1200
610 PRINT "NOW FIND THEM"
630 PRINT "ARE THEY IN"
650 PRINT H$,I$,J$,K$,L$,M$
680 INPUT R$
700 IF R$=T$ THEN GOTO 750
710 GOSUB 1000
740 GOTO 640
750 GOSUB 1200
770 PRINT "NOW RUSH TO SAVE THEM"
790 PRINT "HOW MANY DAYS (1-6)"
810 PRINT "WILL IT TAKE TO GET THERE?"
820 INPUT Z
840 IF Z=A3 THEN GOTO 880
850 GOSUB 1000
860 PRINT "TRY A DIFFERENT NUMBER"
870 GOTO 790
880 GOSUB 1200
890 PRINT "YOU SAVED THE SAFARI"
900 PRINT "HUNTING ";S$;" IN ";T$
    ;" IN ";A3;" DAYS"
910 STOP
1000 CLS
1010 PRINT "WRONG, TRY AGAIN"
1020 RETURN
1200 CLS
1210 PRINT "CORRECT"
1220 RETURN
```

Barrel of Apples

Albert is a fat kid, about as round as that barrel of apples. Oh, that's Albert's barrel by the way. He carts it around with him. Has a new game he likes to play. And play. And play. It's enough to drive you nuts!

Go ahead. Say hello.

Program Listing

```
 10 PRINT "HI",,"I AM ALBERT"
 20 PRINT "WHATS YOUR NAME?"
 30 INPUT L$
 40 CLS
 50 PRINT "HI,";L$
 60 PRINT "WANT TO PLAY A GAME?"
 70 PRINT
 80 PRINT "PRESS ANY KEY"
 90 IF INKEY$="" THEN GOTO 90
100 LET B=Ø
105 LET P=Ø
110 LET Q=Ø
115 LET X=Ø
120 GOSUB 1100
130 CLS
140 GOSUB 1000
150 PRINT
160 PRINT
170 PRINT "THIS BARREL HOLDS LOTS OF
    APPLES"
180 PRINT "IN FACT, ";L$;", UP TO 100
    APPLES"
190 PRINT
200 PRINT "CAN YOU GUESS HOW MANY"
210 PRINT "ITS HOLDING RIGHT NOW?"
220 INPUT P
225 IF P<1 OR P>100 THEN GOTO 220
230 LET B=B+1
240 IF X=P THEN GOTO 300
250 GOTO 500
300 LET Q=Q+1
310 IF B=1 THEN GOTO 450
320 CLS
330 PRINT "YOU GOT IT",,"CONGRATULATIONS"
340 PRINT
350 PRINT "WANT TO PLAY AGAIN?"
360 INPUT R$
370 IF R$="YES" THEN GOTO 400
380 GOTO 800
400 LET X=Ø
```

```
410 LET P=Ø
420 GOTO 120
450 CLS
460 PRINT "WOW",,"RIGHT THE FIRST TIME"
470 PRINT "YOU QUALIFY AS A GENIUS"
480 GOTO 340
500 IF P<X THEN GOTO 600
510 IF P>X THEN GOTO 700
600 CLS
610 PRINT "WRONG",,"THERE ARE MORE"
620 PRINT
630 PRINT "PICK A LARGER NUMBER"
640 INPUT P
650 LET B=B+1
660 GOTO 240
700 CLS
710 PRINT "SORRY",,"TOO MANY"
720 PRINT
730 PRINT "GO FOR A SMALLER NUMBER"
740 INPUT P
750 LET B=B+1
760 GOTO 240
800 CLS
810 PRINT "OKAY, ";L$
820 PRINT "YOU HAD ";Q;" RIGHT"
830 PRINT "IN ";B;" TRIES"
840 LET C=INT ((Q/B)*1000)
850 PRINT
860 PRINT "YOU BATTED ";C
870 PRINT
880 PRINT "BYE BYE, ";L$
900 STOP
1000 FOR H=17 TO 27
1010 FOR Y=43 TO 30 STEP -1
1020 PLOT H,Y
1030 NEXT Y
1040 NEXT H
1050 RETURN
1100 RAND
1110 LET X=INT (101*RND)
1120 IF X<1 OR X>100 THEN GOTO 1110
1130 RETURN
```

The Black Pearl

Loves have been lost for it. Families have been broken by it. Men have killed for it: the infamous Black Pearl from Won Quon Luk temple in the Orient.

One night in 1946, in a fabulous apartment high above Fifth Avenue in New York City, a svelte blonde in black velvet wore a string of 10 superb pearls. At least, nine superb and one ultimate. Nine whites and the black beauty!

The string broke during a lights-out-at-midnight and were lost. Until now, their whereabouts has been a mystery. Until now, that is, because here they are in this leather pouch. Reach in. Take one. Hope you get the Black Pearl!

Program Listing

```
 10 CLEAR
 20 LET C=Ø
 30 LET D=Ø
 40 CLS
 45 PRINT "*********************"
 50 PRINT "* THE BLACK PEARL *"
 55 PRINT "*********************"
 60 PRINT
 65 RAND
 70 PRINT "MY POUCH HAS TEN PEARLS"
 80 PRINT "NINE WHITES AND..."
 90 PRINT "THE BLACK BEAUTY"
100 PRINT
110 PRINT "EACH HAS A TINY GOLD NUMBER"
120 PRINT "FROM ONE TO TEN"
130 PRINT "ETCHED ON ITS SURFACE"
140 PRINT
150 PRINT "TAKE A PEARL AND"
160 PRINT "TELL ME ITS NUMBER"
170 PRINT
180 PRINT "IF IT IS THE BLACK PEARL,"
190 PRINT "YOU WIN"
200 PRINT
210 PRINT "WHICH NUMBER DO YOU HAVE?"
```

```
220 LET X=INT (11*RND)
230 IF X<1 OR X>10 THEN GOTO 220
240 INPUT A
245 LET C=C+1
250 IF X<>A THEN GOTO 300
260 LET D=D+1
270 GOTO 800
300 CLS
310 PRINT "SORRY",,"THAT ONE IS WHITE"
320 PRINT "PLEASE TRY A DIFFERENT PEARL"
330 INPUT B
335 LET C=C+1
340 IF X<>B THEN GOTO 300
350 GOTO 260
800 CLS
820 PRINT "THATS IT",,"YOU HAVE IT"
830 PRINT "THE BLACK PEARL IS NUMBER ";X
840 FOR L=1 TO 5
850 PRINT
860 NEXT L
870 PRINT "WANT TO PLAY AGAIN?"
880 INPUT E$
890 IF E$="YES" THEN GOTO 40
900 IF E$="NO" THEN GOTO 930
910 PRINT "PLEASE ANSWER YES OR NO"
920 GOTO 870
930 LET F=INT ((D/C)*1000)
940 CLS
950 PRINT "OKAY",,"YOUR FINAL SCORE IS ";F
999 STOP
```

Saturn Death

Lights are dimmed to a dull red on the flight deck of the USS Intrepid. Men in your command chatter quietly as their handheld terminal boxes twinkle with vital data. The forward view screen has been showing gigantic Saturn as a tiny ball for days. Now the planet is a giant balloon with the Sun receding from the starboard screens.

Despite the ever-imminent danger in the hostile environment of space, the trip out from Earth Command has been uneventful. Suddenly, the red bullseye flashes on your terminal box. The console under your left elbow brightens and a low buzz emits from its loudspeaker. The ship's main computer sounds an alarm. Life-threatening danger is approaching rapidly. With only seconds to spare, it's you and the computer against the challenge of your life. Death in the frozen void of space lurks nearby.

Program Listing

```
100 CLEAR
110 PRINT "RED ALERT"
130 PRINT "**********"
150 PRINT "EARLY WARNING REPORT",
    "DANGER APPROACHING"
170 RAND
180 GOSUB 1400
200 GOSUB 900
210 PRINT
220 IF W=2 THEN GOTO 400
230 PRINT "ASTEROID CLOSING FAST"
240 GOSUB 900
250 IF W=1 THEN GOTO 310
270 PRINT,,"NO TIME",,"WE ARE HIT"
300 GOTO 1000
310 PRINT "THERE IS TIME",,"BLAST IT"
330 GOSUB 900
340 IF W=1 THEN GOTO 360
350 GOTO 1200
360 CLS
365 PRINT,,"MISSED"
370 GOTO 310
400 PRINT  "ALIEN DEATH PROBE COMING FAST"
410 GOSUB 900
420 IF W=2 THEN GOTO 585
430 GOSUB 1400
460 PRINT,,"TOO LATE",,"HE FIRED TORPEDOS"
480 GOSUB 900
490 IF W=1 THEN GOTO 580
500 PRINT "WE ARE HIT"
520 GOSUB 900
530 IF W=1 THEN GOTO 610
550 PRINT,,"MUCH DAMAGE",,"SHIP EXPLODING"
570 GOTO 1000
```

```
580 CLS
582 PRINT "MISSED"
585 PRINT,,"STANDBY TO FIRE"
590 GOSUB 900
600 GOTO 630
610 PRINT "DAMAGE","WE HAVE POWER"
620 GOTO 585
630 IF W=1 THEN GOTO 690
640 PRINT,,"HIT"
650 GOSUB 900
660 IF W=2 THEN GOTO 710
670 PRINT "DAMAGE BUT HE HAS POWER","WILL
    FIRE AGAIN"
680 GOTO 410
690 PRINT,,"MISSED"
700 GOTO 460
710 GOTO 1200
900 LET W=INT (3*RND)
910 IF W<1 OR W>2 THEN GOTO 900
920 RETURN
1000 GOSUB 1400
1010 CLS
1020 PRINT "THIS IS THE END"
1030 LET A$="TOO BAD"
1040 GOTO 1240
1200 GOSUB 1400
1210 CLS
1220 PRINT "IT IS DESTROYED","ALL ARE SAFE"
1230 LET A$="YOU WIN"
1240 FOR L=1 TO 15
1245 PRINT
1250 NEXT L
1260 PRINT TAB 7;A$
1270 FOR N=1 TO 12
1280 LET X=20-(10*COS (N/6*PI))
1290 LET Y=10+(10*SIN (N/6*PI))
1300 PLOT X,Y
1310 NEXT N
1320 GOTO 1320
1400 FOR L=1 TO 30
1410 NEXT L
1420 RETURN
```

Mystery Clues

Want to create your own murder mystery? Figure out whodunit and write your program backwards from there. When your players make wrong guesses, give them tantalizing clues.

Here's a short program which you can load into your computer in a matter of minutes. Key it in and try it out. It shows how you can add clues to your mysteries.

For simplicity, we assume here the Butler did it. Note that, in line 20, we are making him equal to X$. At line 30, the computer stops to ask you whom you think did it. Your answer is recorded in A$.

In line 40, your answer, lodged in A$, is compared with the computer's already-certain knowledge that the Butler did it. A$ is compared with X$. If they agree, and only if they agree, the computer displays the message, "You guessed it." If you got it right, things will end right there.

If, however, you missed it, program execution (sorry about using that word in a murder mystery!) drops to line 50 where we hear the computer, "Clue: servant." After deftly dropping that clue, the computer moves back to line 10 and runs through the whole affair another time. It will keep running through it until you answer, "Butler," in response to its question in line 30.

Program Listing

```
 10 CLS
 20 LET X$="BUTLER"
 30 PRINT "WHODUNIT ?"
 35 INPUT A$
 40 IF X$=A$ THEN GOTO 100
 45 CLS
 50 PRINT "CLUE: SERVANT"
 60 FOR T=1 TO 100
 70 NEXT T
 80 GOTO 10
100 PRINT "YOU GUESSED IT: BUTLER"
110 PRINT "PRESS ANY KEY TO PLAY AGAIN"
120 IF INKEY$="" THEN GOTO 120
130 GOTO 10
```

Code Groups

Need some secret codes for your latest sensitive mission? How about sets of five random letters for use in Morse code practice?

This program has the computer generate an endless string of random combinations of five letters. It won't stop until you press the BREAK key.

Program Listing

```
 10 RAND
 20 LET A$="ABCDEFGHIJKLMNOPQRSTUVWXYZ"
 30 FOR L=1 TO 5
 40 LET R=INT(100*RND)
 50 IF R<1 OR R>26 THEN GOTO 40
 60 PRINT A$(R);
 70 NEXT L
 80 PRINT
 90 SCROLL
100 GOTO 30
```

Keeping Game Scores

Writing a computer football game? Spelling bee? Cave adventure? No matter what kind of fun you are preparing, you'll need a way to keep score. Here's how.

The wealthy English duke has just been killed in our little mystery game. In lines 10 through 160 of our program listing, below, you play the game, attempting to find out whodunit.

The trick here is in the scorekeeping. Note line 170. If you guessed correctly in response to the query in line 160, at line 170 the computer will give you credit by adding one point to your score stored in memory location R. It does that by comparing your line 160 answer stored in P$ with the correct answer stored in A$.

If you blew it and guessed wrong, the program drops below line 170 to line 180 where it increases your "wrong score" by adding one point to W.

If you got a W+1 at line 190, the program moves back to line 120 and gets you to try again. If you scored a victory and got an R+1 at line 170, the program jumps to line 200 where it stops to display your total right and wrong score. After that, it's back to line 10 for a complete new run-through.

Program Listing

```
 10 CLEAR
 15 LET W=Ø
 20 LET R=Ø
 25 DIM A$(6,7)
 30 DIM P$(7)
 35 LET S=INT(10*RND)
 40 IF S<1 OR S>6 THEN GOTO 30
 60 LET A$(1)="BUTLER"
 70 LET A$(2)="NANNY"
 80 LET A$(3)="MAID"
 90 LET A$(4)="SON"
100 LET A$(5)="COACH"
110 LET A$(6)="WIFE"
120 PRINT "WHO KILLED THE DUKE?"
130 PRINT "WAS IT THE..."
140 FOR L=1 TO 6
145 PRINT A$(L)
150 NEXT L
160 INPUT P$
165 CLS
170 IF A$(S)=P$ THEN GOTO 200
180 PRINT "NOT ";P$
190 LET W=W+1
195 GOTO 120
200 LET R=R+1
210 PRINT P$;" DID IT"
220 PRINT "YOUR SCORE IS..."
230 PRINT R;" RIGHT ";W;" WRONG"
240 PRINT
250 GOTO 10
```

Batting Average

Once you know the number of times you were right and wrong in a game, as in the previous program, it's fun to convert those raw numbers to a batting average. Numbers right and numbers wrong take on a new meaning when changed to a batting average. Folks seem to be able to understand a batting average better.

Our program, starting at line 900, is a partial listing designed to be tacked onto the end of your longer game program to display the final results of play. It will show the number of tries, number of right answers, percentage right, and batting average.

You'll want to test load this program so add lines 10 and 800 as shown. Line 800 will give you the R and T values you'll need going into the program at line 900.

Program Listing

```
 10 CLS
800 LET R=55
810 LET T=100
900 PRINT R;" RIGHT"
910 PRINT "IN ";T;" TRIES"
920 LET D=R/T
930 LET P=100*D
940 LET B=10*P
950 PRINT "THAT IS ";P;" PERCENT"
960 PRINT "BATTING ";B
```

Computer Rating Service

Of course, once you know a player's batting average it still might need some interpretation. In this program, the computer takes a look at a batting average and makes a comment.

Remember that this listing, starting here with line 800, is a partial program to be tacked on the end of a longer game. Note that, at 800, you already have values for G (number right) and E (number of tries). Line 810 converts those raw numbers to a batting average (H).

Then, the computer takes that batting average, stored in H, and compares it with values shown in lines 830 to 870. Depending upon the value of H, a slogan is selected by a jump to one of the lines 880 to 950.

By the way, check line 880. You'll see a special

epitaph for players with batting averages above 900.

Program Listing

```
 10 CLS
700 LET G=55
710 LET E=100
800 PRINT "YOU GOT ";G;" RIGHT IN "
    ;E;" TRIES"
810 LET H=INT(1000*(G/E))
820 PRINT "BATTING ";H
825 PRINT "YOU ARE..."
830 IF H<100 THEN GOTO 910
840 IF H<300 THEN GOTO 920
850 IF H<500 THEN GOTO 930
860 IF H<700 THEN GOTO 940
870 IF H<900 THEN GOTO 950
880 PRINT "QUALIFIED FOR THE HALL OF FAME"
890 GOTO 960
910 PRINT "VERY NEAR THE BOTTOM OF THE
    BARREL"
915 GOTO 960
920 PRINT "POOR"
925 GOTO 960
930 PRINT "AVERAGE"
940 PRINT "TOP NOTCH"
945 GOTO 960
950 PRINT "DAMN NEAR PERFECT"
960 PRINT "YOUR BATTING AVERAGE IS ";H
```

Box Score

To dress up scores during and at the end of a game program, use this method of putting those scores in a box. The box around the score will highlight it and jazz up your video display.

The program here has a temporary substitute for lines 10-40. Normally, you would obtain player's name and score from some larger game program you already have on hand, or are writing. Line 20 gets from you a name and stores it in N$. Line 30 gets a score and stores it in S. If lines 50-230 were a subroutine to a larger program, you would need a RETURN at line 110.

Program Listing

```
 10 DIM A$(10)
 20 PRINT "PLAYERS NAME ?"
 25 INPUT N$
 30 PRINT "PLAYERS SCORE ?"
 35 INPUT S
 40 CLS
 50 LET S$=STR$(S)
 60 LET L=LEN(N$)+LEN(S$)
 70 LET T=L+13
 80 GOSUB 200
 85 PRINT
 90 PRINT "* ";N$;"S SCORE: ";S$;" *"
100 GOSUB 200
110 PRINT
120 PRINT
130 GOTO 20
200 FOR L=1 TO T
210 PRINT "*";
220 NEXT L
230 RETURN
```

Create a Quiz

Quiz data—the computer's storehouse of knowledge—is in lines 100 to 140. Be careful, when you type them in. Spelling and spacing must be exact.

Of course, the quiz can be made much longer. In this example, it could be expanded to encompass all past U.S. presidents.

Program Listing

```
 10 RAND
 20 DIM P$(5,10)
100 LET P$(1)="WASHINGTON"
110 LET P$(2)="ADAMS"
120 LET P$(3)="JEFFERSON"
130 LET P$(4)="MADISON"
140 LET P$(5)="MONROE"
200 LET R=INT(6*RND)
```

```
210 IF R<1 THEN GOTO 200
300 PRINT "WHO WAS PRESIDENT NO. ";R
310 PRINT "OF THE UNITED STATES ?"
320 INPUT A$
330 IF A$="" THEN GOTO 320
340 LET L=LEN A$
350 CLS
360 IF A$=P$(R,1 TO L) THEN GOTO 500
400 PRINT "WRONG"
410 GOTO 510
500 PRINT "CORRECT"
510 PRINT P$(R);" WAS PRESIDENT"
520 PRINT "NUMBER ";R
530 PRINT
540 GOTO 10
```

Killing Time

Sometimes, it may seem to you as if the computer will never get to the result of a job. You understand the processing delay but your non-computer friends may not. They could be confused by the wait and think the computer is "broken."

To keep their minds off the slowness, give them something to look at while the computer is "thinking."

The added, extra lines, numbered 60 and 70, take up more processing time but make for less confusion. Computing may take a bit longer but your fun will be increased.

If you delete lines 60-70 you'll see how the program runs faster but the blank screen is confusing.

Program Listing

```
10 LET X=Ø
20 PRINT "GIVE ME A NUMBER"
30 INPUT N
40 FOR L=1 TO N
50 LET X=X+L
60 CLS
70 PRINT "I AM THINKING"
80 NEXT L
90 CLS
```

```
100 PRINT "I HAVE THE ANSWER"
110 PRINT "THE TOTAL OF ALL NUMBERS"
120 PRINT "FROM 1 TO ";N;" IS ";X
130 PRINT
140 GOTO 10
```

Gee Whiz I: Smart Adder

These six programs, in this section of the book, make up our *Gee Whiz* series. One of the fun ways to use your computer is in wowing your friends. Next time they ask, "But, what can it do?", show them its uncanny abilities at adding, spelling, writing upside down, even cracking jokes. Try these six *Gee Whiz* programs on your friends. You'll love their reactions.

Smart Adder is the first in the series. When your neighbor drops in for a cup of coffee, bring out the computer for a demonstration of its lightning speed.

This program adds long strings of numbers in a flash. You give the computer a number. It starts at 1 and adds all numbers up to and including your number. For instance, if you give it a five, it will add 1 plus 2 plus 3 plus 4 plus 5 and display the result.

Ask your neighbor how fast he or she can add all the numbers to 100. It should take several minutes. While he's working on it, let your computer do it in a split second. Your neighbor's reaction is bound to be, "Gee whiz!"

Program Listing

```
10 PRINT CHR$(147)
20 INPUT"GIVE ME A NUMBER";N
30 IF N<1 THEN 20
40 FOR L=1 TO N:X=X+L:NEXT L
50 PRINT:PRINT"THE TOTAL OF"
60 PRINT"ALL NUMBERS"
70 PRINT"FROM 1 TO";N
80 PRINT"IS";X
90 PRINT:PRINT:PRINT:PRINT
100 CLR:GOTO 20
```

Gee Whiz II: Three-Digit Mystery

Have your neighbor secretly select any three-digit number in which all three digits are the same. Then have him tell the computer only the *sum* of those three digits.

The computer will identify his secret number!

Program Listing

```
10 PRINT CHR$(147)
20 PRINT"SELECT A"
30 PRINT"THREE-DIGIT NUMBER"
40 PRINT"WITH ALL THREE"
50 PRINT"DIGITS THE SAME."
60 PRINT
70 PRINT"ADD THE THREE"
80 PRINT"DIGITS TOGETHER"
90 PRINT
100 PRINT"WHAT IS THE SUM OF"
110 INPUT"THE THREE DIGITS";N
120 IF N<3 OR N>27 THEN 100
130 Q=37*N
140 PRINT:PRINT
150 PRINT"YOUR NUMBER IS";Q
160 FOR L=1 TO 7:PRINT:NEXT L
170 CLR:GOTO 20
```

Gee Whiz III: Up, Down, Back, Forth

"Good golly, what can't it do?", will be the question from your surprised neighbor when you show him this neat trick.

You type in any word. The computer instantly prints it on the video display, both up and down vertically, and backward and forward horizontally. It's great to show how smart your computer is when it comes to spelling!

Program Listing

```
10 HOME
```

```
 20 DIM X$(100)
 30 INPUT"GIVE ME A WORD  ";A$
 40 L=LEN(A$)
 50 FOR J=1 TO L+1
 60 X$(J)=MID$(A$,J,1)
 70 NEXT J
 80 PRINT:PRINT "DOWN:","UP:"
 90 FOR J=1 TO L+1
100 PRINT X$(J),X$(L+1-J)
110 NEXT J
120 PRINT "FORWARD:"
130 PRINT A$
140 FOR J=L+1 TO 1 STEP -1
150 Z$=Z$+MID$(A$,J,1)
160 NEXT J
170 PRINT:PRINT "BACKWARD:"
180 PRINT Z$
190 PRINT:PRINT:CLEAR:GOTO 20
```

Gee Whiz IV: First Alphabet Spotter

There are 26 letters in the alphabet. Each has a number. For instance, number 1 is A. Number 20 is T. This *Gee Whiz* program has the computer ask you for a number from 1 to 26 and then, faster than a jackrabbit, tell you what letter it goes with.

Naturally, you'll know how it works but to your non-computer friends it will seem like the computer is a genius!

Program Listing

```
10 PRINT CHR$(147)
20 PRINT"GIVE ME THE NUMBER"
30 PRINT"OF A LETTER"
40 PRINT"FROM THE ALPHABET"
50 INPUT"FROM 1 TO 26";N
55 IF N<1 OR N>26 THEN 50
60 X=N+64
70 PRINT:PRINT:PRINT
```

```
80 PRINT"LETTER NUMBER";N;"IS ";CHR$(X)
90 FOR L=1 TO 7:PRINT:NEXT L
100 GOTO 20
```

Gee Whiz V: Second Alphabet Spotter

This is a variation on the previous program. This *Gee Whiz* program has the computer ask you for a number from 1 to 26 and then, faster than a jackrabbit, tell you what letter it goes with.

Program Listing

```
10 PRINT CHR$(147)
20 PRINT"GIVE ME THE NUMBER"
30 PRINT"OF A LETTER"
40 PRINT"FROM THE ALPHABET"
50 INPUT"FROM 1 TO 26";N
60 IF N<1 OR N>26 THEN 50
70 FOR L=1 TO N
80 READ A$
90 NEXT L
100 PRINT:PRINT:PRINT
110 PRINT"LETTER NUMBER";N;"IS ";A$
200 FOR L=1 TO 7:PRINT:NEXT L
210 RESTORE
220 GOTO 20
300 DATA A,B,C,D,E,F,G,H,I,J,K,L,M
310 DATA N,O,P,Q,R,S,T,U,V,W,X,Y,Z
```

Gee Whiz VI: Who Is Youngest?

The computer asks for the names and ages of all people in the room. If you are the only person in the room, it will tell you to get someone else to play with you or forget it. After collecting the names and ages, the computer instantly tells which person is youngest.

Program Listing

```
10 HOME
```

```
 20 PRINT"HI":PRINT"I'M YOUR COMPUTER"
 30 INPUT"WHAT'S YOUR NAME ";N$
 40 IF N$="" THEN PRINT"YOU HAVE TO
    HAVE A NAME":GOTO 30
 50 PRINT:PRINT"HI, ";N$
 60 INPUT"HOW MANY PEOPLE ARE IN THE
    ROOM ? ";Q
 70 IF Q<1 OR Q<>INT(Q) THEN 400
 80 IF Q=1 THEN 500
100 PRINT:PRINT"I BET I CAN TELL WHO
    IS YOUNGEST"
110 DIM P$(Q),A(Q)
120 FOR L=1 TO Q
130 IF L>1 THEN 170
140 INPUT"GIVE ME SOMEONE'S NAME "
    ;P$(L)
150 IF P$(L)="" THEN 140
160 IF L=1  THEN 190
170 PRINT:INPUT"GIVE ME ANOTHER NAME "
    ;P$(L)
180 IF P$(L)="" THEN 170
190 PRINT"HOW OLD IS ";P$(L)
200 INPUT A(L)
210 IF L=1 THEN LA=A(L):LN$=P$(L)
    :HA=A(L):HN$=P$(L)
220 IF A(L)<(LA) THEN LA=A(L):LN$=P$(L)
230 IF A(L)>(HA) THEN HA=A(L):HN$=P$(L)
240 NEXT L
250 HOME
260 PRINT N$;", HERE'S WHAT I FIND:"
270 PRINT:PRINT HN$;" IS OLDEST AT ";HA
280 PRINT"AND ";LN$;" IS YOUNGEST AT ";LA
290 PRINT:PRINT"THANKS FOR STOPPING BY,"
300 FOR L=1 TO Q
310 IF L=Q THEN 340
320 PRINT P$(L);","
330 GOTO 350
340 PRINT"AND ";P$(L)
350 NEXT L
360 END
400 PRINT:PRINT"DON'T PLAY AROUND, ";N$
410 PRINT"THERE CAN'T BE ";Q;" PEOPLE"
```

```
420 PRINT"PLEASE TELL THE TRUTH, ";N$
430 PRINT:GOTO 60
500 PRINT:PRINT"WELL, ";N$
510 PRINT"SINCE WE'RE ALL ALONE"
520 PRINT"THERE IS NO ONE TO DEMONSTRATE
    TO"
530 PRINT"SO BRING SOMEONE INTO THIS ROOM"
540 PRINT" OR FORGET IT"
550 PRINT:PRINT"WHICH WILL IT BE"
560 INPUT"GET OR FORGET ? ";G$
570 IF LEFT$(G$,1)="G" THEN PRINT
    :PRINT "OKAY":GOTO 60
580 IF LEFT$(G$,1)="F" THEN PRINT
    :PRINT "OKAY, GOODBYE":END
590 GOTO 560
```

Birthstones

What's your Mother's birthstone? You'd better know! If not, take this little quiz a few times until you get all 12 months memorized.

The computer presents the name of a month. You type in the name of the birthstone (correctly spelled) for that month.

Program Listing

```
 10 CLEAR:CLS
 20 DATA JANUARY,GARNET
 30 DATA FEBRUARY,AMETHYST
 40 DATA MARCH,AQUAMARINE
 50 DATA APRIL,DIAMOND
 60 DATA MAY,EMERALD
 70 DATA JUNE,PEARL
 80 DATA JULY,RUBY
 90 DATA AUGUST,PERIDOT
100 DATA SEPTEMBER,SAPPHIRE
110 DATA OCTOBER,OPAL
120 DATA NOVEMBER,TOPAZ
130 DATA DECEMBER,TURQUOISE
140 PRINT @ 38,STRING$(20,255)
150 PRINT @ 75,"BIRTHSTONES"
```

```
160 PRINT @ 102,STRING$(20,255)
170 PRINT @ 169,"HOW MANY MONTHS"
180 PRINT @ 202,"DO YOU KNOW?"
190 PRINT @ 324,"PRESS ANY KEY TO START"
200 H$=INKEY$
210 IF H$="" THEN 200
220 CLS
230 R=RND(24)
240 IF INT(R/2)=R/2 THEN R=R-1
250 FOR L=1 TO R
260 READ S$
270 NEXT L
280 PRINT:PRINT
290 PRINT "WHAT IS THE BIRTHSTONE"
300 PRINT "FOR THE MONTH OF"
310 PRINT S$
320 READ C$
330 INPUT D$
340 PRINT
350 IF D$=C$ THEN PRINT "*** CORRECT"
    ELSE PRINT "*** WRONG"
360 PRINT "THE BIRTHSTONE FOR ";S$
370 PRINT "IS ";C$
380 RESTORE
390 PRINT:PRINT
400 PRINT"FOR MORE, PRESS M"
410 PRINT"TO STOP, PRESS S"
420 M$=INKEY$
430 IF M$="" THEN 420
440 IF M$="M" THEN CLS:GOTO 220
450 IF M$="S" THEN CLS:GOTO 470
460 GOTO 420
470 PRINT @ 40,STRING$(15,128)
480 PRINT @ 74,"END OF TEST"
490 PRINT @ 104,STRING$(15,243)
500 PRINT @ 170,"THANK YOU !"
510 GOTO 510
999 END
```

Three-Minute Egg Timer

A useful tool, the computer. Set it on the kitchen

counter and it'll even help you make the perfect three-minute egg.

When you have the program typed in, run it. It waits for you to press any key to start the timer. It will sound off at the end of three minutes.

If you make a mistake, press any key to restart the timer at zero.

Program Listing

```
 10 CLEAR:CLS 4
 20 PRINT"PRESS ANY KEY TO START TIMER"
 30 PRINT @ 32,STRING$(32,191)
 40 PRINT @ 64,STRING$(32,175)
 50 PRINT @ 96,STRING$(32,159)
 60 PRINT @ 128,STRING$(32,175)
 70 PRINT @ 160,STRING$(32,255)
 80 PRINT @ 192,STRING$(3,255)
 90 PRINT @ 202,"EGG TIMER"
100 PRINT @ 221,STRING$(3,255)
110 PRINT @ 224,STRING$(32,255)
200 A$=INKEY$
210 IF A$="" THEN 200
220 TIMER=0
230 T=TIMER/3600:DT=3-T
240 TM=INT(DT):TS=INT(60*(DT-TM))
250 PRINT @ 196,TM;" MINUTES"
260 PRINT @ 208,TS
270 PRINT @ 212,"SECONDS"
280 IF TM<1 THEN IF TS<1 THEN SOUND
    150,20:GOTO 320
300 B$=INKEY$
310 IF B$="" THEN 230
320 PRINT @ 196,TM;" MINUTES"
330 PRINT @ 208,TS
340 PRINT @ 212,"SECONDS"
350 PRINT @ 221,STRING$(3,255)
360 PRINT @ 224,STRING$(32,255)
400 C$=INKEY$
410 IF C$="" THEN 400 ELSE 10
```

Membership List

The chore in a membership list is to keep everybody's name separate from everybody else's. In this program, we have set the size of the membership list at 50. You may change that.

The computer asks for information on each member in a familiar pattern: name, address, town, state and zip code, in that order. It takes all information and sorts the list into numerical order by zip code.

Program Listing

```
10 CLS:CLEAR
20 DIM M$(50)
30 FOR L=1 TO 50
40 INPUT"NAME";NM$
50 IF NM$="" THEN 320
60 LN=LEN(NM$)
70 MB=15-LN
80 IF MB<Ø THEN PRINT"NAME TOO LONG"
   :PRINT"PLEASE SHORTEN":NM$="":GOTO 40
90 IF LEN(NM$)<15 THEN NM$=NM$+STRING$
   (MB," ")
100 INPUT"STREET ADDRESS";SA$
110 LA=LEN(SA$)
120 MC=15-LA
130 IF MC<Ø THEN PRINT"STREET ADDRESS
    TOO LONG":PRINT"PLEASE SHORTEN"
    :SA$="":GOTO 100
140 IF LEN(SA$)<15 THEN SA$=SA$+
    STRING$(MC," ")
150 INPUT"TOWN";TW$
160 LT=LEN(TW$)
170 MD=15-LT
180 IF MD<Ø THEN PRINT"TOWN TOO LONG"
    :PRINT"PLEASE SHORTEN":TW$=""
    :GOTO 150
190 IF LEN(TW$)<15 THEN TW$=TW$+
    STRING$(MD," ")
200 INPUT"STATE";ST$
210 LS=LEN(ST$)
```

```
220 ME=2-LS
230 IF ME<Ø THEN PRINT"STATE TOO LONG"
    :PRINT"PLEASE SHORTEN":ST$="":GOTO 200
240 IF LEN(ST$)<2 THEN ST$=ST$+
    STRING$(ME," ")
250 INPUT"ZIP CODE";ZC$
260 LZ=LEN(ZC$)
270 MF=5-LZ
280 IF MF<Ø THEN PRINT"ZIP CODE TOO LONG"
    :PRINT"PLEASE SHORTEN":ZC$=""
    :GOTO 250
290 IF LEN(ZC$)<5 THEN ZC$=ZC$+
    STRING$(MF," ")
300 M$(L)=ZC$+" "+NM$+" "+SA$+" "
    +TW$+" "+ST$
310 NEXT L
320 CLS
330 PRINT"SORTING"
340 T=Ø
350 FOR L=1 TO 49
360 IF M$(L)=M$(L+1) THEN 380
370 E$=M$(L):M$(L)=M$(L+1):M$(L+1)=E$
    :T=1
380 NEXT L
390 IF T=1 THEN 340
400 FOR L=1 TO 50
410 IF M$(L)<>"" THEN PRINT MID$(M$(L)
    ,7,15):PRINT MID$(M$(L),23,15)
    :PRINT MID$(M$(L),39,15)
    :PRINT RIGHT$(M$(L),2),LEFT$
    (M$(L),5)
420 PRINT" "
430 NEXT L
440 Q$=INKEY$
450 IF Q$=""THEN 440
460 GOTO 10
```

Photography
Exposure with Filters

Serious photographers, amateurs and pros, carry an assortment of lens filters in their bags. Lens filters absorb light so cameramen must make exposure corrections when using filters.

The *filter factor* is used in making that correction. The photographer sets the exposure meter for the speed of the film in use without a filter. Then, he modifies the camera settings indicated by the meter.

For example, suppose the filter factor is 2 and the camera setting indicated by the light meter is 1/125 second at f/11. The photographer opens the lens by one full f/stop to f/8.

This computer program displays the proper f/stop correction when a filter factor is known, or the proper filter factor for a particular f/stop correction.

Program Listing

```
 10 "F" CLEAR
 20 PAUSE"WANT FILTER FACTOR OR..."
 30 PAUSE"F/STOP CORRECTION ?"
 40 BEEP 1:INPUT"FILT OR STOP ?",Z$
 50 IF Z$="FILT" THEN 100
 60 IF Z$="STOP" THEN 300
 70 GOTO 40
100 BEEP 1:INPUT"TO CORRECT F/STOP BY +";Y$
    :W=Ø
110 IF Y$="1/3" LET W=1.2
120 IF Y$="2/3" LET W=1.5
130 IF Y$="1" LET W=2
140 IF Y$=1 1/3" LET W=2.5
150 IF Y$="1 2/3" LET W=3
160 IF Y$="2" LET W=4
170 IF Y$="2 1/3" LET W=5
180 IF Y$="2 2/3" LET W=6
190 IF Y$="3" LET W=8
200 IF Y$="3 1/3" LET W=10
210 IF Y$="3 2/3" LET W=12
220 IF Y$="4" LET W=16
230 PRINT "FILTER FACTOR = ";W:GOTO 100
300 BEEP 1:INPUT "FILTER FACTOR = ",X
    :V$="?"
310 IF X=1.2 LET V$="1/3"
320 IF X=1.5 LET V$="2/3"
330 IF X=2 LET V$="1"
```

```
340 IF X=2.5 LET V$="1 1/3"
350 IF X=3 LET V$="1 2/3"
360 IF X=4 LET V$="2"
370 IF X=5 LET V$="2 1/3"
380 IF X=6 LET V$="2 2/3"
390 IF X=8 LET V$="3"
400 IF X=10 LET V$="3 1/3"
410 IF X=12 LET V$="3 2/3"
420 IF X=16 LET V$="4"
430 PRINT "CORRECT F/STOP BY +";V$
440 GOTO 300
```

Photography: Close Ups

For copying and other close-up work with your camera, you extend the camera lens by using bellows or extension tubes. In doing that, you must allow for an effective increase in the normal *f*/number or your picture will be underexposed.

You make such an exposure compensation whenever the subject distance is less than eight times the focal length of your lens.

This program provides a convenient means of determining the effective *f*/number. For example, if the focal length of your camera is 50mm and the lens-to-film distance (focal length plus extension from infinity position) is 100mm, and the normal *f*/stop would be 22, the corrected stop would be *f/11*.

Or, if you are using a 25mm lens, with 50mm lens-to-film distance, a normal *f*/stop of 8 should be corrected to *f/4*. Be sure to keep both focal length and distance in either mm or inches. Don't mix apples and oranges.

Program Listing

```
10 CLS:CLEAR
20 FOR L=Ø TO 200
30 POKE 1024+L,246
40 NEXT L
50 FOR L=1 TO 13
60 DATA 32,16,8,15,20,15,7,18,1,
   16,8,25,32
```

```
 70 READ D
 80 POKE 1224+L,D
 90 NEXT L
100 FOR L=214 TO 511
110 POKE 1024+L,246
120 NEXT L
130 FOR T=1 TO 350:NEXT T
200 CLS:SOUND 200,1
210 PRINT @ 40,"CLOSE UPS"
220 PRINT"CORRECTION FOR LENS EXTENSION"
230 PRINT:PRINT
240 LINE INPUT"NORMAL F/NUMBER: ";F$
250 F=VAL(F$)
260 LINE INPUT"LENS-TO-FILM DISTANCE (MM)
    : ";D$
270 D=VAL(D$):IF D=Ø THEN 260
280 LINE INPUT"LENS FOCAL LENGTH (MM)
    : ";L$
290 L=VAL(L$)
300 N=F*L/D
310 CLS:SOUND 200,1:PRINT:PRINT
320 NN$=STR$(N):L=LEN(NN$)
    :N$=RIGHT$(NN$,L-1)
330 PRINT @ 163,"EFFECTIVE F/NUMBER IS
    F/";N$
400 PRINT @ 355,"FOR ANOTHER, PRESS ANY
    KEY"
410 A$=INKEY$
420 IF A$="" THEN 410 ELSE 200
```

Photography: Flash Exposure

Use your computer to help take better pictures!

The most important factor in pictures shot with flash is the distance from your flash to the subject. Subjects which are close to you will receive a lot of light while subjects farther away will receive less light.

Check your data sheet for the film you are using. Look for the film guide number. Next, make an estimate of the distance in feet from the flash to your subject.

This program determines the proper *f*/stop setting for

your camera. By the way, if the computer tells you to use an *f*/stop setting between two *f*/numbers available on your camera, set your lens opening at the nearest *f*/number or halfway between the two, whichever is closest.

For example, suppose your film has a guide number of 80 and you estimate the flash-to-subject distance at 10 feet. Use *f/8* on your lens.

Program Listing

```
 10 CLS:SOUND 200,1
 20 PRINT @ 102,STRING$(19,255)
 30 PRINT @ 138,"PHOTOGRAPHY"
 40 PRINT @ 166,STRING$(19,255)
 50 PRINT @ 325,"PRESS ANY KEY TO START"
 60 A$=INKEY$
 70 IF A$="" THEN 60
100 CLS:SOUND 200,1
110 PRINT @ 102,STRING$(18,175)
120 PRINT @ 136,"FLASH EXPOSURE"
130 PRINT @ 166,STRING$(18,175)
140 PRINT @ 227,"WHAT IS FILM GUIDE NUMBER ?"
150 LINE INPUT G$:G=VAL(G$)
160 PRINT @ 291,"FLASH-TO-SUBJECT DISTANCE ?"
170 LINE INPUT D$:D=VAL(D$)
180 F=G/D
200 CLS:SOUND 200,1
210 PRINT @ 102,"FILM GUIDE NUMBER:";G
220 PRINT @ 134,"DISTANCE:";D;"FEET"
230 PRINT @ 198,"SHOOT AT F/";F
240 PRINT @ 356,"FOR MORE PRESS ANY KEY"
250 A$=INKEY$
260 IF A$="" THEN 250
270 GOTO 100
```

90-Day Calendar

This program formats and prints out on paper a 90-Day Calendar. It creates a neat, standard calendar design which you'll love to run off upon request from family, friends, co-workers.

Key in your choice of months. Update every three

months or every month if you like.

To change month names in the printout, merely correct lines 100, 200 and 300. Then quickly key in the new day dates in lines 130-180, 230-270, and 330-370.

Naturally, many more months could be added to the program. In fact, it could become a 180-Day calendar or a One-Year Calendar, or whatever you would like to make it.

Program Listing

```
 10 "C" CLEAR
100 PRINT "OCTOBER  1983
110 PRINT "**************"
120 PRINT " S M T W T F S"
130 PRINT "             1"
140 PRINT " 2 3 4 5 6 7 8"
150 PRINT " 9101112131415"
160 PRINT "16171819202122"
170 PRINT "23242526272829"
180 PRINT "3031"
190 PRINT "**************"
195 PRINT " "
200 PRINT "NOVEMBER 1983"
210 PRINT "**************"
220 PRINT " S M T W T F S"
230 PRINT "       1 2 3 4 5"
240 PRINT " 6 7 8 9101112"
250 PRINT "13141516171819"
260 PRINT "20212223242526"
270 PRINT "27282930"
280 PRINT "**************"
290 PRINT " "
300 PRINT "DECEMBER 1983"
310 PRINT "**************"
320 PRINT " S M T W T F S"
330 PRINT "         1 2 3"
340 PRINT " 4 5 6 7 8 910"
350 PRINT "11121314151617"
360 PRINT "18192021222324"
370 PRINT "25262728293031"
380 PRINT "**************"
390 PRINT " "
400 END
```

Alphabet Code

It not only is a lot of fun, but sometimes very useful to create a secret code. An easy way to create a code on your computer is to replace each of the 26 letters of the alphabet with a number. Then, you write secret messages using the code numbers in place of alphabet letters. To decipher messages in the same code, replace numbers with appropriate letters from a chart of this code.

Program Listing

```
10 "A" FOR L=1 TO 26
20 N=N+1:A=NN:Y=(997*X+A)/199:X=Y-INT Y
   :X=X*E 2
30 PRINT USING "####";L;X
40 NEXT L
50 END
```

High/Low Bowling Score

Suppose you bowl with a group of friends, each with a different score or set of scores? This program accepts their scores and sorts out the highest and the lowest bowling scores.

Here's how it works: at line 20 the program is dimensioned to hold data on 10 persons. Lines 30 to 70 take in the info on each person.

Naturally, this kind of sorting could be applied to any game with ranges of scores among different players.

Program Listing

```
 10 CLS
 20 DIM M(10)
 30 FOR L=1 TO 10
 40 PRINT "SCORE: ";
 50 INPUT M(L)
 60 PRINT M(L)
 70 NEXT L
 80 PRINT
 90 PRINT "SORTING"
100 LET T=Ø
```

```
110 FOR L=1 TO 9
120 IF M(L)<=M(L+1) THEN GOTO 170
130 LET E=M(L)
140 LET M(L)=M(L+1)
150 LET M(L+1)=E
160 LET T=1
170 NEXT L
180 IF T=1 THEN GOTO 100
190 CLS
200 PRINT "SCORES IN ORDER:"
210 FOR L=1 TO 10
220 PRINT M(L)
230 NEXT L
```

60-Second Timer

A one-minute timer can be very handy for fun-n-games. This easy-to-use clock "ticks" as it counts off seconds up to 60. When it reaches 60 seconds, it rings an alarm.

The number of seconds counted can be changed by changing the number 60 in line 20.

The clock can be calibrated by changing the number 750 in line 50. Line 50 is a time-delay loop set for approximately one second.

Lines 70-90 provide a rapid burst of five beeps when the clock reaches 60 seconds. To change the length of this alarm, change the number 70 in line 5.

Program Listing

```
10 HOME
20 FOR T=1 TO 60
30 PRINT CHR$(7)
40 PRINT T;" SECONDS"
50 FOR L=1 TO 750:NEXT L
60 NEXT T
70 FOR E=1 TO 5
80 PRINT CHR$(7)
90 NEXT E
```

News Ticker

It's Times Square all over again! This program simulates the crawling message of a news wire.

First the computer will ask for your message. Then it will display that message endlessly (until you press the RESET key).

To speed up, or slow down, the crawl, increase or decrease the number 200 in line 90.

For a test, in answer to the computer's query, "What is the news?", try typing in: The mayor of Smithville today announced he will retire next December.

Program Listing

```
10 HOME
20 PRINT"WHAT IS THE NEWS ?"
30 INPUT N$
40 HOME
50 L=LEN(N$)
60 FOR Y=1 TO L
70 B$=B$+MID$(N$,Y,1)
80 PRINT B$
90 FOR T=1 TO 200:NEXT T
100 HOME
110 NEXT Y
120 B$="":GOTO 80
```

Event Timer

The computer asks how many minutes you want for the event you are timing, and then it sounds a bell when the time has passed.

You can calibrate the clock by changing the value of SP in line 10. A larger number will slow down the clock. A smaller value for SP will speed up the clock. As you can see we have started with an SP value of 16.

If you want to time an event of less than one minute, use a decimal. For instance, when you want to time a 30-second event, respond to the computer's inquiry with .5 or for 45 seconds key in .75. Use .17 for 10 seconds; .25 for 15 seconds.

Program Listing

```
 10 HOME:SP=16
 20 PRINT"EVENT TIMER":PRINT
 30 PRINT"HOW MANY MINUTES"
 40 INPUT"TO THE END OF THE EVENT ";LT
 50 PRINT:PRINT"PRESS ANY KEY"
 60 PRINT"TO START TIMING"
 70 GET ST$
100 HOME
110 C=C+1
120 IF C>(SP*LT*60) THEN 300
130 MN=INT(C/SP/60)
140 SC=INT((C/SP)-(60*MN))
150 PRINT MN;" MINUTES",SC;" SECONDS"
160 GOTO 110
300 HOME:PRINT CHR$(7)
310 PRINT"TIME IS UP"
320 PRINT LT;" MINUTES HAVE PASSED"
330 PRINT:PRINT"TO TIME AGAIN, PRESS
    ANY KEY"
340 CLEAR:GET TA$
350 GOTO 10
```

Day Of The Year

This program reports the number of the day of the year for any day you enter.

Program Listing

```
10 CLEAR
20 GOSUB 500
40 PRINT @ 134,"SELECT ONE:"
50 PRINT @ 168,"TODAY'S DATE (PRESS T)"
60 PRINT @ 208,"OTHER DATE   (PRESS X)"
70 KY$=INKEY$
80 IF KY$="" THEN 70
90 IF KY$="T" THEN 200
100 IF KY$="X" THEN 400
110 PRINT @ 250,"PRESS ONLY T OR X"
120 GOTO 40
200 D$=DATE$
```

```
210 J=VAL(LEFT$(D$,2))
220 K=VAL(MID$(D$,4,2))
230 IF KY$="T" THEN I=VAL("19"+(RIGHT$
    (D$,2)))
235 IF KY$="X" THEN I=VAL(RIGHT$(D$,4))
240 N=INT(3055*(J+2)/100)-91
250 L=0
260 IF I=4*INT(I/4) THEN L=1
270 IF I=100*INT(I/100) THEN L=0
280 IF I=400*INT(I/400) THEN L=1
290 IF J>2 THEN N=N-2+L
300 N=N+K
310 GOTO 600
400 GOSUB 500
410 PRINT @ 126,"TYPE IN DATE AS
    MM/DD/YYYY"
420 PRINT @ 172," ";
430 INPUT D$
440 GOTO 210
500 CLS
510 PRINT @ 51,CHR$(27)+"p";"DAY OF THE
    YEAR";CHR$(27)+"q"
520 LINE(65,7)-(155,15),1,B
530 RETURN
600 GOSUB 500
610 PRINT @ 129,"DAY";K;"OF MONTH";J
620 PRINT @ 161,"IS DAY NUMBER";N
    ;"IN THE YEAR";I
```

Code Breaker

This fancy encoding and decoding program allows you to write secret messages in code and decode secret messages written in the same code. The use of a powerful *code key* format means only the largest computers in the world would have a chance at cracking your code and then only with great difficulty. For all intents and purposes, the code generated by this program is unbreakable.

Next, type in a secret number as a *code key* which only you, and others you tell, will know. The person using this program to decipher your message must have access to the same *code key* number, one way or another.

After you have typed in the *code key* number, the computer will ask you to type in a one-line message.

When the message has been completely entered, press ENTER and the encoded (or decoded) message will be displayed instantly on the screen. If you have encoded a new message, copy it off on paper and send it to a friend. If he has the same software in his computer and knowledge of the *code key* he will be able to type it into his computer and see it instantly decoded.

The same sequence of events happens while decoding as during encoding. Just type in the message to be decoded, press ENTER, and you get an instant translation.

The letter transpositions used in encoding rely on random numbers generated by the computer so the *code key* which controls the random-number generator is vital to being able to decipher someone else's message. It would be extremely difficult, if not impossible, to unravel the letter transpositions without the *code key.*

Program Listing

```
100 CLS:CLEAR
110 DIM M$(255)
120 GOSUB 700
130 PRINT @ 122,"WILL YOU ENCODE OR
    DECODE A MESSAGE?"
140 PRINT @ 211,"TO ENCODE, PRESS E"
150 PRINT @ 251,"TO DECODE, PRESS D"
160 KY$=INKEY$
170 IF KY$="" THEN 160
180 IF KY$="E" OR KY$="D" THEN 200
190 GOTO 160
200 CLS
210 GOSUB 700
220 IF KY$="E" THEN F$="EN"
230 IF KY$="D" THEN F$="DE"
240 PRINT @ 125," ";
250 PRINT"WHAT IS THE ";F$;"CODING KEY";
260 INPUT S
270 FOR L=1 TO S:N=INT(60*RND(1)):NEXT L
280 CLS
300 GOSUB 700
310 PRINT @ 127,"TYPE IN A ONE LINE
    MESSAGE"
```

```
320 PRINT
325 Q=1
330 K$=""
340 K$=INKEY$
350 IF K$="" THEN 340
360 IF ASC(K$)=13 THEN 410
370 PRINT K$;
380 M$(Q)=STR$(ASC(K$))
390 Q=Q+1
400 GOTO 340
410 IF KY$="E" THEN 600
500 PRINT @ 239," ";
505 FOR L=1 TO Q-1
510 Z=VAL(M$(L))-INT(60*RND(1))
520 IF Z<32 THEN Z=Z+59
530 PRINT CHR$(Z);
540 NEXT L
550 IF INKEY$="" THEN 550
560 GOTO 100
600 PRINT @ 239," ";
605 FOR L=1 TO Q-1
610 Z=VAL(M$(L))+INT(60*RND(1))
620 IF Z>90 THEN Z=Z-59
630 PRINT CHR$(Z);
640 NEXT L
650 GOTO 550
700 LINE (80,4)-(158,18),1,B
710 LINE (81,5)-(157,17),1,B
720 PRINT @ 54,"CODE BREAKER"
730 PRINT
740 RETURN
```

Jogger Logger

What a handy way to keep a record of your runs!

The program allows you to add new run records, review old records, erase all records. When you have completed a day's run, simply turn on the computer, select this program, and press A for ADD NEW RUN RECORD at the first menu. The computer will ask you for the run date.

Next the computer will ask for the distance you ran.

When the computer asks for the length of your run time, reply in minutes.

If you wish to review your old records, select that option by pressing the R key at the program's main menu. This will result in a display of your old records, one at a time. Press any key on the keyboard to call up the next record.

If you want to erase your entire log, select that option by pressing E at the main menu.

When you are through using the program, select Q to quit, at the main menu. The run will stop.

Program Listing

```
10 CLS:CLEAR:RV$=CHR$(27)+"p"
   :NV$=CHR$(27)+"q"
100 PRINT @ 54,RV$;"JOGGER LOGGER";NV$
110 LINE(83,7)-(161,15),1,B
120 PRINT @ 125,"ADD NEW RUN RECORD"
    ;SPACE$(5);"PRESS A"
130 PRINT @ 165,"REVIEW OLD RECORDS"
    ;SPACE$(5);"PRESS R"
140 PRINT @ 205,"ERASE ALL RECORDS"
    ;SPACE$(6);"PRESS E"
150 PRINT @ 245,"QUIT";SPACE$(19)
    ;"PRESS Q"
160 BEEP
200 K$=INKEY$
210 IF K$="" THEN 200
220 BEEP
230 IF K$="A" THEN 400
240 IF K$="R" THEN 600
250 IF K$="E" THEN 800
260 IF K$="Q" THEN 1100
270 LINE(83,7)-(161,15),2,B
280 PRINT @ 50,"PRESS ONLY A, R OR Q"
290 GOTO 200
400 CLS
410 PRINT @ 51,RV$;"ADD NEW RUN RECORD"
    ;NV$
420 LINE(65,7)-(173,15),1,B
430 PRINT @ 120,"RUN DATE (MM/DD/YY)";
    :INPUT DT$
440 IF LEN(DT$)<>8 THEN PRINT"PLEASE
    USE MM/DD/YY FORMAT":PRINT @ 141
    ,SPACE$(19):GOTO 430
```

```
445 BEEP
450 PRINT @ 160,"DISTANCE RUN (UP TO
    999 MILES)";:INPUT DS$
455 BEEP
460 PRINT @ 200,"RUN TIME (IN MINUTES)";
    :INPUT TM$
465 BEEP
470 RF$=DT$+SPACE$(4)+DS$+SPACE$(8)+TM$
500 OPEN "RAM:RUNS.DO" FOR APPEND AS 1
510 PRINT#1,RF$
520 CLOSE#1
530 GOTO 10
600 CLS
610 PRINT @ 51,RV$;"REVIEW OLD RECORDS"
    ;NV$
620 LINE(65,7)-(173,15),1,B
700 ON ERROR GOTO 795
705 OPEN "RAM:RUNS.DO" FOR INPUT AS 1
710 PRINT @ 120,"DATE";SPACE$(8);"MILES"
    ;SPACE$(4);"MINUTES"
720 INPUT#1,RF$
730 PRINT @ 160,RF$
750 PRINT @ 240,"PRESS ANY KEY TO
    CONTINUE"
760 IF INKEY$="" THEN 760
765 BEEP
770 PRINT @ 160,SPACE$(39)
775 IF EOF(1) THEN 785
780 GOTO 710
785 CLOSE#1:CLS
790 PRINT @ 120,"THERE ARE NO MORE
    RECORDS":FOR T=1 TO 1000:NEXT T
    :GOTO 10
795 PRINT @ 120,"THERE ARE NO OLD
    RECORDS":FOR T=1 TO 1500:NEXT T
    :GOTO 10
800 CLS
810 FOR L=1 TO 4
815 LINE(95,7)-(137,15),1,B
820 PRINT @ 56,RV$;"WARNING"
825 FOR T=1 TO 250:NEXT T
830 IF L<4 THEN CLS
```

```
835 FOR T=1 TO 50:NEXT T
840 BEEP
845 NEXT L
850 PRINT NV$
860 PRINT @ 123,"YOU WILL ERASE ALL OF
    YOUR RECORDS"
870 PRINT @ 205,"TO ERASE ALL RECORDS
    PRESS E"
880 PRINT @ 245,"TO PREVENT ERASING
    PRESS P"
900 K$=INKEY$
910 IF K$="" THEN 900
915 BEEP
920 IF K$="E" THEN 1000
930 IF K$="P" THEN 10
940 GOTO 900
1000 CLS
1010 LINE(95,7)-(137,15),1,B
1020 PRINT @ 56,RV$;"WARNING"
1030 PRINT NV$
1040 PRINT @ 120,"ARE YOU SURE YOU WANT
     TO ERASE"
1050 INPUT"YES OR NO ";YN$
1055 BEEP
1060 ON ERROR GOTO 1090
1065 IF YN$="YES" THEN KILL "RUNS.DO"
     :GOTO 10
1070 IF YN$="NO" THEN 10
1080 GOTO 1050
1090 CLS:PRINT @ 120,"THERE WERE NO
     RECORDS TO ERASE":FOR T=1 TO 1000
     :NEXT T:GOTO 10
1100 CLS
1110 PRINT @ 55,"END OF RUN"
```

Name 'N Note List

Here's a handy way to keep track of friends' phone numbers or employees' payroll numbers or family charge-account numbers. In fact, this list keeper will be useful anywhere you have a list of pairs of data to be stored together.

The program allows you to type in names and attach

notes to those names. The names, with their attached notes, may be typed in, in any random order. The program automatically arranges the names, with their attached notes, in alphabetical order.

Program Listing

```
10 CLS:CLEAR
15 DIM M$(50):DIM D$(50):DIM Q$(50)
20 FOR L=1 TO 50
25 PRINT @ 43,"TYPE NAME";L;
30 LINE(16,6)-(223,16),1,B
35 INPUT Q$(L)
50 IF Q$(L)="" THEN 90
55 LINE(16,6)-(223,16),2,B
60 PRINT @ 83,"TYPE NOTE";L;
65 LINE(16,6)-(223,24),1,B
70 INPUT D$(L)
75 M$(L)=Q$(L)+"  "+D$(L)
80 CLS
85 NEXT L
90 CLS
95 LINE(75,22)-(145,32),1,B
100 LINE(74,21)-(146,33),1,B
105 PRINT @ 133,"SORTING NOW"
110 T=0
200 FOR L=1 TO 49
210 IF M$(L)<=M$(L+1) THEN 260
220 E$=M$(L)
230 M$(L)=M$(L+1)
240 M$(L+1)=E$
250 T=1
260 NEXT L
270 IF T=1 THEN 110
280 CLS
290 BEEP
300 CLS:PRINT
310 PRINT"WHICH WAY DO YOU WANT THE
    LIST PRINTED?"
315 PRINT
320 PRINT"ON THE DISPLAY PANEL
    (PRESS L)"
330 PRINT"ON PAPER BY THE PRINTER
```

```
    (PRESS P)"
340 K$=INKEY$
350 IF K$="" THEN 340
360 IF K$="L" THEN CLS:GOTO 400
370 IF K$="P" THEN 600
380 PRINT"PRESS ONLY L OR P"
390 GOTO 340
400 FOR L=1 TO 50
410 IF M$(L)<>"" THEN PRINT M$(L):P=P+1
420 IF P<6 THEN 460
430 PRINT"      >>>PRESS ANY KEY TO READ
    MORE<<<"
440 IF INKEY$="" THEN 440
450 P=0
460 NEXT L
470 P=0
500 PRINT "LIST END:PRESS M FOR MORE OR
    Q TO QUIT"
510 K$=INKEY$
520 IF K$="" THEN 510
530 IF K$="M" THEN 300
540 IF K$="Q" THEN END
550 GOTO 500
600 CLS
610 PRINT @ 88,"PLEASE CONNECT A PRINTER"
620 LINE(46,14)-(192,24),1,B
630 PRINT @ 171,"PRESS D WHEN DONE"
640 KZ$=INKEY$
650 IF KZ$<>"D" THEN 640
660 FOR L=1 TO 50
670 IF M$(L)<>"" THEN LPRINT M$(L)
680 NEXT L
690 CLS:PRINT:GOTO 500
```

Great Circle Navigation

If you know the latitudes and longitudes of two points on Earth, the computer can find the shortest distance between those points and the azimuth from north toward east at the starting point.

Distance between the points is expressed in nautical miles. North latitude and east longitude are expressed as positive numbers while south latitude and west longitude are negative numbers. You cannot use 90° north (North Pole) or 90° south (South Pole). Accuracy is less if the distance is under one nautical mile. N1 and E1 are start-points while N2 and E2 are endpoints.

Program Listing

```
 10 WAIT 120
 20 BEEP 1,1
 30 PRINT "*GREAT CIRCLE NAVIGATION*"
 40 INPUT "LATITUDE STARTPOINT",N1
 50 INPUT "LONGITUDE STARTPOINT",E1
 60 INPUT "LATITUDE ENDPOINT",N2
 70 INPUT "LONGITUDE ENDPOINT",E2
 80 PRINT "**PLEASE STAND BY**"
 90 A=N1
100 GOSUB 300
110 N1=A
120 A=N2
130 GOSUB 300
140 N2=A
150 A=E1
160 GOSUB 300
170 E1=A
180 A=E2
190 GOSUB 300
200 E2=A
210 D=60*ACS (SIN N1*SIN N2+COS N1*COS
    N2*COS(E2-E1))
220 S=ACS ((SIN N2-SIN N1*COS (D/60))
    /SIN (D/60)/COS N1)
230 IF SIN (E2-E1)<ØTHEN LET S=360-S
240 BEEP 1,1
250 LPRINT "DISTANCE: ";D
260 LPRINT "START AZIMUTH:";DMS S
270 IF INKEY$ ="" THEN 270
280 CLEAR
290 GOTO 40
300 C=SGN A
310 A=ABS A
320 B=(A-INT A)*100
330 A=INT A+INT B/60+(B-INT B)/36
340 A=A*C
350 RETURN
```

Stopwatch

Now you can leave that chrome-plated stopwatch at home next time you travel to your favorite auto or horse race.

When you RUN the program, the stopwatch will start counting seconds.

You can adjust the accuracy of the seconds count by changing the wait number in line 110. We show it set at 10. To slow down the timer, increase that number. To speed up the clock, decrease the number.

Program Listing

```
 10 PRINT "NUMBER OF SECONDS"
 20 PRINT "TO BE COUNTED DOWN:
 30 INPUT S
 40 PRINT S
 50 PRINT
 60 PRINT "PRESS ANY KEY"
 70 PRINT "TO START TIMING"
 80 IF INKEY$="" THEN GOTO 80
 90 CLS
100 FOR L=S TO 1 STEP -1
110 PAUSE 10
120 PRINT L
130 NEXT L
140 CLS
150 PRINT "TIME IS UP"
160 PRINT S;" SECONDS HAVE ELAPSED"
170 PRINT
180 PRINT
190 GOTO 10
```

Password to Run

A user must enter the right password or the rest of the program won't run.

Program Listing

```
10 INPUT "WHAT IS PASSWORD?",PS$
20 IF PS$<>"GREEN"THEN END
30 PRINT "PROGRAM RUNS"
```

Three-Try Password

This variation gives you three cracks at it. In fact, you can change the number of tries allowed by changing the number 3 in the FOR/NEXT loop statement in line 10.

Program Listing

```
10 FOR L=1 TO 3
20 INPUT "WHAT IS PASSWORD?",PA$
30 IF PA$="RADIO" THEN GOTO 60
40 NEXT L
50 END
60 PRINT "PROGRAM RUNS"
```

Memory Search

Here's a quick way to study the contents of the RAM memory inside your computer.

Key in this simple program, using the powerful PEEK instruction, and your computer will reveal the contents of its memory.

Program Listing

```
10 INPUT "START NUMBER: ";N
20 C=PEEK N
30 WAIT 5
40 PRINT CHR$ C;
50 N=N+1
60 GOTO 20
```

Super Number Reverser

Enter any number and find it reversed on the display!

If you want only to display the reversed number, delete B = VAL(B$) from line 70. Or keep it in if you want to use the reversed number in math.

Program Listing

```
10 CLEAR:INPUT "GIVE ME A NUMBER",N$
```

```
 20 IF N$="" THEN GOTO 10
 30 L=LEN (N$)
 40 FOR Y=L TO 1 STEP -1
 50 B$=B$+MID$ (N$,Y,1)
 60 NEXT Y
 70 B=VAL (B$):BEEP 1
 80 PAUSE "REVERSE D:";B
 90 IF INKEY$="" THEN GOTO 80
100 CLEAR:BEEP 1:GOTO 10
```

Simulated RPN Calculator

The computer can be made to act very much like a calculator with Reverse Polish Notation (RPN).

The only difference here is you must hit the ENTER key after the math operator.

The time delay of display is adjustable at line 1010. If you need to see the total at any time, press R and the ENTER key. Total will be recalled with no math operation done.

To start a run , key in a number and press ENTER. For the remainder of the run, key in a number followed immediately by a math operator symbol. Your choices are limited to + , -, / and *. Don't use other keys except R and BREAK. BREAK ends the run.

You must hit the ENTER key to input your number and math operator, which is how it differs from true RPN.

Program Listing

```
1000 CLS:CLEAR
1010 BEEP 1,1:WAIT 120: PRINT T
1020 INPUT N$
1030 IF N$="R" PRINT T
1040 L=LEN N$
1050 IF ASC (RIGHT$ (N$,1))=42 GOTO 1100
1060 IF ASC (RIGHT$ (N$,1))=43 GOTO 1200
1070 IF ASC (RIGHT$ (N$,1))=45 GOTO 1300
1080 IF ASC (RIGHT$ (N$,1))=47 GOTO 1400
1090 T=T+VAL N$
1095 GOTO 1010
1100 S=VAL (LEFT$ (N$,L-1))
```

```
1110 T=T*S
1120 GOTO 1010
1200 S=VAL (LEFT$ (N$,L-1))
1210 T=T+S
1220 GOTO 1010
1300 S=VAL (LEFT$ (N$,L-1))
1310 T=T-S
1320 GOTO 1010
1400 S=VAL (LEFT$ (N$,L-1))
1410 T=T/S
1420 GOTO 1010
```

Simulated Algebraic Calculator

Similar to the RPN simulator but change all LEFT$ to RIGHT$ and all RIGHT$ to LEFT$ in lines 150 to 180 and lines 1100, 1200, 1300 and 1400.

Now, to enter numbers, put math operator before the number in standard algebraic-entry format. As an option you can choose to eliminate the plus sign math operator.

Program Listing

```
1000 CLS:CLEAR
1010 BEEP 1,1:WAIT 120:PRINT T
1020 INPUT N$
1030 IF N$="R" PRINT T
1040 L=LEN N$
1050 IF ASC (LEFT$ (N$,1))=42 GOTO 1100
1060 IF ASC (LEFT$ (N$,1))=43 GOTO 1200
1070 IF ASC (LEFT$ (N$,1))=45 GOTO 1300
1080 IF ASC (LEFT$ (N$,1))=47 GOTO 1400
1090 T=T+VAL N$
1095 GOTO 1010
1100 S=VAL (RIGHT$ (N$,L-1))
1110 T=T*S
1120 GOTO 1010
1200 S=VAL (RIGHT$ (N$,L-1))
1210 T=T+S
1220 GOTO 1010
1300 S=VAL (RIGHT$ (N$,L-1))
1310 T=T-S
```

```
1320 GOTO 1010
1400 S=VAL (RIGHT$ (N$,L-1))
1410 T=T/S
1420 GOTO 1010
```

Single-Digit Adding Machine

Add as many single-digit numbers as you like. No need to press ENTER after each number since we are using INKEY$.

Program Listing

```
 10 CLEAR:CLS
 20 PRINT @ 72,"ADDING MACHINE"
 30 PRINT @ 104,STRING$(14,"*")
 40 PRINT @ 168,"FIRST NUMBER="
 50 NN$=INKEY$
 60 IF NN$=""THEN50
 70 N=VAL(NN$)
 80 L=L+1
 90 PRINT @ 168,"NUMBER";L;"IS";N
100 T=T+N
110 PRINT @ 233,"TOTAL=";T
120 GOTO 50
```

How Money Grows

My, oh my, how your money grows when you put it in a savings account at a certain annual percentage rate of interest, compounded monthly, for a number of months.

This program asks for information on the initial principal saved, annual interest percentage rate, and number of months. The result is a moving display of the changes in principal as the months pass. The computer holds at the final month's display so you can see what you would have at that time.

Program Listing

```
10 CLS:CLEAR
20 PRINT @ 53,"MONEY GROWTH"
30 LINE (76,6)-(150,16),1,B
40 PRINT:INPUT"PRINCIPAL $                  ";P
```

```
50 INPUT"ANNUAL INTEREST PERCENT ";R
60 INPUT"NUMBER OF MONTHS        ";M
65 PRINT
70 FOR Q=1 TO M
80 I=(P*(0.01*R))/12
90 P=P+I
95 Z=INT(P*100+0.5)/100
100 PRINT "AFTER MONTH ";Q;" = $";Z
110 FOR T=1 TO 250:NEXT T
120 NEXT Q
130 IF INKEY$="" THEN 130
140 GOTO 10
```

Deposit Doubler

There's an old rule of thumb used by some bankers. It holds that money left on deposit in an interest-bearing account will *double* in value as interest compounds.

If you don't take this *Rule of 72nds* too seriously it can be a handy gauge to figure roughly the number of years you need to leave your money in a bank account (or other interest-bearing system) to see it double in value.

The rule holds that the number of years to double is about equal to the number 72 divided by the annual interest rate. The actual conversion is done in line 130 of this program. The rest of the program lines are input and output generators.

Program Listing

```
10 CLS:CLEAR
20 RV$=CHR$(27)+"p":NV$=CHR$(27)+"q"
30 PRINT @ 55,RV$;"DEPOSIT DOUBLER";NV$
40 LINE(90,7)-(179,15),1,B
50 LINE(88,5)-(181,17),1,B
100 PRINT @ 120,"WHAT IS ANNUAL INTEREST
    PERCENT";:INPUT I
110 PRINT @ 120,SPACE$(40)
120 PRINT @ 120,"AT ";I;" PERCENT INTEREST"
130 Y=72/I
140 IF Y>INT(Y) THEN 150 ELSE 180
150 D=Y-INT(Y)
160 IF D>0.5 THEN Y=Y+1
```

```
170 Y=INT(Y)
180 PRINT @ 160,"MONEY DOUBLES IN ABOUT "
    ;Y;" YEARS"
200 PRINT @ 240,"PRESS ";RV$;"ENTER";NV$
 ;" FOR MORE OR ";RV$;"Q";NV$;" TO QUIT"
205 LINE(35,47)-(65,55),1,B
207 LINE(143,47)-(149,55),1,B
210 K$=INKEY$
220 IF K$="" THEN 210
230 IF K$="Q" OR K$="q" THEN 300
240 IF ASC(K$)=13 THEN 10
250 GOTO 210
300 CLS
310 LINE (77,1)-(155,21),1,BF
320 LINE (81,5)-(151,17),2,BF
330 PRINT @ 54,"TERMINATION"
340 END
```

Mortgage Loans

Planning to buy a new home? Thinking of refinancing the old mortgage? This program computes either mortgage payment amount, number of payments or amount borrowed.

When you first run this program, you are presented with a menu of work options. If you wish to find the amount of payment on a certain mortgage, press P. If you wish to compute the number of payments to complete a mortgage, press N. To recall the original loan amount of an existing mortgage, press V.

If you wish to determine the monthly mortgage payment, the computer will ask for the original loan amount in dollars, the percentage interest rate, and the number of months in the life of the mortgage.

To find number of payments, the computer will require the original loan amount, the interest rate, and the monthly payment amount. To recreate the original amount of a mortgage, tell the computer payment, interest rate and number of months in the original agreement.

Program Listing

```
10 CLS:CLEAR
20 TT$="MORTGAGE LOANS"
30 GOSUB 800
```

```
40 PRINT @ 127,"WHICH DO YOU WISH TO FIND?"
50 PRINT @ 163,"MORTGAGE PAYMENT AMOUNT
   (PRESS P)"
60 PRINT @ 203,"NUMBER OF PAYMENTS
   (PRESS N)"
70 PRINT @ 243,"ORIGINAL LOAN AMOUNT
   (PRESS V)"
80 K$=INKEY$
90 IF K$="" THEN 80
100 IF K$="P" THEN 200
110 IF K$="N" THEN 400
120 IF K$="V" THEN 600
130 CLS:BEEP
140 PRINT @ 89,"PRESS ONLY P, N, OR V"
150 GOTO 50
200 TT$="MORTGAGE PAYMENT"
210 GOSUB 800
220 PRINT
230 INPUT"ORIGINAL LOAN AMOUNT $";V
240 INPUT"INTEREST RATE PERCENT ";I
250 LET I=0.01*(I/12)
260 INPUT"NUMBER OF MONTHS       ";N
270 PRINT
280 P=V*(I/(1-(1+I)^-N))
290 P=INT(100*P+0.5)/100
300 PRINT"MORTGAGE PAYMENT       $";P;"<<<"
310 PRINT
320 PRINT"FOR MORE PRESS ANY KEY"
330 K$=INKEY$
340 IF K$="" THEN 330
350 GOTO 10
400 TT$="NUMBER OF PAYMENTS"
410 GOSUB 800
420 PRINT
430 INPUT"ORIGINAL LOAN AMOUNT     $";V
440 INPUT"INTEREST RATE PERCENT    %";I
450 I=0.01*(I/12)
460 INPUT"MORTGAGE PAYMENT AMOUNT $";P
470 PRINT
480 N=-((LOG(1-I*V/P))/(LOG(1+I)))
500 PRINT"NUMBER OF MONTHS ";N;"<<<"
510 GOTO 310
```

```
600 TT$="MORTGAGE LOAN AMOUNT"
610 GOSUB 800
620 PRINT
630 INPUT"MORTGAGE PAYMENT AMOUNT $";P
640 INPUT"INTEREST RATE PERCENT   %";I
650 I=0.01*(I/12)
660 INPUT"NUMBER OF MONTHS         ";N
670 PRINT
680 V=P*((1-(1+I)^-N)/I)
690 V=INT(100*V+0.5)/100
700 PRINT"LOAN AMOUNT              $"
    ;V;"<<<"
710 GOTO 310
790 END
800 CLS:BEEP
810 TL=LEN(TT$)
820 CT=INT((40-TL)/2)
830 BL=TL*6+4
840 BS=(240-BL)/2
850 LINE(BS,6)-(BS+BL-2,16),1,B
860 PRINT @ 40+CT,TT$
870 RETURN
```

Installment Purchase Plan

What can be more confusing than the terms on your credit card? It can be a real hassle trying to get a payment figure from a store or loan company or bank for an installment purchase. With this program, you won't have to call or visit a lender to discover just how much your payment is going to be.

The computer will tell you how much you will have to pay on your installment-credit loan if you give it a few pieces of pertinent information.

Type the program listing below into your computer and RUN it. The computer will ask for the list price of the item you are buying. It will ask for the amount of the down payment you will be making at the time of the purchase. It will ask over how many payments you wish the loan spread. And, finally, it will ask for the annual interest rate percentage of the loan.

After completing its work the computer will tell you the amount of the monthly payment you will have to make on the loan.

Program Listing

```
10 CLS:CLEAR
20 LINE (26,3)-(201,19),1,BF
30 LINE (29,6)-(198,16),2,BF
50 PRINT @ 45,"INSTALLMENT PURCHASE
   PAYMENT"
60 PRINT:PRINT"LIST PRICE $";SPACE$(9);
   :INPUT L
70 PRINT"DOWN PAYMENT $";SPACE$(7);
   :INPUT D
80 PRINT"NUMBER OF PAYMENTS";SPACE$(3);
   :INPUT N
90 PRINT"ANNUAL INPUT PERCENT";SPACE$(1);
   :INPUT I
100 I=(0.01*I)/12
110 P=(L-D)*(I/(1-(1/((1+I)^N))))
120 P=INT(100*P+0.5)/100
130 PRINT
200 PRINT "PAYMENT";SPACE$(14);"$";P
210 IF INKEY$="" THEN 210
220 GOTO 10
```

Rule of 78's Loan Interest Rebate

Paying off your consumer loan? Want to know if you are due a refund on interest and how much it will be? This program will allow the computer to compute the amount of interest you could overpay and the remaining balance of principal you must pay to satisfy the loan.

If you pay off the loan by paying all pre-computed payments, use this program to find how much refund, or *rebate*, is due you. If you haven't paid off the loan yet, use this program to determine the amount of principal to pay off without overpaying interest.

Using what bankers call the *Rule of 78's*, you must supply the number of the current payment, the total number of installment payments for which the loan originally was written, and the original total finance charge or amount of interest dollars.

Program Listing

```
10 CLS:CLEAR
100 INPUT"ORIGINAL NO. OF MONTHS IN LOAN"
    ;N
105 IF N=<0 THEN 100
110 INPUT"PAYMENT NO. WHEN PREPAYMENT
    OCCURS";K
115 IF K>N OR K=<0 THEN 110
120 INPUT"ORIGINAL TOTAL FINANCE CHARGE
    $";P
125 IF P=<0 THEN 120
130 INPUT"MONTHLY PAYMENT $";PM
135 IF PM=<0 THEN 130
200 I=((2*(N-K+1))/(N*(N+1)))*P
210 RB=((N-K)*I)/2
220 BL=((N-K)*PM)-RB
230 II=INT(I*100+0.5)/100
240 R=INT(RB*100+0.5)/100
250 B=INT(BL*100+0.5)/100
300 CLS
310 PRINT"RULE OF 78's LOAN INTEREST
    REBATE"
320 PRINT
330 PRINT"ORIGINAL FINANCE CHARGE $";P
340 PRINT"ORIGINAL NO. PAYMENTS    ";N
350 PRINT"PREPAYMENT MONTH NO.     ";K
360 PRINT"REBATE DUE              $";R
370 PRINT"PRINCIPAL OUTSTANDING   $";B
400 IF INKEY$="" THEN 400
410 GOTO 10
```

Loan Payments

This money program finds the amount of payment to be made on a loan, or the original loan amount, often referred to as *present value,* or the number of payments to be made on a loan.

We use the variable PV for loan amount, or present

value. PY is the amount of the payment and N is the number of months of payments. The annual interest percentage is I.

Program Listing

```
 10 CLEAR
 20 WAIT 120
 30 PRINT "**MONTHLY LOAN REPAYMENT**"
 40 WAIT 60
 50 PRINT "YOU MAY COMPUTE:"
 60 PRINT "LOAN AMOUNT (PRESS A)"
 70 PRINT "PAYMENT (PRESS P)"
 80 PRINT "NUMBER OF MONTHS (PRESS N)"
 90 WAIT Ø
100 PRINT "PRESS A, P OR N"
110 K$=INKEY$
120 IF K$=""THEN GOTO 110
130 IF K$="A"THEN 200
140 IF K$="P"THEN 300
150 IF K$="N"THEN 400
160 GOTO 110
200 GOSUB 600
210 PV=PY*((1-((1+I)^-N))/I)
220 PRINT "LOAN AMT: $";PV
230 GOTO 500
300 GOSUB 600
310 PY=PV*(I/(1-((1+I)^-N)))
320 PRINT "PAYMENT: $";PY
330 GOTO 500
400 GOSUB 600
410 N=-((LN (1-(I*PV)/PY))/(LN (1+I)))
420 PRINT "NO. MONTHS: ";N
500 IF INKEY$ ="" THEN 500
510 CLEAR
520 GOTO 90
600 IF K$="A"THEN INPUT "PAYMENT : $";PY
    :INPUT "NO. MONTHS: ";N:GOTO 630
610 IF K$="P"THEN INPUT "LOAN AMT: $";PV
    :INPUT "NO. MONTHS: ";N:GOTO 630
620 IF K$="N"THEN INPUT "LOAN AMT: $";PV
    :INPUT "PAYMENT: $";PY:GOTO 630
```

```
630 INPUT "ANNUAL INT % :";I
640 I=(.01*I)/12
650 RETURN
```

Checkbook Balancer

One of life's little headaches is reconciling your checkbook register or check stubs with the monthly statement from your bank.

Normally, your checkbook balance will not match the balance shown on your bank statement. That's because you write checks which haven't reached the bank by the time the statement is mailed or make deposits after the bank completed its work on your statement. In other words, there are checks or deposits which haven't cleared by the time the bank mails your statement to you.

This program allows your computer to help you reconcile the difference between the bank's statement and your checkbook balance.

Program Listing

```
 10 REM CHECKBOOK BALANCER
 20 CLEAR
 30 DIM CN(100),CA(100),D(100)
 40 INPUT "NEED INSTRUCTIONS ";I$
 50 IF LEFT$ (I$,1)="Y"THEN GOSUB 500
100 INPUT "BANK BALANCE: ";BB
200 N=N+1
210 INPUT "CHECK NUMBER: ";CN$
220 IF CN$="X"THEN 300
230 CN(N)=VAL (CN$)
240 INPUT "CHECK AMOUNT: ";CA(N)
250 CT=CT+CA(N)
260 GOTO 200
300 L=L+1
310 INPUT "DEPOSIT AMOUNT: ";DA$
320 IF DA$="X"THEN 400
330 D(L)=VAL (DA$)
340 DT=DT+D(L)
350 GOTO 300
400 NB=BB-CT+DT
```

```
410 INPUT "CHECKBOOK BALANCE: ";CB
420 BC=NB-CB
430 PAUSE "NEW BALANCE=$";NB
440 PAUSE "CORRECTION=$";BC
450 GOTO 430
500 PAUSE "ENTER ALL"
510 PAUSE "OUTSTANDING CHECKS"
520 PAUSE "AND DEPOSITS"
530 PAUSE "AMOUNTS AND NUMBERS."
540 PAUSE "ENTER X AFTER LAST ITEM"
550 RETURN
```

Reconciling a N.O.W. Account

N.O.W. stands for *negotiable order of withdrawal.* These accounts have become very popular in banking circles in recent years. Similar to checking accounts, they are more complex in that your money in the account earns interest while on deposit.

Such accounts often also provide for automatic transfers of your money to make car payments, mortgage payments, etc. In addition, interest on certificates of deposit (CDs) and other accounts may be credited to your N.O.W. account by your bank. So, there could be lots of activity in one month in your account to keep track of. This situation is ideal for computer assistance.

Program Listing

```
 10 WAIT Ø
 20 FOR P=25 TO Ø STEP -1
 30 CURSOR (P): PRINT "*";
 40 NEXT P
 50 PRINT "BALANCING N.O.W. ACCOUNT"
 60 FOR T=1 TO 100:NEXT T
 70 INPUT "PREVIOUS BALANCE: ";BL
 80 INPUT "DEPOSIT: ";DP$
 90 IF DP$="X"THEN 120
100 BL=BL+VAL (DP$)
110 GOTO 80
120 INPUT "INTEREST: ";IN$
130 IF IN$="X"THEN 160
```

```
140 BL=BL+VAL (IN$)
150 GOTO 120
160 INPUT "OTHER CREDIT: ";OC$
170 IF OC$="X"THEN 200
180 BL=BL+VAL (OC$)
190 GOTO 160
200 INPUT "SAVINGS WITHDRAWAL: ";SW$
210 IF SW$="X"THEN 240
220 BL=BL-VAL (SW$)
230 GOTO 200
240 INPUT "OTHER WITHDRAWALS: ";OW$
250 IF OW$="X"THEN 280
260 BL=BL-VAL (OW$)
270 GOTO 240
280 INPUT "SERVICE CHARGE: ";SC$
290 IF SC$="X"THEN 320
300 BL=BL-VAL (SC$)
310 GOTO 280
320 INPUT "OUTSTANDING CHECKS: ";OU$
330 IF OU$="X"THEN 360
340 BL=BL-VAL (OU$)
350 GOTO 320
360 BEEP 1,1
370 PRINT "CORRECT BALANCE: $";BL
380 IF INKEY$="" THEN 380
390 CLEAR
400 GOTO 10
```

Finance Charge Refund

Once in a while you get lucky enough to repay an installment loan *before* the final due date. When that happens you may be entitled to a refund of part of the finance charge.

How much rebate is due? The percentage rebate is found in a rebate-schedule table. In this program, we have a portion of such a schedule.

Imbedded in program lines 70 to 200 is data from a rebate-scheduled table. Our table allows loans with lengths of time set at 3, 6, 9, 12, 15 and 18 months. The number of elapsed months runs from 1 to 14.

You type in the original total finance charge on your

installment loan, the original number of months for which the loan was set up, and the number of months the loan has run so far. Be sure to use either 3, 6, 9, 12, 15 or 18 for the original number of months. Use from 1 to 14 for the number of months the loan has run. Use actual dollars for the original total finance charge.

Program Listing

```
 10 WAIT Ø:DIM S(6,14)
 20 FOR P=25 TO Ø STEP -1
 30 CURSOR P
 40 PRINT "*";
 50 NEXT P
 60 PRINT "REFUND OR FINANCE CHARGE"
 70 DATA 50,71.43,80,84.62,87.5,89.47
 80 DATA 16,67,47.62,62.22,70.51,75.83,
    79.53
 90 DATA Ø,28.57,46.67,57.69,65,70.18
100 DATA Ø,14.29,33.33,46.15,55,61.4
110 DATA Ø,4.76,22.22,35.9,45.83,53.22
120 DATA Ø,Ø,13.33,26.92,37.5,45.61
130 DATA Ø,Ø,6.67.19.23,30,38.6
140 DATA Ø,Ø,2.22,12.82,23.33,32.16
150 DATA Ø,Ø,Ø,7.69,17.5,26.32
160 DATA Ø,Ø,Ø,3.85,12.5,21.05
170 DATA Ø,Ø,Ø,1.28,8.33,16.37
180 DATA Ø,Ø,Ø,Ø,5,12.28
190 DATA Ø,Ø,Ø,Ø,2.5,8.77
200 DATA Ø,Ø,Ø,Ø,Ø.83,5.85
210 FOR C=1 TO 14
220 FOR R=1 TO 6
230 READ S(R,C)
240 NEXT R
250 NEXT C
260 INPUT "TOTAL FINANCE CHARGE: ";F
270 INPUT "ORIGINAL LOAN TERM: ";RR
280 INPUT "MONTHS GONE BY: ";C
290 R=RR/3:PD=0.01*S(R,C)
300 RF=INT (100*(PD*F)+0.5/100
310 PRINT "REFUND:$";RF
320 IF INKEY$="" THEN 320
330 GOTO 260
```

Checking Your Charge Account Statement

Do you have credit cards? Charge accounts? Do they send you monthly statements? If the answer is yes to any of these questions, you can use your computer to check up on the companies issuing those statements.

Type in this brief program and RUN it. It will give you a fast and easy check of your statement. Remember, you can do multiple finance charges, new purchases, payments and credits. Use X to exit data-entry loops for these items.

Program Listing

```
10 WAIT Ø
20 FOR P=25 TO Ø STEP -1
30 CURSOR P:PRINT"*";
40 NEXT P
50 PRINT "BALANCING YOUR STATEMENT"
60 FOR T=1 TO 100:NEXT T
70 INPUT "PREVIOUS BALANCE: ";BL
80 INPUT "FINANCE CHARGE: ";FC$
90 IF FC$="X" THEN 120
100 BL=BL+VAL (FC$)
110 GOTO 80
120 INPUT "NEW PURCHASES: ";NP$
130 IF NP$="X" THEN 160
140 BL=BL+VAL (NP$)
150 GOTO 120
160 INPUT "PAYMENTS: ";PY$
170 IF PY$="X" THEN 200
180 BL=BL-VAL (PY$)
190 GOTO 160
200 INPUT "CREDITS: ";CR$
210 IF CR$="X" THEN 240
220 BL=BL-VAL (CR$)
230 GOTO 200
240 BEEP 1,1
250 PRINT "CORRECT BALANCE: ";BL
260 IF INKEY$="" THEN 260
270 CLEAR
280 GOTO 10
```

Average Monthly Expenditures

You can manage your money better by keeping an accurate record of your expenditures each month. You will be able to evaluate your spending habits over the months.

This program accepts monthly total expenditures for a year and gives you the year's total plus the monthly average expenditure.

Program Listing

```
 10 CLEAR :WAIT Ø
 20 FOR P=25 TO Ø STEP -1
 30 CURSOR P:PRINT"*";
 40 NEXT P
 50 PRINT "AVERAGE MONTHLY EXPENSES"
 60 FOR Z=1 TO 100:NEXT Z
 70 DATA "JANUARY","FEBRUARY","MARCH"
 80 DATA "APRIL","MAY","JUNE"
 90 DATA "JULY","AUGUST","SEPTEMBER"
100 DATA "OCTOBER","NOVEMBER","DECEMBER"
110 FOR M=1 TO 12
120 READ N$
130 PRINT  N$;
140 INPUT " EXPENSES: $";E
150 T=T+E
160 CLS
170 NEXT M
180 A=T/12
190 WAIT 40
200 PRINT "TOTAL EXPENSES: $";T
210 PRINT "MONTHLY AVERAGE: $";A
220 IF INKEY$="" THEN 220
230 RESTORE
240 GOTO 10
```

Electric Bill Analysis

Confused by your electric bill? Think you're being stung? Can't figure when you used all that juice? Now you can analyze your bills for a one-year period and see where you are draining the local utility.

The computer will report annual totals, monthly averages of kilowatt hours used, and the cost of those kilowatts. Most folks receive an electric bill every other month and the computer assumes that's the case. It counts on two months of service per bill.

You can give the computer information from your electric bills in any monthly order. The program sorts the monthly bills into chronological order within one year.

Program Listing

```
10 CLEAR:CLS
20 DIM M$(6)
30 FOR L=1 TO 6
40 LINE INPUT"BILLING MONTH: ";MN$
50 IF MN$=""THEN 240
60 LINE INPUT"KILOWATT HOURS: ";KW$
70 LINE INPUT"NUMBER OF DAYS: ";ND$
80 LINE INPUT"UNIT PRICE: ";UP$
90 M$(L)=MN$+"/"+KW$+"KWH/"+ND$+
   "DAYS/"+"$"+UP$
100 N=N+1
110 M=M+2
120 K=VAL(KW$)
130 D=VAL(ND$)
140 P=VAL(UP$)
150 IF N=1 THEN LL=K:LM$=M$(L):HH=K
    :HM$=M$(L)
160 IF K<LL THEN LL=K:LM$=M$(L)
170 IF K>HH THEN HH=K:HM$=M$(L)
180 KK=KK+K
190 DD=DD+D
200 MU=KK/M
210 TC=KK*P
220 MC=TC/M
230 NEXT L
240 CLS
250 PRINT" "
260 PRINT"MONTH/KWH/DAYS/COST"
270 PRINT" "
280 FOR L=1 TO 6
290 IF LEFT$(M$(L),3)="JAN" THEN PRINT M$(L)
```

```
300 NEXT L
310 FOR L=1 TO 6
320 IF LEFT$(M$(L),3)="FEB" THEN PRINT M$(L)
330 NEXT L
340 FOR L=1 TO 6
350 IF LEFT$(M$(L),3)="MAR" THEN PRINT M$(L)
360 NEXT L
370 FOR L=1 TO 6
380 IF LEFT$(M$(L),3)="APR" THEN PRINT M$(L)
390 NEXT L
400 FOR L=1 TO 6
410 IF LEFT$(M$(L),3)="MAY" THEN PRINT M$(L)
420 NEXT L
430 FOR L=1 TO 6
440 IF LEFT$(M$(L),3)="JUN" THEN PRINT M$(L)
450 NEXT L
460 FOR L=1 TO 6
470 IF LEFT$(M$(L),3)="JUL" THEN PRINT M$(L)
480 NEXT L
490 FOR L=1 TO 6
500 IF LEFT$(M$(L),3)="AUG" THEN PRINT M$(L)
510 NEXT L
520 FOR L=1 TO 6
530 IF LEFT$(M$(L),3)="SEP" THEN PRINT M$(L)
540 NEXT L
550 FOR L=1 TO 6
560 IF LEFT$(M$(L),3)="OCT" THEN PRINT M$(L)
570 NEXT L
580 FOR L=1 TO 6
590 IF LEFT$(M$(L),3)="NOV" THEN PRINT M$(L)
600 NEXT L
610 FOR L=1 TO 6
620 IF LEFT$(M$(L),3)="DEC" THEN PRINT M$(L)
630 NEXT L
640 PRINT" "
650 PRINT"FOR BILL ANALYSIS, PRESS A"
660 PRINT"TO QUIT, PRESS Q"
670 AA$=INKEY$
680 IF AA$=""THEN 670
690 IF AA$="A" THEN 720
700 IF AA$="Q" THEN 1040
```

```
710 GOTO 670
720 CLS
730 PRINT" ":PRINT" "
740 PRINT"ELECTRIC BILL ANALYSIS"
750 PRINT N;"BILLS RECEIVED, BIMONTHLY"
760 PRINT" "
770 PRINT"TOTALS OVER";M;"MONTHS"
780 PRINT KK;"KWH USED OVER";M;"MONTHS"
790 PRINT DD;"DAYS IN";M;"MONTHS"
800 PRINT" $";TC;"COST OVER";M;"MONTHS"
810 PRINT" ":PRINT" "
820 PRINT"FOR MONTHLY AVERAGES, PRESS A"
830 AM$=INKEY$
840 IF AM$="" THEN 830
850 IF AM$="A" THEN 870
860 GOTO 830
870 CLS
880 PRINT" "
890 PRINT"AVERAGES PER MONTH"
900 PRINT" "
910 PRINT MU;"KWH AVERAGE USE"
920 PRINT " $";MC;"AVERAGE COST"
930 PRINT " "
940 PRINT "LOWEST-USE BILL":PRINT" ";LM$
950 PRINT "HIGHEST-USE BILL":PRINT" ";HM$
960 PRINT " "
970 PRINT "TO DO ANOTHER SET, PRESS A"
980 PRINT "TO STOP, PRESS S"
990 BB$=INKEY$
1000 IF BB$="" THEN 990
1010 IF BB$="A" THEN 10
1020 IF BB$="S" THEN 1040
1030 GOTO 990
1040 CLS 2
1050 PRINT @ 192,"          THANK YOU"
1060 GOTO 1060
```

Savings Quickie

Want a quick idea of how much your savings account will grow over the years? This program is fast to load and speedy to run.

The computer will ask for initial savings balance, annual interest percentage rate, and number of years. In return, it computes compound interest and displays the savings balance at the end of each year in a handy list.

Program Listing

```
10 CLS:CLEAR
20 INPUT"PRESENT SAVINGS BALANCE";B
30 INPUT"INTEREST RATE";I
40 INPUT"NUMBER OF YEARS";Y
50 FOR L=1 TO Y
60 Z=Z+I*(Z+B)/100
70 PRINT L,Z+B
80 NEXT L
90 END
```

Monthly Loan Payment

Here's a fast computation of the monthly payment on a loan. The amount borrowed, the principle, is stored in memory location P. I is the annual interest rate and N is the number of payments. I is converted to a monthly interest rate and then to a decimal in line 50.

Program Listing

```
10 PRINT "}":REM CLEAR SCREEN
20 PRINT "AMOUNT BORROWED $ ";:INPUT P
30 PRINT "ANNUAL INTEREST % ";:INPUT I
40 PRINT "NUMBER OF PAYMENTS ";:INPUT N
50 I=0.01*(I/12)
60 M=(P*I)/(1-((1+I)^(-N)))
70 PRINT
80 PRINT "MONTHLY PAYMENT IS $";M
90 PRINT :PRINT :PRINT
100 GOTO 20
```

Automobile:

Miles per Gallon and Cost per Mile

With gasoline shortages always a threat, it's important to know just how much gas your car is using to travel a mile—and how much that mile costs in dollars.

This program lets the computer find the total distance you have traveled since the last time you filled your car's gas tank. It reports miles per gallon; gas cost per gallon; and gas cost per mile.

Program Listing

```
 10 CLS
 20 CLEAR
 30 PRINT "CURRENT ODOMETER READING?"
 40 INPUT C
 45 CLS
 50 PRINT "PREVIOUS ODOMETER READING?"
 60 INPUT O
 65 CLS
 70 PRINT "GALLONS OF GAS?"
 80 INPUT G
 85 CLS
 90 PRINT "TOTAL PRICE ?"
100 INPUT P
110 LET A=P/G
115 LET A=INT (100*A+0.5)/100
120 LET M=C-O
130 LET N=M/G
135 LET N=INT (100*N+0.5)/100
140 LET L=P/M
145 LET L=INT (100*L+0.5)/100
150 CLS
160 PRINT "MILES TRAVELED: ";M
170 PRINT "MILES PER GALLON: ";N
180 PRINT "GAS: $";A;" PER GALLON"
190 PRINT "GAS: $";L;" PER MILE"
200 PRINT
210 PRINT
220 PRINT
230 PRINT
240 PRINT "PRESS ENTER FOR MORE"
250 INPUT K$
260 GOTO 10
```

Automobile:
Miles Left in Gas Tank

Make a conservative estimate of the number of miles per gallon you have been getting out of your car recently. Check the car's owners manual for information about the capacity of the gas tank. Recall the odometer reading at the last gas fill-up. Using this information, the computer will be able to tell you how many miles you can drive before your gas tank runs dry.

Program Listing

```
 10 CLS
 20 CLEAR
 30 PRINT "CURRENT ODOMETER READING?"
 40 INPUT O
 45 CLS
 50 PRINT "PREVIOUS ODOMETER READING?"
 60 INPUT P
 65 CLS
 70 PRINT "MILES PER GALLON"
 80 INPUT M
 85 CLS
 90 PRINT "GAS TANK CAPACITY?"
100 INPUT T
110 LET D=O-P
120 LET R=M*T
130 LET L=R-D
140 CLS
150 PRINT "MAXIMUM RANGE: ";R
160 PRINT "DISTANCE SO FAR: ";D
170 PRINT "MILES REMAINING: ";L
200 PRINT
210 PRINT
220 PRINT
230 PRINT
240 PRINT "PRESS ENTER FOR MORE"
250 INPUT K$
260 GOTO 10
```

Car Payments

Shopping for a new car? Use your Computer to compute quickly the potential monthly car payment on various models.

Program Listing

```
 10 LET P=Ø
 20 PRINT "CAR PAYMENT"
 30 FOR L=1 TO 11
 40 PRINT "*";
 50 NEXT L
 60 PRINT
100 PRINT "PURCHASE PRICE ?"
110 INPUT T
120 CLS
130 PRINT "DOWN PAYMENT ?"
140 INPUT R
150 CLS
160 PRINT "NUMBER OF MONTHS ?"
170 INPUT N
180 CLS
190 PRINT "ANNUAL INTEREST ?"
200 INPUT I
210 LET I=(0.01*I)/12
220 CLS
230 LET P= (T-R)*I/(1-1/(1+I)**N)
240 LET P=INT(100*P+.5)/100
250 PRINT "PAYMENT WILL BE"
260 PRINT "$";P;" A MONTH"
```

Simple Interest

My savings account has $400 in it. The bank pays me 7.5 percent interest on the account. If I leave the money in that account for 12 years, how much interest will I have earned after 12 years? What will the new amount total in the account?

Program Listing

```
 10 CLS
 15 CLEAR
 20 PRINT "PRESENT VALUE $";
 25 INPUT P
 27 PRINT P
 30 PRINT "ANNUAL INTEREST PERCENT?";
 35 INPUT I
 37 PRINT I
 40 PRINT "NUMBER OF YEARS?";
 45 INPUT Y
 50 LET I=0.01*I
 55 LET X=P*I*Y
 60 CLS
 65 PRINT Y;" YEARS INTEREST"
 70 PRINT "TOTALS $";X
 75 LET A=P+X
 80 PRINT "PRINCIPAL = $";A
 85 PRINT
 90 PRINT
 95 PRINT
100 PRINT "TO DO ANOTHER..."
110 PRINT
120 GOTO 15
```

Compound Interest: Present Value

Using this program, the computer can tell you how much money to deposit in your savings account today, at what interest rate, and how long to leave it in that account to get a specific amount you require in that account at a point in the future.

Program Listing

```
10 CLS
15 CLEAR
20 PRINT "FUTURE VALUE?";
25 INPUT F
30 PRINT " $";F
35 PRINT "ANNUAL INTEREST PERCENT?";
```

```
40 INPUT I
45 PRINT I
50 PRINT "NUMBER OF YEARS?";
55 INPUT Y
60 PRINT Y
65 LET I=0.01*I
70 LET P=F/(1+I)**Y
75 PRINT
77 LET P=INT (100*P+0.5)/100
80 PRINT "PRESENT VALUE $";P
85 PRINT
90 PRINT
95 PRINT
100 PRINT "PRESS ENTER TO DO ANOTHER"
110 INPUT K$
120 GOTO 10
```

Compound Interest: Future Value

(Annual Compounding)

Here the computer uses the present value of your savings account, the annual interest rate and the number of years you plan to leave the money in the account to compute the future value of the account with annual compounding.

Program Listing

```
10 CLS
15 CLEAR
20 PRINT "PRESENT VALUE? ";
25 INPUT P
30 PRINT "$";P
35 PRINT "ANNUAL INTEREST PERCENT? ";
40 INPUT I
45 PRINT I
50 PRINT "NUMBER OF YEARS? ";
60 INPUT Y
65 PRINT Y;" YEARS"
70 LET I=0.01*I
75 LET F=P*(1+I)**Y
```

```
 77 LET F=INT (100*F+0.5)/100
 80 PRINT
 90 PRINT "FUTURE VALUE $";F
 95 PRINT
100 PRINT
105 PRINT
110 PRINT "PRESS ENTER TO DO MORE"
115 INPUT K$
120 GOTO 10
```

Compound Interest: Future Value

(Quarterly Compounding)

If you know how much you have in a savings account, how much interest you are earning, and how many years you plan to leave the money in the account, the computer will tell you how many quarters are in those years and compute the future total value of the account.

Program Listing

```
 10 CLS
 20 CLEAR
 30 PRINT "PRESENT VALUE? ";
 40 INPUT P
 50 PRINT "$";P
 60 PRINT "ANNUAL INTEREST? ";
 70 INPUT I
 80 PRINT I;" PERCENT"
 90 PRINT "NUMBER OF YEARS? ";
100 INPUT Y
110 PRINT Y
120 LET Q=4*Y
130 LET I=0.01*(I/4)
140 LET F=P*(1+I)**Q
150 LET F=INT (100*F+0.5)/100
160 PRINT
170 PRINT Q;" QUARTERS"
180 PRINT "FUTURE VALUE $";F
190 PRINT
200 PRINT
```

```
210 PRINT
220 PRINT "PRESS ENTER TO DO MORE"
230 INPUT K$
240 GOTO 10
```

Compound Interest: Future Value
(Showing Intermediate Years)

Here the computer uses the present value of your savings account, the interest rate, and the number of years you plan to leave the money in the account. It then lists the total amount in the account after each year through the period you plan to maintain the account.

Program Listing

```
 10 CLS
 20 CLEAR
 30 PRINT "PRESENT VALUE? ";
 40 INPUT P
 50 PRINT "$";P
 60 PRINT "INTEREST RATE? ";
 70 INPUT I
 80 PRINT I;" PERCENT"
 90 LET L=I/100+1
100 PRINT "NUMBER OF YEARS? ";
110 INPUT Y
120 PRINT Y
130 PRINT
140 PRINT
150 PRINT "STARTING WITH $";P
155 PRINT
160 FOR K=1 TO Y
170 LET P=P*L
180 PRINT "AFTER ";K;" YEARS"
190 PRINT "PRINCIPAL=$";P
200 PRINT
210 NEXT K
220 PRINT
230 PRINT
240 PRINT "TO DO MORE PRESS ANY KEY"
```

```
250 LET K$=INKEY$
260 IF K$="" THEN GOTO 250
270 GOTO 10
```

Bank Loans

This handy program will allow you to compute payment, length of time or amount borrowed for your next bank loan.

If you know the amount you want to borrow, the interest rate you will be charged, and the length of time you need the money, the computer will figure your payment.

If you know how much you can pay, the current interest rate, and the length of time you will need to repay, the computer will tell you how much you can borrow.

Or, if you know the amount of payment, the interest rate, and the original amount you borrowed, it will compute the number of payments.

Program Listing

```
 10 LET T$="BANK LOANS"
 15 GOSUB 700
 20 PRINT
 25 PRINT "WHICH TO FIND:"
 30 PRINT
 35 PRINT "PAYMENT AMOUNT (P)"
 40 PRINT "NUMBER OF PAYMENTS (N)"
 45 PRINT "AMOUNT OF LOAN (A)"
 50 GOSUB 900
 55 CLS
 60 IF M$="P" THEN GOTO 100
 65 IF M$="N" THEN GOTO 300
 70 IF M$="A" THEN GOTO 500
 75 CLS
 80 GOTO 10
100 LET T$="PAYMENT"
110 GOSUB 700
120 PRINT
130 PRINT "LOAN AMOUNT ? ";
140 INPUT V
150 PRINT "$";V
```

```
160 PRINT"ANNUAL INTEREST RATE ? ";
170 INPUT I
180 PRINT I;" PCT"
190 PRINT "NUMBER OF PAYMENTS ? ";
200 INPUT N
210 PRINT N
220 LET I=0.01*I/12
230 LET P=V*(I/(1-(1+I)**-N))
240 LET P=INT (100*P+0.5)/100
250 PRINT
260 PRINT "PAYMENT $";P
270 CLEAR
280 GOSUB 1000
300 LET T$="NUMBER OF PAYMENTS"
310 GOSUB 700.
320 PRINT
330 PRINT "LOAN AMOUNT ? ";
340 INPUT V
350 PRINT "$";V
360 PRINT "ANNUAL INTEREST RATE ? ";
370 INPUT I
380 PRINT I;" PCT"
390 PRINT"PAYMENT ? ";
400 INPUT P
410 PRINT "$";P
420 LET I=0.01*I/12
430 LET N=-((LN(1-(I*V/P))/LN 10)/
    ((LN (1+I))/LN 10))
450 PRINT
460 PRINT "NUMBER OF MONTHS ";N
470 GOTO 270
500 LET T$="AMOUNT OF LOAN"
510 GOSUB 700
520 PRINT
530 PRINT "PAYMENT ? ";
540 INPUT P
550 PRINT "$";P
560 PRINT "ANNUAL INTEREST RATE ? ";
570 INPUT I
580 PRINT I;" PCT"
590 PRINT "NUMBER OF PAYMENTS ? ";
```

```
600 INPUT N
610 PRINT N
620 LET I=0.01*I/12
630 LET V=P*((1-(1+I)**-N)/I)
640 LET V=INT (100*V+0.5)/100
650 PRINT
660 PRINT "LOAN AMOUNT $";V
670 GOTO 270
700 LET K=LEN T$
710 FOR L=1 TO K
720 PRINT CHR$128;
730 NEXT L
740 PRINT
750 PRINT T$
760 FOR L=1 TO K
770 PRINT CHR$128;
780 NEXT L
790 PRINT
800 CLEAR
810 RETURN
900 LET M$=INKEY$
910 IF M$="" THEN GOTO 900
920 RETURN
1000 FOR L=1 TO 7
1010 PRINT
1020 NEXT L
1030 PRINT "FOR MORE PRESS ANY KEY"
1040 LET H$=INKEY$
1050 IF H$="" THEN GOTO 1040
1060 CLS
1070 CLEAR
1080 GOTO 10
```

Checking Account Monthly Balancer

On the first day Man created the computer. On the second day, he created the High-Low Numbers game. On the third day, he created check-balancing software.

This handy program does the whole bit, including

warnings of impending overdrafts and service- charge deductions.

Program Listing

```
410 "B" CLEAR
420 FOR X=1 TO 3
    :PAUSE" * CHECKBOOK BALANCER *"
    :NEXT X
430 IF B THEN 460
440 BEEP 1:INPUT"OPENING BALANCE = $";B
445 IF B THEN 460
450 BEEP 3
    :PAUSE"ACCOUNT BALANCE = ZERO"
455 PRINT"ACCOUNT CANCELLED":GOTO440
460 BEEP 1:PAUSE"CHECK OR DEPOSIT ?"
470 INPUT" C OR D ?",A$
480 PAUSE" THANK YOU"
490 IF A$="C" THEN 600
500 BEEP1:INPUT"DEPOSIT AMOUNT = $";D
510 B=B+D
520 GOTO 900
600 BEEP 1:INPUT"AMOUNT OF CHECK = $";C
610 B=B-C
620 GOTO 800
700 IF B>=300 PAUSE"NO SERVICE CHARGE"
710 IF B<300 LET B=B-1
    :PAUSE"BALANCE UNDER $300"
    :PAUSE"$1 SERVICE CHARGE"
720 IF B<200 LET B=B-1
    :PAUSE"BALANCE UNDER $200"
    :PAUSE"$1 MORE SERVICE CHARGE"
730 IF B<100 LET B=B-1
    :PAUSE"BALANCE UNDER $100"
    :PAUSE"$1 MORE SERVICE CHARGE"
800 IF B<Ø THEN 820
810 GOTO 870
820 BEEP 3:FOR Z=1 TO 3:BEEP 1
    :PAUSE"OVERDRAFT":NEXT Z
830 PAUSE"$5 OVERDRAFT FEE PAID"
    :W=W+1
840 B=B-5:E=INT((ABS B)+1)
```

```
850 IF W>2 PAUSE"EXCESSIVE OVERDRAFTS"
    :GOTO455
860 PAUSE"DEPOSIT $";E;" IMMEDIATELY"
    :GOTO 500
870 IF B =Ø BEEP 3:PAUSE"BALANCE = ZERO"
    :PAUSE"DEPOSIT $1 IMMEDIATELY"
    :GOTO 500
900 BEEP 2:PRINT"YOUR NEW BALANCE = $";B
910 BEEP 1:PAUSE"WANT TO DEDUCT..."
920 INPUT"SERVICE CHARGES ? ",F$
930 IF F$="YES" THEN 700
940 GOTO 445
```

Decreasing Debts

Ever wonder how many months it will take to pay off all your bills? Got several credit cards, all with balances requiring monthly payments? Using this program, the computer accepts information from you about those balances and payments. It computes the ratio of payment to balance and then uses that ratio to estimate future balances and payment amounts for the coming months.

It's very useful in estimating just how quickly the balances on your credit cards will go down and how the payments on revolving accounts will drop each month as you make payments on accounts.

Remember this is only an estimate—but a handy one!

Program Listing

```
 10 "B" CLEAR
 20 INPUT "OPENING BALANCE $";B
 30 INPUT "KNOWN PAYMENT $";P
 40 R=P/B
 50 FOR K=1 TO 999
 60 B=B-P:P=RB
 70 PAUSE "AFTER ";K;" MONTHS..."
 80 PRINT "NEW BALANCE = $";B
 90 PRINT "NEW PAYMENT = $";P
100 NEXT K
110 GOTO 20
```

Savings Accumulation

Like to see your money grow in a savings account or investment paying interest? Here's a way to know just how much it will grow over the years.

Suppose you make a deposit of the same amount each month for several years. How much will you have at the end of those years?

This program instructs the computer to accept information about the amount of money in the account and the amount added each month. It computes the total amount in the account after each year. You must leave both principle and interest in the account to accumulate, of course.

The program is good up to 999 years.

We store the initial principle amount in memory location P; amount added each month is S; and the annual interest rate in I.

Program Listing

```
 10 "A" CLEAR
 20 INPUT "INITIAL $";P
 30 INPUT "MONTHLY SAVING $";S
 40 INPUT "INTEREST % ";I
 50 L=I/100+1
 60 PAUSE "STARTING WITH $";P;"..."
 70 FOR K=1 TO 999
 80 P=PL+12S
 90 PAUSE "AFTER ";K;" YRS..."
100 PRINT "PRINCPLE = $";P
110 NEXT K
120 GOTO 20
```

Shopper's Friend

Take your computer along the next time you go shopping!

This program finds the computer asking for certain information and then telling you which product brand name is the best buy.

The computer wil ask for the brand name of a product, the quantity in the product package, and the price of the package. Then it will ask for the name, quantity and price for a second product.

After digesting all this information, it will tell you the brand name of the best-buy product and show you the unit prices for both brand names so you can agree with the computer's judgment.

Program Listing

```
 10 PRINT "SHOPPERS FRIEND"
 20 FOR L=1 TO 15
 30 PRINT "*";
 40 NEXT L
 50 PRINT
100 PRINT "FIRST BRAND NAME:"
110 INPUT X$
120 PRINT X$
130 PRINT "QUANTITY: ";
140 INPUT M
150 PRINT M
160 PRINT "PRICE: $";
170 INPUT N
180 PRINT N
200 PRINT "SECOND BRAND NAME:"
210 INPUT Y$
220 PRINT Y$
230 PRINT "QUANTITY: ";
240 INPUT Q
250 PRINT Q
260 PRINT "PRICE: ";
270 INPUT R
280 PRINT R
300 IF N/M=R/Q THEN GOTO 600
310 IF N/M<R/Q THEN GOTO 400
320 PRINT Y$;" IS BEST BUY"
330 GOTO 500
400 PRINT X$;" IS BEST BUY"
500 PRINT X$;" UNIT = $";N/M
510 PRINT Y$;" UNIT = $";R/Q
520 PRINT
530 STOP
600 PRINT X$;" = ";Y$
610 GOTO 500
```

Temperature Converter

Convert Celsius to Fahrenheit or Kelvin. Change Fahrenheit to Celsius or Kelvin. See Kelvin temperatures in Celsius or Fahrenheit degrees. This handy program makes the necessary conversions.

Program Listing

```
10 CLS:CLEAR
20 PRINT @ 49,"TEMPERATURE CONVERTER"
30 LINE(52,6)-(180,16),1,B
40 PRINT @ 121,"PLEASE SELECT DIRECTION
   OF CONVERSION:"
50 PRINT @ 168,"FROM FAHRENHEIT, PRESS F"
60 PRINT @ 208,"FROM CELSIUS,    PRESS C"
70 PRINT @ 248,"FROM KELVIN,     PRESS K"
80 KY$=INKEY$
90 IF KY$="" THEN 80
100 IF KY$="F" THEN 200
110 IF KY$="C" THEN 300
120 IF KY$="K" THEN 400
130 CLS
140 PRINT @ 126,">>> PRESS ONLY F, C OR
    K <<<"
150 GOTO 50
200 FOR Z=121 TO 279:PRINT CHR$(127);
    :NEXT Z
210 PRINT @ 128,"FAHRENHEIT TEMPERATURE ";
    :INPUT F
220 C=(F-32)/1.8
230 K=(F+459.67)/1.8
240 GOTO 500
300 FOR Z=121 TO 279:PRINT CHR$(127);
    :NEXT Z
310 PRINT @ 129,"CELSIUS TEMPERATURE ";
    :INPUT C
320 F=1.8*C+32
330 K=C+273.15
340 GOTO 500
400 FOR Z=121 TO 279:PRINT CHR$(127);
    :NEXT Z
410 PRINT @ 130,"KELVIN TEMPERATURE ";
```

```
    :INPUT K
420 F=1.8*K-459.67
430 C=K-273.15
500 CLS
510 PRINT @ 49,"CONVERTED TEMPERATURE"
520 LINE(52,6)-(180,16),1,B
530 PRINT @ 130,"FAHRENHEIT:";F;CHR$(166)
540 PRINT @ 170,"CELSIUS:    ";C;CHR$(166)
550 PRINT @ 210,"KELVIN:     ";K;CHR$(166)
600 IF INKEY$="" THEN 600
610 GOTO 10
```

Foreign Capitals

Here's a learning quiz we'll bet you haven't seen anywhere else. This program tests your knowledge of foreign countries. The more you play, the more you learn!

You must tell the computer the correct name of the capital of the country it presents. And you must spell the name of that city correctly.

Program Listing

```
10 RANDOMIZE
15 CALL CLEAR
20 DATA AFGHANISTAN,KABUL
30 DATA ALBANIA,TIRANA
40 DATA ALGERIA,ALGIERS
50 DATA ARGENTINA,BUENOS AIRES
60 DATA AUSTRALIA,CANBERRA
70 DATA AUSTRIA,VIENNA
80 DATA BAHRAIN,MANAMA
90 DATA BANGLADESH,DACCA
100 DATA BELGIUM,BRUSSELS
110 DATA BOLIVIA,LA PAZ
120 DATA BRAZIL,BRASILIA
130 DATA BULGARIA,SOFIA
140 DATA BURMA,RANGOON
150 DATA CHILE,SANTIAGO
160 DATA COLOMBIA,BOGOTA
170 DATA CUBA,HAVANA
180 DATA CZECHOSLOVAKIA,PRAGUE
```

```
190 DATA DENMARK,COPENHAGEN
200 DATA EGYPT,CAIRO
210 DATA FINLAND,HELSINKI
220 DATA FRANCE,PARIS
230 DATA GERMANY EAST,EAST BERLIN
240 DATA GERMANY WEST,BONN
250 DATA GREECE,ATHENS
260 DATA HAITI,PORT-AU-PRINCE
270 DATA HUNGARY,BUDAPEST
280 DATA ICELAND,REYKJAVIK
290 DATA INDIA,NEW DELHI
300 DATA IRAN,TEHRAN
310 DATA ITALY,ROME
320 DATA JAPAN,TOKYO
330 DATA KUWAIT,KUWAIT
340 DATA LIBYA,TRIPOLI
350 DATA MEXICO,MEXICO CITY
360 DATA NEPAL,KATHMANDU
370 DATA NEW ZEALAND,WELLINGTON
380 DATA NORWAY,OSLO
390 DATA OMAN,MUSCAT
400 DATA PERU,LIMA
410 DATA POLAND,WARSAW
420 DATA QATAR,DOHA
430 DATA ROMANIA,BUCHAREST
440 DATA SPAIN,MADRID
450 DATA SUDAN,KHARTOUM
460 DATA SWEDEN,STOCKHOLM
470 DATA SWITZERLAND,BERN
480 DATA TURKEY,ANKARA
490 DATA U.S.S.R.,MOSCOW
500 DATA UNITED KINGDOM,LONDON
510 DATA VENEZUELA,CARACAS
520 DATA YUGOSLAVIA,BELGRADE
530 DATA ZAIRE,KINSHASA
540 DATA ZAMBIA,LUSAKA
550 PRINT "*****FOREIGN CAPITALS*****"
560 R=INT(106*RND)
570 IF R<1 THEN 560
580 IF INT(R/2)=(R/2)THEN 600
590 GOTO 610
600 R=R-1
```

```
610 FOR L=1 TO R
620 READ S$
630 NEXT L
640 PRINT
650 PRINT
660 PRINT "COUNTRY: ";S$
670 READ C$
680 INPUT "WHAT IS THE CAPITAL ":D$
690 IF D$=C$ THEN 710
700 GOTO 730
710 PRINT "RIGHT"
720 GOTO 740
730 PRINT "WRONG"
740 PRINT "CAPITAL OF ";S$;" IS ";C$
750 RESTORE
760 PRINT
770 PRINT
780 GOTO 560
```

Number Of Days In A Month

Here's a cute teacher for your elementary-age kids. This program displays the name of a month and asks how many days in that month. If the correct number of days is entered, the computer says "correct." If an incorrect number of days is entered, the computer says "wrong." In either case, the correct answer is displayed. The educational game can go on forever if needed.

Program Listing

```
10 CALL CLEAR
15 RANDOMIZE
20 DATA JANUARY,31
30 DATA FEBRUARY,28
40 DATA MARCH,31
50 DATA APRIL,30
60 DATA MAY,31
70 DATA JUNE,30
80 DATA JULY,31
90 DATA AUGUST,31
100 DATA SEPTEMBER,30
```

```
110 DATA OCTOBER,31
120 DATA NOVEMBER,30
130 DATA DECEMBER,31
140 R=INT(25*RND)
150 IF INT(R/2)=(R/2)THEN 170
160 GOTO 180
170 R=R-1
180 FOR L=1 TO R
190 READ S$
200 NEXT L
210 PRINT "MONTH IS ";S$
220 READ C$
230 INPUT "HOW MANY DAYS?":D$
240 IF D$=C$ THEN 270
250 PRINT "WRONG"
260 GOTO 280
270 PRINT "RIGHT"
280 PRINT "NUMBER OF DAYS IS ";C$
290 RESTORE
300 PRINT
310 GOTO 140
```

Bubble Sort

This program sorts names, labels, words, letters into alphabetical order, A to Z. As written here it will accept up to 26 items, sort them, and print a list of those names horizontally across the screen in alphabetical order. Then it prints the list in original entry order for comparison. It shows that the items really were sorted and none were lost!

You may type in a list of up to 26 items. If you type in fewer than 26, press ENTER without data to exit the entry loop and get on with sorting.

Program Listing

```
10 CLS:CLEAR
20 DIM M$(26):DIM D$(26)
30 FOR L=1 TO 26
40 INPUT "NAME";M$(L)
50 IF M$(L)="" THEN 70
55 D$(L)=M$(L)
```

```
60 NEXT L
70 CLS
80 PRINT"SORTING NOW"
90 T=0
100 FOR L=1 TO 25
110 IF M$(L)<=M$(L+1) THEN 160
120 E$=M$(L)
130 M$(L)=M$(L+1)
140 M$(L+1)=E$
150 T=1
160 NEXT L
170 IF T=1 THEN 90
180 CLS
190 BEEP
200 FOR L=1 TO 26
210 IF M$(L)<>"" THEN PRINT M$(L);" ";
220 NEXT L
225 PRINT
230 FOR L=1 TO 26
240 IF D$(L)<>"" THEN PRINT D$(L);" ";
250 NEXT L
300 IF INKEY$="" THEN 300
310 GOTO 10
```

Astronomy
Lightyears/Distance Conversions

For students of astronomy everywhere, here's how to plug your computer into your hobby: use the machine to discover distances across the Universe!

This program converts lightyears to kilometers or kilometers to lightyears or lightyears to miles or miles to lightyears. It's hard to visualize distances in lightyears. Run this program and you'll be better able to grasp the vast expanse of the Cosmos with your mind.

Of course, all distances are approximate. We use 365.86 days per year and, thus, 9.4830912×10^{12}km/ly or $5.892792872 \times 10^{12}$mi/ly.

Program Listing

```
10 CALL CLEAR
```

```
20 GOSUB 410
30 PRINT "LIGHTYRS/DISTANCE CONVERSION"
40 GOSUB 410
50 PRINT
60 PRINT "YOUR CHOICES ARE:"
70 PRINT "(1) LIGHTYRS TO KILOMETERS"
80 PRINT "(2) LIGHTYRS TO MILES"
90 PRINT "(3) KILOMETERS TO LIGHTYRS"
100 PRINT "(4) MILES TO LIGHTYRS"
110 GOSUB 410
120 PRINT "WHICH CONVERSION: 1,2,3,4?"
130 CALL KEY(0,C,X)
140 IF X=0 THEN 130
150 IF C<49 THEN 120
160 IF C>52 THEN 120
170 IF C>50 THEN 310
180 PRINT
190 INPUT "LIGHTYEARS: ":L
200 K=L*(9.4830912*(10^12))
210 M=L*(5.89279287*(10^12))
220 CALL CLEAR
230 PRINT "LIGHTYEARS: ";L
240 IF C=50 THEN 290
250 PRINT "KILOMETERS: ";K
260 PRINT
270 PRINT
280 GOTO 50
290 PRINT "MILES:       ";M
300 GOTO 50
310 CALL CLEAR
320 IF C=52 THEN 370
330 INPUT "KILOMETERS: ":K
340 L=K/(9.4830912*(10^12))
350 PRINT "LIGHTYEARS:";L
360 GOTO 50
370 INPUT "MILES:       ":M
380 L=M/(5.89279287*(10^12))
390 GOTO 350
400 END
410 FOR Z=1 TO 28
420 PRINT "+";
430 NEXT Z
440 RETURN
```

State Geographic Centers

This mind bender tests your knowledge of geographic locations of cities and towns in the United States. These are special places since, in each case, they are the town nearest to the geographic center of its state.

Program Listing

```
10 CALL CLEAR
20 DATA CLANTON,ALABAMA
30 DATA MT. McKINLEY,ALASKA
40 DATA PRESCOTT,ARIZONA
50 DATA LITTLE ROCK,ARKANSAS
60 DATA MADERA,CALIFORNIA
70 DATA PIKES PEAK,COLORADO
80 DATA EAST BERLIN,CONNECTICUT
90 DATA DOVER,DELAWARE
100 DATA BROOKSVILLE,FLORIDA
110 DATA MACON,GEORGIA
120 DATA MAUI ISLAND,HAWAII
130 DATA CHALLIS,IDAHO
140 DATA SPRINGFIELD,ILLINOIS
150 DATA INDIANAPOLIS,INDIANA
160 DATA AMES,IOWA
170 DATA GREAT BANK,KANSAS
180 DATA LEBANON,KENTUCKY
190 DATA MARKSVILLE,LOUISIANA
200 DATA DOVER/FOXCROFT,MAINE
210 DATA DAVIDSONVILLE,MARYLAND
220 DATA WORCESTER,MASSACHUSETTS
230 DATA CADILLAC,MICHIGAN
240 DATA BRAINERD,MINNESOTA
250 DATA CARTHAGE,MISSISSIPPI
260 DATA JEFFERSON CITY,MISSOURI
270 DATA LEWISTOWN,MONTANA
280 DATA BROKEN BOW,NEBRASKA
290 DATA AUSTIN,NEVADA
300 DATA ASHLAND,NEW HAMPSHIRE
310 DATA TRENTON,NEW JERSEY
320 DATA WILLARD,NEW MEXICO
330 DATA ONEIDA,NEW YORK
```

```
340 DATA SANFORD,NORTH CAROLINA
350 DATA McCLUSKY,NORTH DAKOTA
360 DATA COLUMBUS,OHIO
370 DATA OKLAHOMA CITY,OKLAHOMA
380 DATA PRINEVILLE,OREGON
390 DATA BELLEFONTE,PENNSYLVANIA
400 DATA CROMPTON,RHODE ISLAND
410 DATA COLUMBIA,SOUTH CAROLINA
420 DATA PIERRE,SOUTH DAKOTA
430 DATA MURFREESBORO,TENNESSEE
440 DATA BRADY,TEXAS
450 DATA MANTI,UTAH
460 DATA ROXBURY,VERMONT
470 DATA BUCKINGHAM,VIRGINIA
480 DATA WENATCHEE,WASHINGTON
490 DATA SUTTON,WEST VIRGINIA
500 DATA MARSHFIELD,WISCONSIN
510 DATA LANDER,WYOMING
520 PRINT "FOR HOW MANY STATES"
530 PRINT "CAN YOU NAME"
540 PRINT "THE GEOGRAPHICAL CENTER?"
550 RANDOMIZE
560 R=INT(100*RND)
570 IF R<1 THEN 560
580 IF INT(R/2)=(R/2)THEN 600
590 GOTO 610
600 R=R-1
610 FOR L=1 TO R
620 READ S$
630 NEXT L
640 PRINT
650 PRINT
660 PRINT "WHICH STATE HAS ITS"
670 PRINT "GEOGRAPHIC CENTER NEAR"
680 PRINT S$
690 READ C$
700 INPUT D$
710 PRINT
720 IF C$=D$ THEN 740
730 GOTO 760
740 PRINT "THAT IS CORRECT"
750 GOTO 770
```

```
760 PRINT "SORRY, WRONG"
770 PRINT "THE CENTER OF ";C$
780 PRINT "IS ";S$
790 RESTORE
800 PRINT
810 PRINT
820 PRINT
830 GOTO 560
```

U.S. Presidents

Fourteenth. Let's see, that was Franklin Pierce. *Correct. The fourteenth president was Franklin Pierce*. Let's try another. *Thirty-fourth*. John F. Kennedy. *Wrong. The thirty-fourth president was Dwight D. Eisenhower*.

How many of the 40 U.S. presidents can you name? Bet not as many as you would like!

This program tests not only your knowledge of the name of each president and his number in rank, but also the spelling of his name.

Program Listing

```
10 CALL CLEAR
20 RANDOMIZE
30 DATA FIRST,GEORGE WASHINGTON
40 DATA SECOND,JOHN ADAMS
50 DATA THIRD,THOMAS JEFFERSON
60 DATA FOURTH,JAMES MADISON
70 DATA FIFTH,JAMES MONROE
80 DATA SIXTH,JOHN QUINCY ADAMS
90 DATA SEVENTH,ANDREW JACKSON
100 DATA EIGHTH,MARTIN VAN BUREN
110 DATA NINTH,WILLIAM H. HARRISON
120 DATA TENTH,JOHN TYLER
130 DATA ELEVENTH,JAMES K. POLK
140 DATA TWELFTH,ZACHARY TAYLOR
150 DATA THIRTEENTH,MILLARD FILLMORE
160 DATA FOURTEENTH,FRANKLIN PIERCE
170 DATA FIFTEENTH,JAMES BUCHANAN
180 DATA SIXTEENTH,ABRAHAM LINCOLN
190 DATA SEVENTEENTH,ANDREW JOHNSON
```

```
200 DATA EIGHTEENTH,ULYSSES S. GRANT
210 DATA NINTEENTH,RUTHERFORD B. HAYES
220 DATA TWENTIETH,JAMES A. GARFIELD
230 DATA TWENTY-FIRST,CHESTER A. ARTHUR
240 DATA TWENTY-SECOND,GROVER CLEVELAND
250 DATA TWENTY-THIRD,BENJAMIN HARRISON
260 DATA TWENTY-FOURTH,GROVER CLEVELAND
270 DATA TWENTY-FIFTH,WILLIAM MCKINLEY
280 DATA TWENTY-SIXTH,THEODORE ROOSEVELT
290 DATA TWENTY-SEVENTH,WILLIAM H. TAFT
300 DATA TWENTY-EIGHTH,WOODROW WILSON
310 DATA TWENTY-NINTH,WARREN G. HARDING
320 DATA THIRTIETH,CALVIN COOLIDGE
330 DATA THIRTY-FIRST,HERBERT HOOVER
340 DATA THIRTY-SECOND,FRANKLIN D. ROOSEVELT
350 DATA THIRTY-THIRD,HARRY S TRUMAN
360 DATA THIRTY-FOURTH,DWIGHT D. EISENHOWER
370 DATA THIRTY-FIFTH,JOHN F. KENNEDY
380 DATA THIRTY-SIXTH,LYNDON B. JOHNSON
390 DATA THIRTY-SEVENTH,RICHARD M. NIXON
400 DATA THIRTY-EIGHTH,GERALD R. FORD
410 DATA THIRTY-NINTH,JIMMY CARTER
420 DATA FOURTIETH,RONALD REAGAN
430 PRINT "*******************"
440 PRINT "* U.S. PRESIDENTS *"
450 PRINT "*******************"
460 PRINT
470 PRINT "HOW MANY CAN YOU NAME?"
480 FOR Q=1 TO 11
490 PRINT
500 NEXT Q
510 PRINT "PRESS ANY KEY TO START"
520 CALL KEY(0,Z,X)
530 IF X=0 THEN 520
540 CALL CLEAR
550 R=INT(81*RND)
560 IF R<1 THEN 550
570 IF INT(R/2)=(R/2)THEN 590
580 GOTO 600
590 R=R-1
600 FOR L=1 TO R
610 READ S$
```

```
620 NEXT L
630 PRINT "WHO WAS THE"
640 PRINT S$
650 PRINT "PRESIDENT OF THE"
660 READ C$
670 INPUT "UNITED STATES? ":D$
680 PRINT
690 PRINT
700 IF D$=C$ THEN 730
710 PRINT "WRONG"
720 GOTO 740
730 PRINT "CORRECT"
740 PRINT "THE ";S$;" PRESIDENT"
750 PRINT "WAS ";C$
760 RESTORE
770 PRINT
780 PRINT
790 PRINT "FOR MORE, PRESS M"
800 PRINT "TO QUIT,  PRESS Q"
810 CALL KEY(0,Z,X)
820 IF X=0 THEN 810
830 IF Z=77 THEN 540
840 IF Z=81 THEN 860
850 GOTO 780
860 CALL CLEAR
870 PRINT "END OF TEST"
880 PRINT "***********"
890 PRINT "THANK YOU"
900 PRINT
910 PRINT
```

Ohm's Law

Here's a complete Ohm's Law program for engineers, scientists, students, repairmen, installers, hams, technicians, experimenters and anybody who needs an easy-to-carry fast-use computer.

If you know current, resistance, voltage or power, the computer can find current, resistance, voltage or power very, very quickly.

Program Listing

```
30000 WAIT 60
30010 PRINT "TO FIND OHMS, PRESS O"
30020 PRINT "TO FIND VOLTS, PRESS V"
30030 PRINT "TO FIND AMPS, PRESS A"
30040 PRINT "TO FIND WATTS, PRESS W"
30050 PRINT "PRESS O, V, A, OR W"
30060 K$=INKEY$
30070 IF K$=""THEN 30060
30080 IF K$="O" THEN 31000
30090 IF K$="V" THEN 32000
30100 IF K$="A" THEN 33000
30110 IF K$="W" THEN 34000
30120 GOTO 30060
31000 INPUT "VOLTS=";V$
31010 INPUT "AMPS=";A$
31020 INPUT "WATTS=";W$
31025 WAIT 300
31030 IF V$<>""AND A$<>""THEN LET O=
      (VAL V$)/(VAL A$):PRINT O;" OHMS"
      :GOTO 34060
31040 IF A$<>""AND W$<>""THEN LET O=
      (VAL W$)/((VAL A$)^2):PRINT O;" OHMS"
      :GOTO 34060
31050 IF W$<>""AND V$<>""THEN LET O=
      ((VAL V$)^2)/(VAL W$):PRINT O;" OHMS"
      :GOTO 34060
31060 GOTO 34060
32000 INPUT "OHMS=";O$
32010 INPUT "AMPS=";A$
32020 INPUT "WATTS=";W$
32025 WAIT 300
32030 IF O$<>""AND A$<>""THEN LET V=(VAL
      O$)*(VAL A$):PRINT V;" VOLTS"
      :GOTO 34060
32040 IF A$<>""AND W$<>""THEN LET V=(VAL
      W$)/(VAL A$):PRINT V;" VOLTS"
      :GOTO 34060
32050 IF W$<>""AND O$<>""THEN LET V=√
      ((VAL W$)*(VAL O$)):PRINT V;" VOLTS"
      :GOTO 34060
```

```
32060 GOTO 34060
33000 INPUT "VOLTS=";V$
33010 INPUT "OHMS=";O$
33020 INPUT "WATTS=";W$
33025 WAIT 300
33030 IF V$<>""AND O$<>""THEN LET A=
      (VAL V$)/(VAL O$):PRINT A;" AMPS"
      :GOTO 34060
33040 IF O$<>""AND W$<>""THEN LET A=√
      ((VAL W$)/(VAL O$)):PRINT A;" AMPS"
      :GOTO 34060
33050 IF W$<>""AND V$<>""THEN LET A=
      (VAL W$)/(VAL V$):PRINT A;" AMPS"
      :GOTO 34060
33060 GOTO 34060
34000 INPUT "VOLTS=";V$
34010 INPUT "AMPS=";A$
34020 INPUT "OHMS=";O$
34025 WAIT 300
34030 IF V$<>""AND A$<>""THEN LET W=
      (VAL V$)*(VAL A$):PRINT W;" WATTS"
      :GOTO 34060
34040 IF A$<>""AND O$<>""THEN LET W=
      ((VAL A$)∧2)*(VAL O$):PRINT W
      ;" WATTS":GOTO 34060
34050 IF O$<>""AND V$<>""THEN LET W=
      ((VAL V$)∧2)/(VAL O$):PRINT W
      ;" WATTS"
34060 CLEAR
34070 GOTO 30050
```

Designing Active Filters

Design your own low-pass and high-pass active filters. For electronics experimenters, technicians, electrical engineers, the computer takes the drudgery out of resistance, capacitance, frequency an other computations.

Program Listing

```
10 WAIT 120
```

```
 20 PRINT "******ACTIVE FILTERS******"
 30 PRINT "HI-PASS OR LO-PASS"
 40 PRINT "PRESS H OR L"
 50 WAIT Ø
 60 K$=INKEY$
 70 IF K$=""THEN 60
 80 IF K$="H"THEN 200
 90 IF K$="L"THEN 400
100 GOTO 60
200 INPUT "FC (HZ) = ";F
210 INPUT "HØ=";H
220 INPUT "C (MICROFD) = ";C
230 INPUT "A=";A
240 C=C/(10∧6)
250 B=2*π*F
260 WAIT 120
270 PRINT "R1=";(2*H+1)/(A*B*C)
280 PRINT "R2=";A/(B*C*(2+1/H))
290 PRINT "C=";C/H
300 GOTO 40
400 INPUT "FC (HZ) = ";F
410 INPUT "AF = ";A
420 INPUT "C1 (MICROFD) = ";C
430 C=C/(10∧6)
440 R=√2/4/A/π/F/C
450 S=A*R
460 T=S/(A+1)
470 U=2*(A+1)*C*(10∧6)
480 WAIT 120
490 PRINT "R1=";R
500 PRINT "R2=";S
510 PRINT "R3=";T
520 PRINT "C2=";U
530 GOTO 40
```

Major U.S. Cities

Here's a variety we'll bet you haven't seen anywhere else. This program tests knowledge of geographic locations of major U.S. cities.

In what state is New Orleans? Seattle? Salt Lake City?

You not only have to name the state but spell its name correctly. It can be very tough!

Program Listing

```
 10 CLEAR:CLS
 20 DATA ALBUQUERQUE,NEW MEXICO
 30 DATA ATLANTA,GEORGIA
 40 DATA BALTIMORE,MARYLAND
 50 DATA BIRMINGHAM,ALABAMA
 60 DATA BOSTON,MASSACHUSETTS
 70 DATA BUFFALO,NEW YORK
 80 DATA CHARLESTON,SOUTH CAROLINA
 90 DATA CHICAGO,ILLINOIS
100 DATA CINCINNATI,OHIO
110 DATA CLEVELAND,OHIO
120 DATA COLUMBUS,OHIO
130 DATA DALLAS,TEXAS
140 DATA DENVER,COLORADO
150 DATA DETROIT,MICHIGAN
160 DATA FORT WORTH,TEXAS
170 DATA HONOLULU,HAWAII
180 DATA HOUSTON,TEXAS
190 DATA INDIANAPOLIS,INDIANA
200 DATA KANSAS CITY,KANSAS
210 DATA LOS ANGELES,CALIFORNIA
220 DATA LOUISVILLE,KENTUCKY
230 DATA MEMPHIS,TENNESSEE
240 DATA MIAMI,FLORIDA
250 DATA MILWAUKEE,WISCONSIN
260 DATA MINNEAPOLIS,MINNESOTA
270 DATA NEWARK,NEW JERSEY
280 DATA NEW ORLEANS,LOUISIANA
290 DATA NEW YORK CITY,NEW YORK
300 DATA OKLAHOMA CITY,OKLAHOMA
310 DATA OMAHA,NEBRASKA
320 DATA PHILADELPHIA,PENNSYLVANIA
330 DATA PHOENIX,ARIZONA
340 DATA PITTSBURGH,PENNSYLVANIA
350 DATA PORTLAND,OREGON
360 DATA PROVIDENCE,RHODE ISLAND
370 DATA ROCHESTER,NEW YORK
380 DATA SACRAMENTO,CALIFORNIA
```

```
390 DATA ST. LOUIS,MISSOURI
400 DATA ST. PAUL,MINNESOTA
410 DATA SALT LAKE CITY,UTAH
420 DATA SAN ANTONIA,TEXAS
430 DATA SAN DIEGO,CALIFORNIA
440 DATA SAN FRANCISCO,CALIFORNIA
450 DATA SAN JOSE,CALIFORNIA
460 DATA SEATTLE,WASHINGTON
470 DATA TAMPA,FLORIDA
480 DATA WASHINGTON,DISTRICT OF COLUMBIA
490 DATA WILMINGTON,DELAWARE
500 PRINT @ 39,STRING$(17,"*")
510 PRINT @ 71,"MAJOR U.S. CITIES"
520 PRINT @ 103,STRING$(17."*")
530 PRINT @ 164,"CAN YOU NAME THEIR STATES?"
540 PRINT @ 260,"PRESS ANY KEY TO START"
550 H$=INKEY$
560 IF H$=""THEN 550
570 CLS
580 R=RND(96)
590 IF INT(R/2)=R/2 THEN R=R-1
600 FOR L=1 TO R
610 READ $
620 NEXT L
630 PRINT" ":PRINT" "
640 PRINT"CITY IS: "S$
650 READ C$
660 INPUT"WHAT IS STATE";D$
670 IF D$=C$ THEN PRINT "CORRECT"
    ELSE PRINT "WRONG"
680 PRINT"STATE IS: "C$
690 RESTORE
700 PRINT" ":PRINT" "
710 PRINT"FOR MORE, PRESS M"
720 PRINT"TO STOP, PRESS S"
730 M$=INKEY$
740 IF M$="" THEN 730
750 IF M$="M" THEN CLS:GOTO 580
760 IF M$="S" THEN CLS:GOTO 780
770 GOTO 730
780 PRINT @ 40,STRING$(15,"*")
```

```
790 PRINT @ 74,"END OF TEST"
800 PRINT @ 104,STRING$(15,"*")
810 PRINT @ 170,"THANK YOU !"
820 GOTO 820
```

Body Surface Area

This medical program finds the surface area of a human body, using DuBois's formula and Boyde's formula.

BSA is Body Surface Area. BSA(D) is the area computed via DuBois's formula. BSA(B) is found by Boyde's formula. The DuBois formula produced significant errors when computing area of a child's body of smaller than $0.6m^2$. In that case, the Boyde formula is used.

For this program, heighth is figured in centimeters and weight in kilograms. If BSA(D) is less than 0.6, use BSA(B).

Program Listing

```
 10 WAIT 120
 20 PRINT "****BODY SURFACE AREA****"
 30 INPUT "HEIGHTH (CM): ";H
 40 INPUT "WEIGHT (KG): ";W
 50 BD=(H∧.725)*(W∧.425)*(71.84*(10∧-4))
 60 WAIT 300
 70 PRINT "B.S.A.(D):";BD
 80 W=W*(10∧3)
 90 BB=(H∧.3)*(W∧(.7285-(.0188*LOG W)))
    *(3.207*10∧-4)
100 PRINT "B.S.A.(B):";BB
110 IF INKEY$ ="" THEN 110
120 CLEAR
130 GOTO 30
```

Urea Removal

There is another medical program, this time finding the rate of generation of urine by a human body.

The program causes the computer to correct automatically for body surface area, depending upon whether you key in a zero or BSA in response to the prompt.

Program Listing

```
 10 INPUT "VT=";V
 20 INPUT "U=";U
 30 INPUT "B=";B
 40 INPUT "ENTER ZERO OR BSA: ";F
 50 IF F<>ØTHEN LET V=(1.73/F)*V
    :PRINT "V*=";V
 60 GOSUB SGN (SGN(V-2)-1)*10+110
 70 PRINT "CS=";C
 80 PRINT "<CS>=";D
 90 GOTO 10
100 C=(U*√V)/B:D=1.85*C:RETURN
110 C=(U*V)/B:D=1.33*C:RETURN
```

Canadian Provinces

Another interesting learning experience. Test your knowledge of the Canadian provinces.

You must correctly identify the name of each capital and spell it properly.

Program Listing

```
 10 CLEAR:CLS
 20 DATA ALBERTA,EDMONTON
 30 DATA BRITISH COLUMBIA,VICTORIA
 40 DATA MANITOBA,WINNIPEG
 50 DATA NEW BRUNSWICK,FREDERICTON
 60 DATA NEWFOUNDLAND,ST. JOHN'S
 70 DATA NOVA SCOTIA,HALIFAX
 80 DATA ONTARIO,TORONTO
 90 DATA PRINCE EDWARD ISLAND,CHARLOTTETOWN
100 DATA QUEBEC, QUEBEC
110 DATA SASKATCHEWAN,REGINA
120 PRINT @ 39,STRING$(18,"*")
130 PRINT @ 71,"CANADIAN PROVINCES"
140 PRINT @ 103,STRING$(18,"*")
150 PRINT @ 162,"CAN YOU NAME THEIR
    CAPITALS?"
```

```
160 PRINT @ 261,"PRESS ANY KEY TO START"
170 H$=INKEY$
180 IF H$="" THEN 170
190 CLS
200 R=RND(20)
210 IF INT(R/2)=R/2 THEN R=R-1
220 FOR L=1 TO R
230 READ S$
240 NEXT L
250 PRINT" ":PRINT" "
260 PRINT"PROVINCE IS "S$
270 READ C$
280 INPUT"WHAT IS CAPITAL";D$
290 IF D$=C$ THEN PRINT "CORRECT"
    ELSE PRINT "WRONG"
300 PRINT"CAPITAL IS "C$
310 RESTORE
320 PRINT" ":PRINT" "
330 PRINT"FOR MORE, PRESS M"
340 PRINT"TO STOP, PRESS S"
350 M$=INKEY$
360 IF M$="" THEN 350
370 IF M$="M" THEN CLS:GOTO 200
380 IF M$="S" THEN CLS:GOTO 400
390 GOTO 350
400 PRINT @ 40,STRING$(15,"*")
410 PRINT @ 74,"END OF TEST"
420 PRINT @ 104,STRING$(15,"*")
430 PRINT @ 170,"THANK YOU !"
440 GOTO 440
```

Thermal Stress

Mechanical engineers can use the computer to find thermal stress, including linear expansion coefficient, elastic constant and cross section.

Program Listing

```
10 WAIT 120
20 PRINT "******THERMAL STRESS******"
30 INPUT "L1=";L
40 INPUT "L2=";M
```

```
 50 INPUT "E1=";E
 60 INPUT "E2=";F
 70 INPUT "A1=";A
 80 INPUT "A2=";B
 90 INPUT "T=";T
100 C=E*F*(L-M)*T
110 C=C/(E*A+F*B)
120 R=-(B*C)
130 S=A*C
140 PRINT "S1=";R
150 PRINT "S2=";S
160 GOTO 10
```

Radio Frequency & Wavelength

Let your computer convert frequency to wavelength and wavelength to frequency. Upon running this program, press F to compute frequency or W to compute wavelength. After conversion press M to do more. The program will run continuously until you press the BREAK key.

Program Listing

```
10 CLS:CLEAR
20 GOSUB 800
30 PRINT @ 125,"COMPUTE FREQUENCY"
   ;SPACE$(4);"PRESS F"
40 PRINT @ 165,"COMPUTE WAVELENGTH"
   ;SPACE$(3);"PRESS W"
50 K$=INKEY$
60 IF K$="" THEN 50
70 IF K$="W" THEN 200
80 IF K$="F" THEN 500
90 PRINT @ 250,"PRESS ONLY F OR W"
100 GOTO 50
200 CLS:GOSUB 800
210 PRINT @ 125,"FREQUENCY (MHz)"
    ;SPACE$(4);:INPUT F
220 W=300/F
230 PRINT @ 165,F;"MHz =";W;"METERS"
240 PRINT @ 245,"PRESS M FOR MORE"
250 IF INKEY$="" THEN 250
260 GOTO 10
```

```
500 CLS:GOSUB 800
510 PRINT @ 125,"WAVELENGTH (METERS)"
    ;SPACE$(1);:INPUT W
520 F=300/W
530 PRINT @ 165,W;"METERS =";F;"MHz"
540 GOTO 240
800 LINE(24,2)-(202,20),1,BF
810 LINE(28,6)-(198,16),2,BF
820 PRINT @ 45,"RADIO FREQUENCY &
    WAVELENGTH"
830 RETURN
```

Receiver Sensitivity

Sensitivity is the ability of a radio receiver to respond to signals. Published sensitivity ratings for your receiver, in microvolts, can be converted to power ratings by changing microvolts (uV) to dBf.

This program computes dBf when uV are known. A 300-ohm antenna input to the receiver is assumed. Note that, in hi-fi, sensitivity is not the same for monaural and stereo so stereo tuners and receivers should include separate dBf figures for each.

In this program, we store microvolts in memory location V and, after computation, dBf is in D.

Program Listing

```
 10 CLS
 20 CLEAR
 30 FOR L=1 TO 32
 40 PRINT CHR$ 131;
 50 NEXT L
 60 PRINT
 70 PRINT CHR$ 133;" RECEIVER SENSITIVITY "
    ;CHR$ 5
 80 FOR L=1 TO 32
 90 PRINT CHR$ 3;
100 NEXT L
110 PRINT
120 PRINT "ENTER DATA:"
```

```
130 PRINT
140 PRINT "SENSITIVITY MICROVOLTS ?"
150 INPUT V
160 CLS
165 PRINT
170 PRINT V;" MICROVOLTS"
180 LET D=20*((LN (V/.55))/(LN 10))
190 PRINT "DBF";D
200 FOR L=1 TO 5
210 PRINT
220 NEXT L
240 GOTO 20
```

Horsepower

Horsepower can be converted to watts. Watts can be changed to horsepower. This set of instructions will let you have your choice on the computer. And, if you are converting horsepower to watts, you get a conversion of watts to kilowatts as a bonus.

We use one horsepower as equal to 746 watts or as equal to 550 foot-pounds per second. One watt then is 1/746 horsepower which is 0.00134 horsepower.

Program Listing

```
 10 CLS
 20 CLEAR
 30 FOR L=1 TO 32
 40 PRINT CHR$ 136;
 50 NEXT L
 60 PRINT
 70 PRINT  CHR$ 136;" HORSEPOWER "
    ;CHR$ 136
 80 FOR L=1 TO 32
 90 PRINT CHR$ 136;
100 NEXT L
110 PRINT
120 PRINT
130 PRINT "DO YOU WANT TO FIND"
140 PRINT
150 PRINT "WATTS (W)"
```

```
160 PRINT "HORSEPOWER (H)"
170 LET K$=INKEY$
180 IF K$="" THEN GOTO 170
190 IF K$="W" THEN GOTO 300
200 IF K$="H" THEN GOTO 500
210 GOTO 170
300 CLS
310 PRINT
320 PRINT "PLEASE ENTER HORSEPOWER "
330 INPUT H
340 CLS
350 LET W=746*H
360 LET K=0.001*W
370 PRINT H;" HORSEPOWER"
380 PRINT W;" WATTS"
390 PRINT K;" KILOWATTS"
400 PRINT
410 PRINT
420 PRINT
430 GOTO 20
500 CLS
510 PRINT
520 PRINT "PLEASE ENTER NUMBER OF WATTS"
530 INPUT W
540 CLS
550 LET H=W/746
560 LET K=0.001*W
570 GOTO 370
```

Math Flasher

Flash cards for memorizing and practicing math problems have been around since Grandpa was a boy. They used to be printed cards which you manually displayed to the testee. Now, the computer does the job and all you have to do is sit by and watch.

With this program, you select addition, subtraction, multiplication or division. The computer randomly selects a pair of numbers and creates the necessary math problem.

We assume it is desirable to *not* have negative numbers

as results of subtraction. We want subtraction problems which result in answers of zero, one, two and higher. None below zero such as -1, -2, -3 or lower. The program will present only pairs of numbers which result in the desired values.

Also, in division, we want whole-number answers like 2, 11 or 26. Not 1.81, 9.7, or 21.334. The program controls for the desired answers.

Program Listing

```
 10 PRINT "ADDITION"
 20 FOR L=1 TO 8
 30 PRINT "*";
 40 NEXT L
 50 PRINT
 60 PRINT
100 LET P=INT(10*RND)
110 LET Q=INT(10*RND)
200 PRINT P;" PLUS ";Q
210 INPUT R
220 CLS
300 IF R=P+Q THEN GOTO 400
310 PRINT "WRONG"
320 GOTO 410
400 PRINT "CORRECT"
410 PRINT P;" PLUS ";Q;" = ";P+Q
500 PRINT
510 PRINT
520 GOTO 10
```

Program Listing

```
 10 PRINT "SUBTRACTION"
 20 FOR L=1 TO 11
 30 PRINT "*";
 40 NEXT L
 50 PRINT
 60 PRINT
100 LET P=INT(10*RND)
110 LET Q=INT(10*RND)
120 IF P-Q<Ø THEN GOTO 100
200 PRINT "SUBTRACT ";Q;" FROM ";P
```

```
210 INPUT R
220 CLS
300 IF R=P-Q THEN GOTO 400
310 PRINT "WRONG"
320 GOTO 410
400 PRINT "CORRECT"
410 PRINT P;" MINUS ";Q;" = ";P-Q
500 PRINT
510 PRINT
520 GOTO 10
```

Program Listing

```
 10 PRINT "MULTIPLICATION"
 20 FOR L=1 TO 14
 30 PRINT "*";
 40 NEXT L
 50 PRINT
 60 PRINT
100 LET P=INT(10*RND)
110 LET Q=INT(10*RND)
200 PRINT "MULTIPLY ";P;" TIMES ";Q
210 INPUT R
220 CLS
300 IF R=P*Q THEN GOTO 400
310 PRINT "WRONG"
320 GOTO 410
400 PRINT "CORRECT"
410 PRINT P;" TIMES ";Q;" = ";P*Q
500 PRINT
510 PRINT
520 GOTO 10
```

Program Listing

```
 10 PRINT "DIVISION"
 20 FOR L=1 TO 8
 30 PRINT "*";
 40 NEXT L
 50 PRINT
 60 PRINT
100 LET P=INT(10*RND)
```

```
110 LET Q=INT(10*RND)
120 IF Q<1 THEN GOTO 110
130 IF P/Q <> INT(P/Q) THEN GOTO 100
200 PRINT "DIVIDE ";P;" BY ";Q
210 INPUT R
220 CLS
300 IF R=P/Q THEN GOTO 400
310 PRINT "WRONG"
320 GOTO 410
400 PRINT "CORRECT"
410 PRINT P;" DIVIDED BY ";Q;" = ";P/Q
500 PRINT
510 PRINT
520 GOTO 10
```

Advanced Math Flasher

Similar to the previous Math Flasher program, this version permits negative numbers and decimal answers.

Program Listing

```
 10 PRINT "ADDITION"
 20 FOR L=1 TO 8
 30 PRINT "*";
 40 NEXT L
 50 PRINT
 60 PRINT
100 LET P=INT(100*RND)
110 LET Q=INT(100*RND)
200 PRINT "ADD ";P;" PLUS ";Q
210 INPUT R
220 CLS
300 IF R=P+Q THEN GOTO 400
310 PRINT "WRONG"
320 GOTO 410
400 PRINT "CORRECT"
410 PRINT P;" PLUS ";Q;" = ";P+Q
500 PRINT
510 PRINT
520 GOTO 10
```

Program Listing

```
 10 PRINT "SUBTRACTION"
 20 FOR L=1 TO 11
 30 PRINT "*";
 40 NEXT L
 50 PRINT
 60 PRINT
100 LET P=INT(100*RND)
110 LET Q=INT(100*RND)
200 PRINT "SUBTRACT ";Q;" FROM ";P
210 INPUT R
220 CLS
300 IF R=P-Q THEN GOTO 400
310 PRINT "WRONG"
320 GOTO 410
400 PRINT "CORRECT"
410 PRINT P;" MINUS ";Q;" = ";P-Q
500 PRINT
510 PRINT
520 GOTO 10
```

Program Listing

```
 10 PRINT "MULTIPLICATION"
 20 FOR L=1 TO 14
 30 PRINT "*";
 40 NEXT L
 50 PRINT
 60 PRINT
100 LET P=INT(100*RND)
110 LET Q=INT(100*RND)
200 PRINT "MULTIPLY ";P;" TIMES ";Q
210 INPUT R
220 CLS
300 IF R=P*Q THEN GOTO 400
310 PRINT "WRONG"
320 GOTO 410
400 PRINT "CORRECT"
410 PRINT P;" TIMES ";Q;" = ";P*Q
500 PRINT
510 PRINT
520 GOTO 10
```

Program Listing

```
10 PRINT "DIVISION"
20 FOR L=1 TO 8
30 PRINT "*";
40 NEXT L
50 PRINT
60 PRINT
100 LET P=INT(100*RND)
110 LET Q=INT(100*RND)
120 IF Q=Ø THEN GOTO 110
200 PRINT "DIVIDE ";P;" BY ";Q
210 INPUT R
220 CLS
300 IF R=P/Q THEN GOTO 400
310 PRINT "WRONG"
320 GOTO 410
400 PRINT "CORRECT"
410 PRINT P;" DIVIDED BY ";Q;" = ";P/Q
500 PRINT
510 PRINT
520 GOTO 10
```

Weights & Measures

How many inches in a centimeter? Ounces in a tablespoon? Cubic feet of firewood in a cord? Run this program and you'll not only test your existing knowledge of weights and measurements but learn more.

Program Listing

```
10 HOME
20 DATA MILE IN FEET,5280
30 DATA MILE IN KILOMETERS,1.609
40 DATA NAUTICAL MILE IN STATUTE
   MILES,1.151
50 DATA MILLIMETER IN INCHES,.03937
60 DATA POINT(TYPOGRAPHY) IN
   INCHES,.013837
70 DATA ROD IN YARDS,5.5
80 DATA ACRE IN SQUARE YARDS,4840
```

```
 90 DATA ACRE IN SQUARE FEET,43560
100 DATA HECTARE IN ACRES,2.471
110 DATA CENTIMETER IN INCHES,0.3937
120 DATA SURVEYOR'S CHAIN IN FEET,66
130 DATA ENGINEER'S CHAIN IN FEET,100
140 DATA FATHOM IN FEET,6
150 DATA FOOT IN METERS,0.3048
160 DATA FURLONG IN FEET,660
170 DATA FURLONG IN YARDS,220
180 DATA FURLONG IN METERS,201.168
190 DATA HAND IN INCHES,4
200 DATA INCH IN CENTIMETERS,2.54
210 DATA KILOMETER IN MILES,0.621
220 DATA LEAGUE IN MILES,3
230 DATA METER IN INCHES,39.37
240 DATA METER IN YARDS,1.094
250 DATA SQ. FOOT IN SQ. CENTIMETERS,
    929.030
260 DATA SQ. METER IN SQ. YARDS,1.196
270 DATA SQUARE MILE IN HECTARES,258.999
280 DATA SQ. YARD IN SQUARE METERS,0.836
290 DATA BUSHEL IN CUBIC INCHES,2150.42
300 DATA CORD FIREWOOD IN CUBIC FEET,128
310 DATA CUBIC FOOT IN GALLONS,7.481
320 DATA CUP IN FLUID OUNCES,8
330 DATA CUP LIQUID IN PINTS,0.5
340 DATA U.S. GALLON IN LITERS,3.785
350 DATA LITER LIQUID IN QUARTS,1.057
360 DATA FLUID OUNCE IN MILLILITERS,29.574
370 DATA PECK IN LITERS,8.810
380 DATA DRY PINT IN CUBIC INCHES,33.6
390 DATA PINT LIQUID IN LITERS,0.473
400 DATA DRY QUART IN CUBIC INCHES,67.201
410 DATA QUART LIQUID IN LITERS,0.946
420 DATA TABLESPOON IN TEASPOONS,3
430 DATA TABLESPOON IN FLUID OUNCES,0.5
440 DATA TEASPOON IN TABLESPOONS,0.3333333
450 DATA GRAM IN OUNCES,0.035
460 DATA KILOGRAM IN POUNDS,2.205
470 DATA OUNCE IN GRAMS,28.350
480 DATA PENNYWEIGHT IN GRAMS,1.555
490 DATA POUND IN GRAMS,453.59237
```

```
500 DATA TON(NET OR SHORT) IN POUNDS,2000
510 DATA TON(METRIC) IN POUNDS,2204.623
520 PRINT"HOW MANY EQUIVALENTS OF"
530 PRINT"WEIGHTS AND MEASURES DO YOU
    KNOW ?"
540 R=INT(100*(RND(1)))
550 IF R<1 THEN 540
560 IF INT(R/2)=R/2 THEN R=R-1
570 FOR L=1 TO R
580 READ S$
590 NEXT L
600 PRINT:PRINT
610 PRINT"WHAT IS THE EQUIVALENT OF 1"
    ;S$
620 READ C$
630 INPUT D$
640 PRINT
650 IF D$=C$ THEN PRINT "CORRECT"
    :GOTO 670
660 PRINT "WRONG"
670 PRINT"THE CORRECT ANSWER IS ";C$
680 RESTORE
690 PRINT:PRINT
700 GOTO 540
```

Lakes of the World

Sure, Lake of the Woods and the Great Salt Lake are in North America. But where is Lake Van, Lake Onega, Lake Reindeer, or Lake Nyasa?

The computer asks you which continent is the location of a major large lake.

Program Listing

```
10 HOME
20 DATA CASPIAN SEA,ASIA/EUROPE
30 DATA SUPERIOR,NORTH AMERICA
40 DATA VICTORIA,AFRICA
50 DATA ARAL SEA,ASIA
60 DATA HURON,NORTH AMERICA
70 DATA MICHIGAN,NORTH AMERICA
```

```
 80 DATA TANGANYIKA,AFRICA
 90 DATA BAYKAL,ASIA
100 DATA GREAT BEAR,NORTH AMERICA
110 DATA NYASA (MALAWI),AFRICA
120 DATA GREAT SLAVE,NORTH AMERICA
130 DATA CHAD,AFRICA
140 DATA ERIE,NORTH AMERICA
150 DATA WINNIPEG,NORTH AMERICA
160 DATA ONTARIO,NORTH AMERICA
170 DATA LADOGA,EUROPE
180 DATA BALKHASH,ASIA
190 DATA MARACAIBO,SOUTH AMERICA
200 DATA BANGWEULU,AFRICA
210 DATA TUNGTING,ASIA
220 DATA ONEGA,EUROPE
230 DATA EYRE,AUSTRALIA
240 DATA TITICACA,SOUTH AMERICA
250 DATA NICARAGUA,NORTH AMERICA
260 DATA ATHABASCA,NORTH AMERICA
270 DATA REINDEER,NORTH AMERICA
280 DATA TONLE SAP,ASIA
290 DATA TURKANA (RUDOLF),AFRICA
300 DATA ISSYK-KUL',ASIA
310 DATA URMIA,ASIA
320 DATA TORRENS,AUSTRALIA
330 DATA VANERN,EUROPE
340 DATA WINNIPEGOSIS,NORTH AMERICA
350 DATA ALBERT,AFRICA
360 DATA KARIBA,AFRICA
370 DATA NETTILLING,NORTH AMERICA
380 DATA CHANY,ASIA
390 DATA NIPIGON,NORTH AMERICA
400 DATA GAIRDNER,AUSTRALIA
410 DATA MWERU,AFRICA
420 DATA MANITOBA,NORTH AMERICA
430 DATA TAYMYR,ASIA
440 DATA KYOGA,AFRICA
450 DATA KHANKA,ASIA
460 DATA LAKE OF THE WOODS,NORTH AMERICA
470 DATA PEIPUS,EUROPE
480 DATA KOKO NOR,ASIA
490 DATA NASSER-NUBIA,AFRICA
```

```
500 DATA DUBAWNT,NORTH AMERICA
510 DATA VAN,ASIA
520 DATA WOLLASTON,NORTH AMERICA
530 DATA GREAT SALT LAKE,NORTH AMERICA
540 PRINT"HOW MANY FAMOUS LAKES OF THE
    WORLD CAN YOU LOCATE ?"
550 R=INT(104*(RND(1)))
560 IF R<1 THEN 550
570 IF INT(R/2)=R/2 THEN R=R-1
580 FOR L=1 TO R
590 READ S$
600 NEXT L
610 PRINT:PRINT
620 PRINT S$;" IS A LARGE LAKE"
630 READ C$
640 INPUT"ON WHAT CONTINENT OR CONTINENTS
    IS IT LOCATED";D$
650 IF D$=C$ THEN PRINT"CORRECT"
    :GOTO 670
660 PRINT"WRONG"
670 PRINT"THE CONTINENT IS ";C$
680 RESTORE
690 PRINT:PRINT
700 GOTO 550
```

Deserts of the World

If lakes are too wet for you, how about something more in the dry line? Deserts!

There are many major ones around the world. You may have heard of the Sahara or Death Valley. But where are they? On what continents? And where is Atacama, Gibson, Nefud or Sechura?

Program Listing

```
10 HOME
20 DATA ARABIAN,AFRICA
30 DATA ATACAMA,SOUTH AMERICA
40 DATA COLORADO,NORTH AMERICA
50 DATA DASHT-I-KAVIR,ASIA
60 DATA DASHT-I-LUT,ASIA
```

```
 70 DATA DEATH VALLEY,NORTH AMERICA
 80 DATA GIBSON,AUSTRALIA
 90 DATA GOBI,ASIA
100 DATA GREAT SALT LAKE,NORTH AMERICA
110 DATA GREAT SANDY,AUSTRALIA
120 DATA GREAT VICTORIA,AUSTRALIA
130 DATA KALAHARI,AFRICA
140 DATA KARA-KUM,ASIA
150 DATA KYZYL-KUM,ASIA
160 DATA MOJAVE,NORTH AMERICA
170 DATA NAMIB,AFRICA
180 DATA NEFUD (AN NAFUD),ASIA
190 DATA NEGEV,ASIA
200 DATA NUBIAN,AFRICA
210 DATA RUB AL KHALI,ASIA
220 DATA SAHARA,AFRICA
230 DATA SECHURA,SOUTH AMERICA
240 DATA SIMPSON,AUSTRALIA
250 DATA SYRIAN (EL HAMAD),ASIA
260 DATA TAKLAMAKAN,ASIA
270 DATA THAR (GREAT INDIAN),ASIA
280 DATA VIZCAINO,NORTH AMERICA
290 PRINT"HOW MANY DESERTS OF THE WORLD
    CAN YOU LOCATE ?"
300 R=INT(54*(RND(1)))
310 IF R<1 THEN 300
320 IF INT(R/2)=R/2 THEN R=R-1
330 FOR L=1 TO R
340 READ S$
350 NEXT L
360 PRINT:PRINT
370 PRINT S$
380 PRINT"IS ONE OF"
390 PRINT"WORLD'S GREAT DESERTS"
400 READ C$
410 PRINT:PRINT"ON WHAT CONTINENT"
420 INPUT"IS IT LOCATED";D$
430 IF D$=C$ THEN PRINT"CORRECT"
    :GOTO 450
440 PRINT"WRONG"
450 PRINT"CONTINENT IS ";C$
460 RESTORE
```

```
470 PRINT:PRINT
480 GOTO 300
```

Volcanoes of the World

In what country does the lava flow? Where is the active volcano we know as Mauna Loa? Lascar? Fogo? Torbert?

The computer names a volcano and you name the country, except in the one case in Antarctica which is a continent.

Program Listing

```
 10 HOME
 20 DATA KILIMANJARO,TANZANIA
 30 DATA EREBUS,ANTARCTICA
 40 DATA KLYUCHEVSKAYA,USSR
 50 DATA MAUNA KEA,USA
 60 DATA ETNA,ITALY
 70 DATA POPOCATEPETL,MEXICO
 80 DATA GUALLATIRI,CHILE
 90 DATA CAMEROON MT.,CAMEROON
100 DATA KERINTJI,INDONESIA
110 DATA MAUNA LOA,USA
120 DATA COLIMA,MEXICA
130 DATA TAJUMULCO,GUATEMALA
140 DATA LASCAR,CHILE
150 DATA FUJI,JAPAN
160 DATA WRANGELL,USA
170 DATA COTOPAXI,ECUADOR
180 DATA NYIRAGONGO,CONGO
190 DATA TOLBACHIK,USSR
200 DATA TORBERT,USA
210 DATA SPURR,USA
220 DATA LASSEN,USA
230 DATA TACANA,GUATEMALA
240 DATA IRAZU,COSTA RICA
250 DATA MISTI,PERU
260 DATA PURACE,COLOMBIA
270 DATA EL TEIDE,CANARY ISLANDS
280 DATA FOGO,CAPE VERDE ISLANDS
```

```
290 PRINT"HOW MANY VOLCANOES OF THE WORLD"
300 PRINT"CAN YOU LOCATE ?"
310 R=INT(54*(RND(1)))
320 IF R<1 THEN 310
330 IF INT(R/2)=R/2 THEN R=R-1
340 FOR L=1 TO R
350 READ S$
360 NEXT L
370 PRINT:PRINT
380 PRINT S$
390 PRINT"IS ONE OF THE"
400 PRINT"WORLD'S HIGHEST VOLCANOES"
410 READ C$
420 PRINT"IN WHAT COUNTRY"
430 INPUT"IS IT LOCATED";D$
440 IF D$=C$ THEN PRINT"CORRECT"
    :GOTO 460
450 PRINT:PRINT"WRONG"
460 PRINT"COUNTRY IS ";C$
470 RESTORE
480 PRINT:PRINT
490 GOTO 310
```

Chemistry: Elements and their Symbols

Here's a great drill for the chemistry student. The computer displays one of the chemical symbols and you must reply with the correct name of the element. And it must be spelled correctly!

Program Listing

```
10 HOME
20 DATA AC,ACTINIUM
30 DATA AL,ALUMINUM
40 DATA AM,AMERICIUM
50 DATA SB,ANTIMONY
60 DATA AR,ARGON
70 DATA AS,ARSENIC
80 DATA AT,ASTATINE
```

```
 90 DATA BA,BARIUM
100 DATA BK,BERKELIUM
110 DATA BE,BERYLLIUM
120 DATA BI,BISMUTH
130 DATA B,BORON
140 DATA BR,BROMINE
150 DATA CD,CADMIUM
160 DATA CA,CALCIUM
170 DATA CF,CALIFORNIUM
180 DATA C,CARBON
190 DATA CE,CERIUM
200 DATA CS,CESIUM
210 DATA CL,CHLORINE
220 DATA CR,CHROMIUM
230 DATA CO,COBALT
240 DATA CU,COPPER
250 DATA CM,CURIUM
260 DATA DY,DYSPROSIUM
270 DATA ES,EINSTEINIUM
280 DATA ER,ERBIUM
290 DATA EU,EUROPIUM
300 DATA FM,FERMIUM
310 DATA F,FLUORINE
320 DATA FR,FRANCIUM
330 DATA GD,GADOLINIUM
340 DATA GA,GALLIUM
350 DATA GE,GERMANIUM
360 DATA AU,GOLD
370 DATA HF,HAFNIUM
380 DATA HE,HELIUM
390 DATA HO,HOLMIUM
400 DATA H,HYDROGEN
410 DATA IN,INDIUM
420 DATA I,IODINE
430 DATA IR,IRIDIUM
440 DATA FE,IRON
450 DATA KR,KRYPTON
460 DATA LA,LANTHANUM
470 DATA LR,LAWRENCIUM
480 DATA PB,LEAD
490 DATA LI,LITHIUM
500 DATA LU,LUTETIUM
```

```
510 DATA MG,MAGNESIUM
520 DATA MN,MANGANESE
530 DATA MD,MENDELEVIUM
540 DATA HG,MERCURY
550 DATA MO,MOLYBDENUM
560 DATA ND,NEODYMIUM
570 DATA NE,NEON
580 DATA NP,NEPTUNIUM
590 DATA NI,NICKEL
600 DATA NB,NIOBIUM
610 DATA N,NITROGEN
620 DATA NO,NOBELIUM
630 DATA OS,OSMIUM
640 DATA O,OXYGEN
650 DATA PD,PALLADIUM
660 DATA P,PHOSPHORUS
670 DATA PT,PLATINUM
680 DATA PU,PLUTONIUM
690 DATA PO,POLONIUM
700 DATA K,POTASSIUM
710 DATA PR,PRASEODYMIUM
720 DATA PM,PROMETHIUM
730 DATA PA,PROTACTINIUM
740 DATA RA,RADIUM
750 DARA RN,RADON
760 DATA RE,RHENIUM
770 DATA RH,RHODIUM
780 DATA RB,RUBIDIUM
790 DATA RU,RUTHENIUM
800 DATA SM,SAMARIUM
810 DATA SC,SCANDIUM
820 DATA SE,SELENIUM
830 DATA SI,SILICON
840 DATA AG,SILVER
850 DATA NA,SODIUM
860 DATA SR,STRONTIUM
870 DATA S,SULFUR
880 DATA TA,TANTALUM
890 DATA TC,TECHNETIUM
900 DATA TE,TELLURIUM
910 DATA TB,TERBIUM
920 DATA TL,THALLIUM
```

```
 930 DATA TH,THORIUM
 940 DATA TM,THULIUM
 950 DATA SN,TIN
 960 DATA TI,TITANIUM
 970 DATA W,TUNGSTEN
 980 DATA U,URANIUM
 990 DATA V,VANADIUM
1000 DATA XE,XENON
1010 DATA YB,YTTERBIUM
1020 DATA Y,YTTRIUM
1030 DATA ZN,ZINC
1040 DATA ZR,ZIRCONIUM
1050 PRINT"FOR HOW MANY CHEMICAL ELEMENTS"
1060 PRINT"DO YOU KNOW THE SYMBOLS ?"
1070 R=INT(206*(RND(1)))
1080 IF R<1 THEN 1070
1090 IF INT(R/2)=R/2 THEN R=R-1
1100 FOR L=1 TO R
1110 READ S$
1120 NEXT L
1130 PRINT:PRINT
1140 PRINT S$;" IS THE SYMBOL"
1150 PRINT "WHAT IS THE ELEMENT"
1160 READ C$
1170 INPUT D$
1180 PRINT
1190 IF D$=C$ THEN PRINT"CORRECT"
     :GOTO 1210
1200 PRINT"WRONG"
1210 PRINT"THE ELEMENT IS ";C$
1220 RESTORE
1230 PRINT:PRINT
1240 GOTO 1070
```

Chemistry: Periodic Table of Elements

How many atomic numbers do you know? What is the atomic number of gold? Silver? Oxygen? Uranium? Neodymium? Ytterbium?

Program Listing

```
 10 HOME
 20 DATA ACTINIUM,89
 30 DATA ALUMINUM,13
 40 DATA AMERICIUM,95
 50 DATA ANTIMONY,51
 60 DATA ARGON,18
 70 DATA ARSENIC,33
 80 DATA ASTATINE,85
 90 DATA BARIUM,56
100 DATA BERKELIUM,97
110 DATA BERYLLIUM,4
120 DATA BISMUTH,83
130 DATA BORON,5
140 DATA BROMINE,35
150 DATA CADMIUM,48
160 DATA CALCIUM,20
170 DATA CALIFORNIUM,98
180 DATA CARBON,6
190 DATA CERIUM,58
200 DATA CESIUM,55
210 DATA CHLORINE,17
220 DATA CHROMIUM,24
230 DATA COBALT,27
240 DATA COPPER,29
250 DATA CURIUM,96
260 DATA DYSPROSIUM,66
270 DATA EINSTEINIUM,99
280 DATA ERBIUM,68
290 DATA EUROPIUM,63
300 DATA FERMIUM,100
310 DATA FLUORINE,9
320 DATA FRANCIUM,87
330 DATA GADOLINIUM,64
340 DATA GALLIUM,31
350 DATA GERMANIUM,32
360 DATA GOLD,79
370 DATA HAFNIUM,2
380 DATA HELIUM,2
390 DATA HOLMIUM,67
400 DATA HYDROGEN,1
```

```
410 DATA INDIUM,49
420 DATA IODINE,53
430 DATA IRIDIUM,77
440 DATA IRON,26
450 DATA KRYPTON,36
460 DATA LANTHANUM,57
470 DATA LAWRENCIUM,103
480 DATA LEAD,82
490 DATA LITHIUM,3
500 DATA LUTETIUM,71
510 DATA MAGNESIUM,12
520 DATA MANGANESE,25
530 DATA MENDELEVIUM,101
540 DATA MERCURY,80
550 DATA MOLYBDENUM,42
560 DATA NEODYMIUM,60
570 DATA NEON,10
580 DATA NEPTUNIUM,93
590 DATA NICKEL,28
600 DATA NIOBIUM,41
610 DATA NITROGEN,7
620 DATA NOBELIUM,102
630 DATA OSMIUM,76
640 DATA OXYGEN,8
650 DATA PALLADIUM,46
660 DATA PHOSPHORUS,15
670 DATA PLATINUM,78
680 DATA PLUTONIUM,94
690 DATA POLONIUM,84
700 DATA POTASSIUM,19
710 DATA PRASEODYMIUM,59
720 DATA PROMETHIUM,61
730 DATA PROTACTINIUM,91
740 DATA RADIUM,88
750 DATA RADON,86
760 DATA RHENIUM,75
770 DATA RHODIUM,45
780 DATA RUBIDIUM,37
790 DATA RUTHENIUM,44
800 DATA SAMARIUM,62
810 DATA SCANDIUM,21
820 DATA SELENIUM,34
```

```
 830 DATA SILICON,14
 840 DATA SILVER,47
 850 DATA SODIUM,11
 860 DATA STRONTIUM,38
 870 DATA SULFUR,16
 880 DATA TANTALUM,73
 890 DATA TECHNETIUM,43
 900 DATA TELLURIUM,52
 910 DATA TERBIUM,65
 920 DATA THALLIUM,81
 930 DATA THORIUM,90
 940 DATA THULIUM,69
 950 DATA TIN,50
 960 DATA TITANIUM,22
 970 DATA TUNGSTEN,74
 980 DATA URANIUM,92
 990 DATA VANADIUM,23
1000 DATA XENON,54
1010 DATA YTTERBIUM,70
1020 DATA YTTRIUM,39
1030 DATA ZINC,30
1040 DATA ZIRCONIUM,40
1050 PRINT"IN THE PERIODIC TABLE OF
     ELEMENTS"
1060 PRINT"HOW MANY ATOMIC NUMBERS DO
     YOU KNOW ?"
1070 R=INT(206*(RND(1)))
1080 IF R<1 THEN 1070
1090 IF INT(R/2)=R/2 THEN R=R-1
1100 FOR L=1 TO R
1110 READ S$
1120 NEXT L
1130 PRINT:PRINT
1140 PRINT"WHAT IS THE"
1150 PRINT"ATOMIC NUMBER OF"
1160 PRINT S$
1170 READ C$
1180 INPUT D$
1190 PRINT
1200 IF D$=C$ THEN PRINT"CORRECT"
     :GOTO 1220
1210 PRINT"WRONG"
```

```
1220 PRINT C$;"IS THE ATOMIC NUMBER FOR "
     ;S$
1230 RESTORE
1240 PRINT:PRINT
1250 GOTO 1070
```

Class Roll Sorter

Here's a simple sorting routine which you can use to keep your class roll in order. Suppose it's the first day of classes and you have been handed an unorganized list of student names. Merely key those names into the computer and it will use this "bubble sort" program to put the list in alphabetical order. As set up, it accepts up to 20 names.

Program Listing

```
10 CALL CLEAR
20 DIM M$(20)
30 FOR L=1 TO 20
40 INPUT "NAME: ":M$(L)
50 IF M$(L)="" THEN 70
60 NEXT L
70 CALL CLEAR
80 PRINT "SORTING NOW"
90 T=0
100 FOR L=1 TO 19
110 IF M$(L)<=M$(L+1)THEN 160
120 E$=M$(L)
130 M$(L)=M$(L+1)
140 M$(L+1)=E$
150 T=1
160 NEXT L
170 IF T=1 THEN 90
180 CALL CLEAR
190 CALL SOUND(2,1000,1)
200 FOR L=1 TO 20
210 IF M$(L)<>"" THEN 230
220 GOTO 240
230 PRINT M$(L)
240 NEXT L
```

Exam Score Sorting

The final number scores of a large number of test results can be categorized and thereby cut down into a smaller quantity of numbers easily.

This program accepts exam scores and divides them into ranges we have labeled A, B, C, D and F. The program looks for test scores in a range of zero to 100. The predetermined grade ranges are F=0 to 59; D=60 to 69; C=70 to 79; B=80 to 89; and A=90 to 100.

Program Listing

```
10 CALL CLEAR
20 PRINT "ENTER A GROUP OF SCORES"
30 PRINT "RANGING FROM ZERO TO 100"
40 PRINT "ONE AT A TIME."
50 PRINT
60 PRINT "ENTER X AFTER LAST SCORE"
70 PRINT
80 INPUT "SCORE: ":G$
90 IF G$="X" THEN 600
100 G=VAL(G$)
110 N=N+1
120 IF G<60 THEN 140
130 GOTO 160
140 F=F+1
150 GOTO 300
160 IF G<70 THEN 180
170 GOTO 200
180 D=D+1
190 GOTO 300
200 IF G<80 THEN 220
210 GOTO 240
220 C=C+1
230 GOTO 300
240 IF G<90 THEN 260
250 GOTO 280
260 B=B+1
270 GOTO 300
280 A=A+1
300 IF N=1 THEN 320
```

```
310 GOTO 350
320 L=G
330 H=G
340 GOTO 500
350 IF G<L THEN 370
360 GOTO 390
370 L=G
380 GOTO 500
390 IF G>H THEN 410
400 GOTO 500
410 H=G
500 S=S+G
510 GOTO 80
600 P=S/N
610 M=L+((H-L)/2)
700 CALL CLEAR
710 PRINT "A TOTAL OF ";N;" SCORES"
720 PRINT "RANGING FROM ";L;" TO ";H
730 PRINT "MID-RANGE SCORE IS ";M
740 PRINT "AVERAGE SCORE IS ";P
750 PRINT
760 PRINT "TOTALS FOR EACH LETTER:"
770 PRINT "A: ";A
780 PRINT "B: ";B
790 PRINT "C: ";C
800 PRINT "D: ";D
810 PRINT "F: ";F
900 PRINT
910 PRINT
920 PRINT
930 INPUT "TO DO MORE, PRESS RETURN":KY$
940 A=0
950 B=0
960 C=0
970 D=0
980 F=0
990 N=0
1000 L=0
1010 H=0
1020 M=0
1030 P=0
1040 G=0
```

```
1050 S=0
1060 G$=""
1070 GOTO 10
```

Teacher's Grade-Curve Graph

The computer asks the teacher for the quantity of grades in each of the letters, A, B, C, D and F. Then a vertical bar braph is created on the display screen.

The range of quantities you can use for each letter grade must be from zero to 50.

Program Listing

```
10 CLS:CLEAR
20 GOSUB 1000
30 PRINT"TYPE IN THE TOTAL NUMBER FOR
   EACH GRADE"
40 PRINT"A,B,C,D,F        0 TO 50 PER
   LETTER GRADE"
100 GOSUB 1100
110 INPUT"NUMBER OF A's";A
120 GOSUB 1100
130 INPUT"NUMBER OF B's";B
140 GOSUB 1100
150 INPUT"NUMBER OF C's";C
160 GOSUB 1100
170 INPUT"NUMBER OF D's";D
180 GOSUB 1100
190 INPUT"NUMBER OF F's";F
200 CLS
210 PRINT @ 160,CHR$(147);"  ";
220 GOSUB 1010
230 LINE(95,1)-(95,62)
240 LINE -(163,62)
245 LINE -(163,1)
250 PRINT @ 17,"A B C D F"
260 LINE(102,62)-(108,62-A),1,BF
270 LINE(114,62)-(120,62-B),1,BF
280 LINE(126,62)-(132,62-C),1,BF
290 LINE(138,62)-(144,62-D),1,BF
300 LINE(150,62)-(156,62-F),1,BF
```

```
400 IF INKEY$="" THEN 400
410 GOTO 10
990 END
1000 PRINT SPACE$(14);
1010 PRINT"GRADE CURVE"
1020 RETURN
1100 PRINT @ 226," "
1110 PRINT @ 210,CHR$(154);
1120 RETURN
```

ASCII Conversion

Here's a fast conversion, either to or from an ASCII value.

Program Listing

```
 10 CLS:CLEAR
 20 PRINT"SELECT:ASCII-TO-CHARACTER (A)"
 30 PRINT"OR CHARACTER-TO-ASCII (C)"
 40 PRINT"A OR C ?"
 50 C$=INKEY$
 60 IF C$="" THEN 50
 70 IF C$="A" THEN 100
 80 IF C$="C" THEN 200
 90 GOTO 50
100 INPUT"ASCII VALUE: ";A
110 PRINT CHR$(A)
120 PRINT" "
130 GOTO 20
200 INPUT"CHARACTER: ";CH$
210 PRINT ASC(CH$)
220 PRINT" "
230 GOTO 20
```

Sentence Writer

Practice your English!

Exhibit your knowledge of nouns and verbs. This program leads the computer to solicit individual words from you and use those words to create sentences.

Besides helping you better understand verbs, nouns and simple declarative sentence structures, the program demonstrates the computer's ability to simulate conversation and communication.

Program Listing

```
10 PRINT "A PLURAL NOUN = ?";
20 INPUT N$
25 PRINT "A VERB = ?";
30 INPUT V$
35 PRINT "A SINGULAR NOUN = ?";
40 INPUT S$
50 CLS
60 PRINT "THE "+N$+" "+V$+" "+S$+"."
65 PRINT
70 GOTO 10
```

Resistance

Here's just what the electronics hobbyist or technician has always needed: a program to compute total resistances among resistors in parallel or in series.

Program Listing

```
 10 "L" CLEAR
 20 PRINT "TOTALING RESISTORS..."
 30 PRINT "IN SERIES OR PARALLEL"
 40 INPUT " S OR P ? ";X$
 50 IF X$="S" THEN 120
 60 INPUT "OHMS = ";R
 70 IF R=Ø THEN 100
 80 A=A+1/R:T=1/A:R=Ø
 90 GOTO 60
100 PRINT "TOTAL =";T
110 T=Ø:A=Ø:GOTO 40
120 INPUT "OHMS = ";R
130 IF R=Ø THEN 160
140 T=T+R:R=Ø
150 GOTO 120
160 PRINT"TOTAL OHMS = ";T
170 T=Ø:GOTO 40
```

Time Constants
Series RL and Series RC

In electronics, in RL circuits, the time it takes a current to reach 63.2 percent of peak is important. If you know the impedance in henrys and the resistance in ohms, this program will compute the RL time constant in seconds.

Time also is important in RC circuits. Time, that is, for the voltage across a capacitor to reach 63.2 percent of peak. If you know the resistance in ohms and the capacitance in farads, this program computes the time constant in seconds.

Program Listing

```
 10 "S" CLEAR
 20 PRINT "TIME CONSTANT"
 30 PRINT "FOR SERIES RL OR RC..."
 40 INPUT " RL OR RC ?",X$
 50 INPUT "OHMS = ";R
 60 IF X$="RL" THEN 100
 70 IF X$="RC" THEN 200
 80 GOTO 20
100 INPUT"HENRYS = ";L
110 T=L/R
120 PRINT "SECONDS = ";T
130 GOTO 20
200 INPUT"FARADS = ";C
210 T=RC
220 PRINT "SECONDS = ";T
230 GOTO 20
```

Heating Effect of Current

Current passing through a wire generates heat. How much? This program computes that heat in calories-per-second if resistance in ohms is known.

We store the number of ohms in memory location R and, after computation, the heat in H.

Program Listing

```
10 "H" CLEAR
20 INPUT "OHMS RESISTANCE =",R
30 H=.057168R
40 PRINT "CALORIES/SEC HEAT=";H
50 GOTO 10
```

Diagonal of a Square

This handy programming quickie computes the length of the diagonal of any square.

The length of any side of the square is stored in memory location L. The diagonal length is computed and stored in D. For instance, if you have a square with sides each 36 units long, the diagonal of the square is 50.904 units.

Program Listing

```
10 "D" CLEAR
20 INPUT "SIDE LENGTH = ";L
30 D=1/414L
40 PRINT "DIAGONAL = ";D
50 GOTO 10
```

dB

Here's a handy quickie for engineers, radio technicians, electronics buffs, hams, shortwave listeners and others who know how many bels there are in a decibel.

Program Listing

```
10 "DB" CLEAR
20 BEEP 1:INPUT"INPUT POWER = ";I
30 BEEP 1:INPUT"OUTPUT POWER = ";O
40 D=10*LOG(O+I)
50 BEEP 2:PRINT D;" DB"
60 GOTO 10
```

State Capitals

Idaho. Let's see. Boise. *Correct. Capital is Boise. Minnesota.* Minneapolis. *Wrong. Capital is St. Paul.* How many of the 50 state capitals can you name? Bet not as many as you would like!

This program tests not only knowledge of the name of each state capital but also the correct spelling of that name. The test goes on forever until you BREAK.

Program Listing

```
10 CLEAR:CLS
20 DATA ALABAMA,MONTGOMERY
30 DATA ALASKA,JUNEAU
40 DATA ARIZONA,PHOENIX
50 DATA ARKANSAS,LITTLE ROCK
60 DATA CALIFORNIA,SACRAMENTO
70 DATA COLORADO,DENVER
80 DATA CONNECTICUT,HARTFORD
90 DATA DELAWARE,DOVER
100 DATA FLORIDA,TALLAHASSEE
110 DATA GEORGIA,ATLANTA
120 DATA HAWAII,HONOLULU
130 DATA IDAHO,BOISE
140 DATA ILLINOIS,SPRINGFIELD
150 DATA INDIANA,INDIANAPOLIS
160 DATA IOWA,DES MOINES
170 DATA KANSAS,TOPEKA
180 DATA KENTUCKY,FRANKFORT
190 DATA LOUISIANA,BATON ROUGE
200 DATA MAINE,AUGUSTA
210 DATA MARYLAND,ANNAPOLIS
220 DATA MASSACHUSETTS,BOSTON
230 DATA MICHIGAN,LANSING
240 DATA MINNESOTA,ST. PAUL
250 DATA MISSISSIPPI,JACKSON
260 DATA MISSOURI,JEFFERSON CITY
270 DATA MONTANA,HELENA
280 DATA NEBRASKA,LINCOLN
290 DATA NEVADA,CARSON CITY
300 DATA NEW HAMPSHIRE,CONCORD
```

```
310 DATA NEW JERSEY,TRENTON
320 DATA NEW MEXICO,SANTA FE
330 DATA NEW YORK,ALBANY
340 DATA NORTH CAROLINA,RALEIGH
350 DATA NORTH DAKOTA,BISMARCK
360 DATA OHIO,COLUMBUS
370 DATA OKLAHOMA,OKLAHOMA CITY
380 DATA OREGON,SALEM
390 DATA PENNSYLVANIA,HARRISBURG
400 DATA RHODE ISLAND,PROVIDENCE
410 DATA SOUTH CAROLINA,COLUMBIA
420 DATA SOUTH DAKOTA,PIERRE
430 DATA TENNESSEE,NASHVILLE
440 DATA TEXAS,AUSTIN
450 DATA UTAH,SALT LAKE CITY
460 DATA VERMONT,MONTPELIER
470 DATA VIRGINIA,RICHMOND
480 DATA WASHINGTON,OLYMPIA
490 DATA WEST VIRGINIA,CHARLESTON
500 DATA WISCONSIN,MADISON
510 DATA WYOMING,CHEYENNE
520 PRINT @ 40,STRING$(14,"*")
530 PRINT @ 72,"STATE CAPITALS"
540 PRINT @ 104,STRING$(14,"*")
550 PRINT @ 164,"HOW MANY CAN YOU NAME?"
560 PRINT @ 260,"PRESS ANY KEY TO START"
570 H$=INKEY$
580 IF H$="" THEN 570
590 CLS
600 R=RND(100)
610 IF INT(R/2)=R/2 THEN R=R-1
620 FOR L=1 TO R
630 READ S$
640 NEXT L
650 PRINT" ":PRINT" "
660 PRINT"STATE IS: "S$
670 READ C$
680 INPUT"WHAT IS CAPITAL";D$
690 IF D$=C$ THEN PRINT "CORRECT" ELSE
    PRINT "WRONG"
700 PRINT"CAPITAL IS: "C$
710 RESTORE
```

```
720 PRINT" ":PRINT" "
730 PRINT"FOR MORE, PRESS M"
740 PRINT"TO STOP, PRESS S"
750 M$=INKEY$
760 IF M$="" THEN 750
770 IF M$="M" THEN CLS:GOTO 600
780 IF M$="S" THEN CLS:GOTO 800
790 GOTO 750
800 PRINT @ 40,STRING$(15,"*")
810 PRINT @ 74,"END OF TEST"
820 PRINT @ 104,STRING$(15,"*")
830 PRINT @ 170,"THANK YOU !"
840 GOTO 840
```

History of Invention

When was the zipper invented? The sprinkler? The light bulb? The elevator? The aerosol spray? Here's an endless source of pleasure in a solid learning experience, a quiz on your knowledge of the history of science, technology and invention.

You must identify correctly the year the invention was made.

Program Listing

```
 10 CLEAR:CLS
 20 DATA ADDING MACHINE,1642
 30 DATA AEROSOL SPRAY,1941
 40 DATA AIR CONDITIONING,1911
 50 DATA AIRPLANE,1903
 60 DATA AUTOMOBILE,1887
 70 DATA BALLOON,1783
 80 DATA BARBED WIRE,1874
 90 DATA BAROMETER,1643
100 DATA BATTERY,1800
110 DATA BICYCLE,1816
120 DATA BULLDOZER,1923
130 DATA BULLET,1849
140 DATA CALCULATOR,1823
150 DATA CAMERA,1822
160 DATA CARBURETOR,1892
```

```
170 DATA CASH REGISTER,1879
180 DATA CEMENT,1824
190 DATA CLOCK,1656
200 DATA COMPUTER,1928
210 DATA CONDENSED MILK,1853
220 DATA COTTON GIN,1793
230 DATA DYNAMITE,1866
240 DATA ELECTRIC MOTOR,1822
250 DATA VACUUM CLEANER,1907
260 DATA ELEVATOR,1852
270 DATA FM RADIO,1933
280 DATA GEIGER COUNTER,1913
290 DATA IRON LUNG,1928
300 DATA KALEIDOSCOPE,1816
310 DATA LIGHTBULB,1879
320 DATA LASER,1960
330 DATA LIFE PRESERVER,1805
340 DATA LIGHTNING ROD,1752
350 DATA LINOLEUM,1860
360 DATA MACHINE GUN,1862
370 DATA MATCH,1855
380 DATA MICROSCOPE,1590
390 DATA MOVIES,1872
400 DATA MOTORCYCLE,1885
410 DATA NYLON,1935
420 DATA OLEO,1868
430 DATA PARACHUTE,1783
440 DATA PARKING METER,1935
450 DATA RADIO,1895
460 DATA REFRIGERATOR,1858
470 DATA RIFLE,1520
480 DATA SAFETY PIN,1849
490 DATA SEWING MACHINE,1790
500 DATA SPRINKLER,1723
510 DATA STEAMBOAT,1783
520 DATA STOCK TICKER,1870
530 DATA STREET CAR,1834
540 DATA SWITCHBOARD,1877
550 DATA TANK,1914
560 DATA TELEPHONE,1876
570 DATA TELESCOPE,1608
```

```
580 DATA TELEVISION,1926
590 DATA THERMOMETER,1592
600 DATA TOASTER,1918
610 DATA TRACTOR,1825
620 DATA TRANSISTOR,1948
630 DATA TYPEWRITER,1714
640 DATA WASHING MACHINE,1858
650 DATA ZIPPER,1893
660 PRINT @ 38,STRING$(21,"*")
670 PRINT @ 70,"HISTORY OF INVENTIONS"
680 PRINT @ 102,STRING$(21,"*")
690 PRINT @ 164,"CAN YOU NAME THEIR DATES?"
700 PRINT @ 261,"PRESS ANY KEY TO START"
710 H$=INKEY$
720 IF H$="" THEN 710
730 CLS
740 R=RND(128)
750 IF INT(R/2)=R/2 THEN R=R-1
760 FOR L=1 TO R
770 READ S$
780 NEXT L
790 PRINT" ":PRINT" "
800 PRINT"INVENTION: "S$
810 READ C$
820 INPUT"WHAT WAS YEAR";D$
830 IF D$=C$ THEN PRINT "CORRECT"
    ELSE PRINT "WRONG"
840 PRINT"YEAR WAS "C$
850 RESTORE
860 PRINT" ":PRINT" "
870 PRINT"FOR MORE, PRESS M"
880 PRINT"TO STOP, PRESS S"
890 M$=INKEY$
900 IF M$="" THEN 890
910 IF M$="M" THEN CLS:GOTO 740
920 IF M$="S" THEN CLS:GOTO 940
930 GOTO 890
940 PRINT @ 40,STRING$(15,"*")
950 PRINT @ 74,"END OF TEST"
960 PRINT @ 104,STRING$(15,"*")
970 PRINT @ 170,"THANK YOU !"
980 GOTO 980
```

Alphabetizing Test Evaluation

Here's a more elaborate exam-score evaluation. As set here, you may enter scores for up to 50 students. The computer asks for last name, first name, and score number for each student.

The machine sorts students so it can present an alphabetized list at the end.

Again we assume zero to 59, F; 60-69, D; 70-79, C; 80-89, B; and 90-100, A. You can change those ranges in lines 1110-1150.

Program Listing

```
1000 CLEAR 5000:CLS
1010 DIM M$(50)
1020 FOR L=1 TO 50
1030 LINE INPUT "LAST NAME: ";P$
1040 IF P$=""THEN 1300
1050 LINE INPUT "FIRST NAME: ";Q$
1060 LINE INPUT "GRADE: ";G$
1100 X=VAL(G$)
1110 IF X<60 THEN F=F+1:GOTO 1160
1120 IF X<70 THEN D=D+1:GOTO 1160
1130 IF X<80 THEN C=C+1:GOTO 1160
1140 IF X<90 THEN B=B+1:GOTO 1160
1150 A=A+1
1160 Y=Y+X
1170 Z=Z+1
1180 IF Z=1 THEN J=X:K=X
1190 IF X<J THEN J=X
1200 IF X>K THEN K=X
1210 I=I+X
1220 H=I/Z:MM=J+((K-J)/2)
1230 M$(L)=P$+" "+Q$+" "+"GRADE: "+G$
1240 NEXT L
1300 CLS
1310 PRINT "SORTING"
1320 T=Ø
1330 FOR L=1 TO 49
1340 IF M$(L)<=M$(L+1) THEN 1360
1350 E$=M$(L):M$(L)=M$(L+1):M$(L+1)=E$
```

```
     :T=1
1360 NEXT L
1370 IF T=1 THEN 1320
1400 CLS
1410 PRINT "LAST NAME/FIRST NAME/GRADE"
1420 PRINT " "
1425 FOR L=1 TO 50
1430 IF M$(L)<>"" THEN PRINT M$(L)
1435 NEXT L
1440 PRINT" "
1450 PRINT"FOR STATISTICS, PRESS S"
1455 PRINT"TO QUIT, PRESS Q"
1460 AA$=INKEY$
1470 IF AA$="" THEN 1460
1480 IF AA$="S" THEN 1500
1485 IF AA$="Q" THEN 1800
1490 GOTO 1460
1500 CLS
1510 PRINT @ 37,"TEST SCORE STATISTICS"
1520 PRINT " "
1530 PRINT "SCORES RANGE";J;"TO";K
1540 PRINT "MID-RANGE SCORE IS";MM
1550 PRINT "AVERAGE SCORE IS";H
1560 PRINT "TOTALS FOR EACH LETTER GRADE:"
1570 PRINT A;"A"
1580 PRINT B;"B"
1590 PRINT C;"C"
1600 PRINT D;"D"
1610 PRINT F;"F"
1620 PRINT "A TOTAL OF";Z;"SCORES"
1630 PRINT " "
1640 PRINT "TO DO ANOTHER SET, PRESS A"
1650 PRINT "TO STOP, PRESS S"
1660 BB$=INKEY$
1670 IF BB$="" THEN 1660
1680 IF BB$="A" THEN 1000
1690 IF BB$="S" THEN 1800
1700 GOTO 1660
1800 CLS 2
1810 PRINT @ 192,"              THANK YOU"
1820 GOTO 1820
```

Foreign Measurements

The computer names a country and one of its unique measurements. You tell the common U.S. equivalent measure. A great way to learn international cultures!

Program Listing

```
 10 CLEAR:CLS
 20 DATA EGYPTIAN ARDEB,43.55 GALLONS
 30 DATA LAOTIAN BAK,57.9 GRAINS
 40 DATA IRANIAN BATMAN,6.546 POUNDS
 50 DATA CUBAN BOCOY,18.214 BUSHELS
 60 DATA JAPANESE BU,0.011930 INCH
 70 DATA BRITISH CABLE,200 YARDS
 80 DATA BURMESE CANDY,18000 POUNDS
 90 DATA SOUTH AFRICAN CAPE INCH,1.033 INCHES
100 DATA MEXICAN CARGA,308.6 POUNDS
110 DATA SAMOAN CASE OF BANANAS,72 POUNDS
120 DATA INDONESIAN CATTY,1.3616 POUNDS
130 DATA MONGOLIAN CHANG,3.5 YARDS
140 DATA HONG KONG CHEUNG,4.063 YARDS
150 DATA KOREAN CHI,1.423 SQUARE INCHES
160 DATA JAPANESE CHO,119.3 YARDS
170 DATA MALAYSIAN CHUM,1.475 INCHES
180 DATA ETHIOPIAN DAWULLA,220.46 POUNDS
190 DATA BULGARIAN DEKARE,0.247 ACRES
200 DATA ISRAELI DONUM,1196 SQUARE YARDS
210 DATA GERMAN DOPPELZENTNER,220.462 POUNDS
220 DATA JORDANIAN DRA,26.8 INCHES
230 DATA MONGOLIAN DU,5.72 QUARTS
240 DATA SURINAM EL,2.26 FEET
250 DATA CHINESE FAN CHE,1.19599 SQ. FEET
260 DATA TANZANIAN FRASILA,36 POUNDS
270 DATA GERMAN FUDER,220 GALLONS
280 DATA HONG KONG FUN,0.14625 INCH
290 DATA GERMAN FUSS,12.36 INCHES
300 DATA VIETNAMESE GANG,0.4306 SQ. FEET
310 DATA HONG KONG GUN,1.333 POUNDS
320 DATA BRITISH HAND,4 INCHES
330 DATA HUNGARIAN HOLD,1.422 ACRES
340 DATA PHILIPPINES KILATES,3.09 GRAINS
```

```
350 DATA NEPALESE KOSH,2 MILES
360 DATA POLISH KWINTAL,220.46 POUNDS
370 DATA SOUTH AFRICAN LEAGUER,127 GALLONS
380 DATA SPANISH LIBRA,1.014 POUNDS
390 DATA SIERRA LEONE COCOA LOAD,60 POUNDS
400 DATA HONG KONG MA(CHINESE YD),35.1 INCHES
410 DATA ADEN MAUND,82.28 POUNDS
420 DATA SWEDISH MIL,6.214 MILES
430 DATA DUTCH MUD,2.471 ACRES
440 DATA NIGERIAN RICE MUDU,2.5 POUNDS
450 DATA SAUDI ARABIAN OKE,2.8 POUNDS
460 DATA ARGENTINIAN PIE,1 FOOT
470 DATA SURINAM POND,1.102 POUNDS
480 DATA RUSSIAN GRAIN POUD,36.11 POUNDS
490 DATA JAPANESE RI,2.44 MILES
500 DATA CYPRIOT TEXTILE ROUPI,3 INCHES
510 DATA GERMAN RUTE,4.12 YARDS
520 DATA LIBYAN SAA,26.13 GALLONS
530 DATA COLUMBIAN COFFEE SACO,137.8 POUNDS
540 DATA NEPALESE SEER,2.057 POUNDS
550 DATA ICELANDIC SILDARMAL,4.12 BUSHELS
560 DATA ECUADORIAN SOLAR,0.43 ACRES
570 DATA BRITISH STONE,14 POUNDS
580 DATA DUTCH BEER STOOP,1.32 GALLONS
590 DATA JAPANESE SUN,1.19303 INCHES
600 DATA CAMBODIAN TAEL,1.323 OUNCES
610 DATA THAI TANAN,0.88 QUART
620 DATA INDONESIAN OPIUM THAIL,1.241 OUNCES
630 DATA PAKISTANI TOLA,180 GRAINS
640 DATA DANISH TOMME,1.03 INCHES
650 DATA GERMAN TONNE,1.35 ACRES
660 DATA PERUVIAN TOPO,0.86 ACRES
670 DATA FINNISH TUUMA,1 INCH
680 DATA SUDAN UD,2.54 YARDS
690 DATA ADEN WAR,1 YARD
700 DATA BARBADOS WINE GALLON,0.83267 GALLONS
710 DATA MALTESE WIZNA,8.75 POUNDS
720 DATA KOREAN YANG,1.32 OUNCES
730 DATA VIETNAMESE YEN,13.33 POUNDS
740 DATA AUSTRIAN ZENTNER,220.46 POUNDS
750 DATA GERMAN ZOLL,1.03 INCHES
760 PRINT @ 38,STRING$(20,218)
```

```
770 PRINT @ 70,"FOREIGN MEASUREMENTS"
780 PRINT @ 102,STRING$(20,218)
790 PRINT @ 164,"HOW MANY U.S.EQUIVALENTS"
800 PRINT @ 202,"DO YOU KNOW?"
810 PRINT @ 324,"PRESS ANY KEY TO START"
820 H$=INKEY$
830 IF H$="" THEN 820
840 CLS
850 R=RND(148)
860 IF INT(R/2)=R/2 THEN R=R-1
870 FOR L=1 TO R
880 READ S$
890 NEXT L
900 PRINT:PRINT
910 PRINT "WHAT IS THE"
920 PRINT "U.S. EQUIVALENT OF"
930 PRINT "1 ";S$
940 READ C$
950 INPUT D$
960 PRINT
970 IF D$=C$ THEN PRINT "*** CORRECT"
    ELSE PRINT "*** WRONG"
980 PRINT "1 ";S$
981 PRINT "EQUALS ";C$
990 RESTORE
1000 PRINT:PRINT
1010 PRINT"FOR MORE, PRESS M"
1020 PRINT"TO STOP, PRESS S"
1030 M$=INKEY$
1040 IF M$="" THEN 1030
1050 IF M$="M" THEN CLS:GOTO 840
1060 IF M$="S" THEN CLS:GOTO 1080
1070 GOTO 1030
1080 PRINT @ 40,STRING$(15,243)
1090 PRINT @ 74,"END OF TEST"
1100 PRINT @ 104,STRING$(15,243)
1110 PRINT @ 170,"THANK YOU !"
1120 GOTO 1120
1999 END
```

World's Hottest Places

No, you don't have to know the exact temperatures. The computer mentions a continent and a temperature. You must identify which country on that continent holds that particular high-temperature record.

Program Listing

```
 10 CLEAR:CLS
 20 DATA AFRICA AT 120,LIBYA
 30 DATA NORTH AMERICA AT 134,CALIFORNIA
 40 DATA ASIA AT 129,ISRAEL
 50 DATA AUSTRALIA AT 128,QUEENSLAND
 60 DATA EUROPE AT 122,SPAIN
 70 DATA SOUTH AMERICA AT 120,ARGENTINA
 80 DATA OCEANIA AT 108,PHILIPPINES
 90 DATA ANTARCTICA AT 58,PALMER PENINSULA
100 PRINT @ 36,STRING$(22,"[")
110 PRINT @ 68,"WORLD'S HOTTEST PLACES"
120 PRINT @ 100,STRING$(22,"]")
130 PRINT @ 164,"HOW MANY CAN YOU IDENTIFY ?"
140 PRINT @ 260,"PRESS ANY KEY TO START"
150 H$=INKEY$
160 IF H$="" THEN 150
170 CLS
180 R=RND(16)
190 IF INT(R/2)=R/2 THEN R=R-1
200 FOR L=1 TO R
210 READ S$
220 NEXT L
230 PRINT:PRINT
240 PRINT "THE HOTTEST COUNTRY (OR STATE)"
250 PRINT "ON THE CONTINENT OF"
260 PRINT S$;" DEGREES"
270 READ C$
280 INPUT "IS";D$
290 IF D$=C$ THEN PRINT "*** CORRECT"
    ELSE PRINT "*** WRONG"
300 PRINT "LOCATION IS: ",C$
310 RESTORE
```

```
320 PRINT:PRINT
330 PRINT"FOR MORE, PRESS M"
340 PRINT"TO STOP, PRESS S"
350 M$=INKEY$
360 IF M$="" THEN 350
370 IF M$="M" THEN CLS:GOTO 170
380 IF M$="S" THEN CLS:GOTO 400
390 GOTO 350
400 PRINT @ 40,STRING$(15,"/")
410 PRINT @ 74,"END OF TEST"
420 PRINT @ 104,STRING$(15,"/")
430 PRINT @ 170,"THANK YOU !"
440 GOTO 440
450 END
```

World's Coldest Places

Here, the computer names a continent and a record low temperature. You must specify which country holds that low-temperature record. Clue: to stay warm stay near the equator.

Program Listing

```
 10 CLEAR:CLS
 20 DATA AFRICA AT -11,MOROCCO
 30 DATA NORTH AMERICA AT -81,YUKON
 40 DATA ASIA AT -90,USSR
 50 DATA AUSTRALIA AT -8,NEW SOUTH WALES
 60 DATA EUROPE AT -67,USSR
 70 DATA SOUTH AMERICA AT -27,ARGENTINA
 80 DATA GREENLAND AT -87,NORTHICE STATION
 90 DATA ANTARCTICA AT -127,VOSTOK STATION
100 PRINT @ 36,STRING$(22,79)
110 PRINT @ 68,"WORLD'S COLDEST PLACES"
120 PRINT @ 100,STRING$(22,79)
130 PRINT @ 163,"HOW MANY CAN YOU IDENTIFY ?"
140 PRINT @ 260,"PRESS ANY KEY TO START"
150 H$=INKEY$
160 IF H$="" THEN 150
170 CLS
180 R=RND(16)
190 IF INT(R/2)=R/2 THEN R=R-1
```

```
200 FOR L=1 TO R
210 READ S$
220 NEXT L
230 PRINT:PRINT
240 PRINT "THE COLDEST COUNTRY (OR STATE)"
250 PRINT "ON THE LAND MASS OF"
260 PRINT S$;" DEGREES"
270 READ C$
280 INPUT "IS";D$
290 IF D$=C$ THEN PRINT "*** CORRECT"
    ELSE PRINT "*** WRONG"
300 PRINT "LOCATION IS: ",C$
310 RESTORE
320 PRINT:PRINT
330 PRINT"FOR MORE, PRESS M"
340 PRINT"TO STOP, PRESS S"
350 M$=INKEY$
360 IF M$="" THEN 350
370 IF M$="M" THEN CLS:GOTO 170
380 IF M$="S" THEN CLS:GOTO 400
390 GOTO 350
400 PRINT @ 40,STRING$(15,79)
410 PRINT @ 74,"END OF TEST"
420 PRINT @ 104,STRING$(15,79)
430 PRINT @ 170,"THANK YOU !"
440 GOTO 440
999 END
```

Earth's Extremes

What country or state is wettest? Coldest? Southernmost? Has the biggest meteor crater? Not one of these correct answers is Texas.

The computer lists the extreme and you place it.

Program Listing

```
10 CLEAR:CLS
20 DATA WETTEST (AT 460 INCHES RAIN PER
   YEAR),HAWAII
30 DATA DRIEST,CHILE
```

```
 40 DATA COLDEST (AT -127 DEGREES),
    ANTARCTICA
 50 DATA HOTTEST (AT 136 DEGREES),LIBYA
 60 DATA NORTHERNMOST TOWN (SPITSBERGEN),
    NORWAY
 70 DATA SOUTHERNMOST TOWN (PUERTO
    WILLIAMS),CHILE
 80 DATA HIGHEST TOWN (AT 17500 FEET),
    CHILE
 90 DATA LARGEST GORGE (277 MILES LONG/20
    MILES WIDE/1 MILE DEEP),ARIZONA
100 DATA DEEPEST GORGE (AT 7900 FEET),
    IDAHO
110 DATA STRONGEST SURFACE WIND (AT 231
    MPH),NEW HAMPSHIRE
120 DATA GREATEST TIDES (AT 53 FEET),
    NOVA SCOTIA
130 DATA BIGGEST METEOR CRATER (AT 2
    MILES WIDE),CANADA
140 DATA LARGEST ISLAND,GREENLAND
150 DATA HIGHEST VOLCANO (AT 19882 FEET),
    CHILE
160 PRINT @ 36,STRING$(22,79)
170 PRINT @ 71,"EARTH'S EXTREMES"
180 PRINT @ 100,STRING$(22,79)
190 PRINT @ 163,"HOW MANY CAN YOU PLACE ?"
200 PRINT @ 260,"PRESS ANY KEY TO START"
210 H$=INKEY$
220 IF H$="" THEN 210
230 CLS
240 R=RND(28)
250 IF INT(R/2)=R/2 THEN R=R-1
260 FOR L=1 TO R
270 READ S$
280 NEXT L
290 PRINT:PRINT
300 PRINT "WHICH COUNTRY (OR STATE)"
310 PRINT "HAS THIS WORLD RECORD:"
320 PRINT S$
330 READ C$
```

```
340 INPUT D$
350 IF D$=C$ THEN PRINT "*** CORRECT"
    ELSE PRINT "*** WRONG"
360 PRINT "LOCATION IS: ",C$
370 RESTORE
380 PRINT:PRINT
390 PRINT"FOR MORE, PRESS M"
400 PRINT"TO STOP, PRESS S"
410 M$=INKEY$
420 IF M$="" THEN 410
430 IF M$="M" THEN CLS:GOTO 230
440 IF M$="S" THEN CLS:GOTO 460
450 GOTO 410
460 PRINT @ 40,STRING$(15,79)
470 PRINT @ 74,"END OF TEST"
480 PRINT @ 104,STRING$(15,79)
490 PRINT @ 170,"THANK YOU !"
500 GOTO 500
999 END
```

Test Timer

Place your computer in the corner and let it time your exams. Good for home self-testing as well as in the classroom.

Program Listing

```
10 CLEAR:CLS 4
20 PRINT" "
30 PRINT @ 11,"TEST TIMER"
40 PRINT" "
50 PRINT @ 43,STRING$(10,159)
60 PRINT" "
70 PRINT @ 69,"PRESS ANY KEY TO START"
80 PRINT" "
90 PRINT @ 101,STRING$(22,175)
100 PRINT"THEN PRESS ANY KEY TO STOP TIMER"
110 PRINT @ 160,STRING$(32,255)
200 A$=INKEY$
210 IF A$="" THEN 200
```

```
220 TIMER=0
230 T=TIMER/3600
240 TM=INT(T):TS=INT(60*(T-TM))
250 PRINT @ 196,TM;" MINUTES"
260 PRINT @ 208,TS
270 PRINT @ 212,"SECONDS"
280 IF TM=20 THEN SOUND 100,20:GOTO 320
300 B$=INKEY$
310 IF B$="" THEN 230
320 PRINT @ 196,TM;" MINUTES"
330 PRINT @ 208,TS
340 PRINT @ 212,"SECONDS"
400 C$=INKEY$
410 IF C$="" THEN 400 ELSE 10
```

Screen Full

Fill your video screen with square dots, starting from the upper left, moving down and across to the lower right. Line 200 is a freeze frame.

Program Listing

```
 10 CLS
100 FOR X=1 TO 21 STEP 2
110 FOR Y=1 TO 21 STEP 2
120 PRINT AT X,Y;CHR$ 128
130 NEXT Y
140 NEXT X
200 GOTO 200
```

Sine Wave

Note that some complex screen art can be created with only a few program lines. You will want to refine these programs to make them even shorter.

Program Listing

```
10 CLS
20 FOR X=1 TO 63
30 LET Y=SIN X + 10
40 PLOT X,Y
50 NEXT X
60 GOTO 60
```

Create A Table

This program generates a table of values, as a demonstration on how to set up a table on the video display.

Program Listing

```
  5 RAND
 10 LET A=Ø
 20 LET B=Ø
 30 LET T=Ø
 40 PRINT CHR$ 166,CHR$ 167
 50 GOSUB 900
 60 IF X>50 THEN LET A=A+1
 70 IF X>50 THEN GOTO 50
 80 GOSUB 900
 90 IF X>50 THEN LET B=B+1
100 IF X>50 THEN GOTO 80
110 PRINT A,B
120 IF T=10 THEN STOP
130 LET A=Ø
140 LET B=Ø
150 LET T=T+1
160 GOTO 20
900 LET X=INT(100*RND)
910 RETURN
```

Centered Message

The computer will highlight your message by centering it on the video screen.

Use this handy centering program for titles and other important parts of longer programs.

Program Listing

```
 10 LET A$=""
100 PRINT "MESSAGE:"
110 INPUT M$
200 LET L=LEN M$
210 LET T=L+4
220 FOR Z=1 TO T
230 LET A$=A$+"*"
```

```
240 NEXT Z
250 LET P=(40-T)/2
260 CLS
300 PRINT TAB P;A$
310 PRINT TAB P;"* ";M$;" *"
320 PRINT TAB P;A$
```

Beautiful Braided Rug

Just goes to show that some of the most attractive computer graphics require some of the shortest programs.

Program Listing

```
10 FOR X=1 TO 20 STEP 2
20 FOR Y=1 TO 20 STEP 2
30 PRINT AT X,Y;CHR$ 8
40 PRINT AT X+1,Y+1;CHR$ 128
50 NEXT Y
60 NEXT X
```

Eyeball Scrambler

Blink. Blink. Blink. It's enough to make your eyeballs hurt!

The screen is filled with all the many printable keyboard characters. Some flash on and off. Some do not. Creates a very lively display!

Program Listing

```
10 LET X=INT(30*RND)
20 LET Y=INT(20*RND)
30 LET C=INT(256*RND)
40 PRINT AT Y,X;CHR$ C
50 GOTO 10
```

Draw A Line

There are different ways to draw a line on the Computer screen.

Program Listing

```
10 LET A$=""
20 FOR L=1 TO 30
30 LET A$=A$+"*"
40 NEXT L
50 PRINT A$
```

Program Listing

```
10 FOR L=1 TO 30
20 PRINT CHR$ 128
30 NEXT L
```

Program Listing

```
10 FOR X=1 TO 50
20 PLOT X,10
30 NEXT X
```

Program Listing

```
10 FOR Y=1 TO 25
20 PLOT 20,Y
30 NEXT Y
```

Draw Bar Graphs

Drawing graphs on the video screen are a popular form of communication today. This program establishes a bar graph on the display.

We have selected the business-like example, shown here, to demonstrate how you go about setting up a bar graph on the TV screen.

Program Listing

```
10 PRINT "1979 PROFITS"
20 INPUT A
30 CLS
40 PRINT "1980 PROFITS"
50 INPUT B
60 CLS
70 PRINT "1981 PROFITS"
80 INPUT C
```

```
 90 CLS
100 LET X$=""
110 PRINT TAB 9;"PROFITS"
200 PRINT AT 3,Ø;"1979 ";
210 FOR L=1 TO A
220 LET X$=X$+CHR$ 128
230 NEXT L
240 PRINT X$
250 LET X$=""
300 PRINT AT 5,Ø;"1980 ";
310 FOR L=1 TO B
320 LET X$=X$+CHR$ 128
330 NEXT L
340 PRINT X$
350 LET X$=""
400 PRINT AT 7,Ø;"1981 ";
410 FOR L=1 TO C
420 LET X$=X$+CHR$ 128
430 NEXT L
440 PRINT X$
```

Random Bar Graph

If you don't have any particular data to display, but would like to see how these bar graphs work, try this program.

Program Listing

```
 10 RAND
 20 LET X$=""
 30 PRINT TAB 9;"PROFITS"
 40 PRINT AT 3,Ø;"1978 ";
 50 GOSUB 400
 60 PRINT AT 5,Ø;"1979 ";
 70 GOSUB 400
 80 PRINT AT 7,Ø;"1980 ";
 90 GOSUB 400
100 STOP
400 FOR L=1 TO INT(27*RND)
410 LET X$=X$+CHR$ 128
420 NEXT L
430 PRINT X$
```

```
440 LET X$=""
450 RETURN
```

Number reverser

Give the computer any three-digit number and, as a result of using this particular small programming trick, it will reverse the original number.

Program Listing

```
10 "N" CLEAR
20 INPUT"GIVE ME 3-DIGIT NUMBER",N
30 IF N<1 THEN 20
40 IF N>999 THEN 20
50 A=INT(N/100)
60 B=INT(10*(N/100-A))
70 C=INT(10*(N/10-INT(N/10)))
80 PRINT USING"##";C;B;A
90 GOTO 10
```

Changing signs

This technique changes a negative number to a positive number. It also deletes either a plus-sign or a minus-sign, using the ABS function.

Program Listing

```
10 INPUT A
20 B=ABS A
30 PRINT B
40 GOTO 10
```

Fraction Inverter

Just for fun, and to demonstrate the power tucked into the INSTR function, we take fractions and turn them up-sidedown.

Program Listing

```
10 CLS
20 LINE INPUT"FRACTION ";FR$
30 DV=INSTR(FR$,"/")
```

```
 40 SL=LEN(FR$)
 50 NU$=LEFT$(FR$,DV-1)
 60 DE$=RIGHT$(FR$,SL-DV)
 70 N=VAL(NU$)
 80 D=VAL(DE$)
 90 PRINT D;"/";N
100 PRINT D/N
110 GOTO 20
```

Making Change

A penny saved is a penny earned. Every businessman is aware of pennies, nickels, dimes, even quarters lost by sales people who can't make correct change. If you have sales people accepting cash away from your register, or if you're too small to have a cash register, use this program to make *correct* change.

Program Listing

```
10 CLS:CLEAR
20 INPUT"NEW SALE AMOUNT IN CENTS ";X
30 INPUT"AMOUNT TENDERED IN CENTS ";T
40 PRINT
90 A=T-X
100 IF A<25 THEN 140
110 Q=Q+1
120 A=A-25
130 GOTO 100
140 IF A<10 THEN 180
150 D=D+1
160 A=A-10
170 GOTO 140
180 IF A<5 THEN 220
190 N=N+1
200 A=A-5
210 GOTO 180
220 P=A
230 PRINT"CORRECT CHANGE IS:"
240 PRINT Q;" QUARTERS"
250 PRINT D;" DIMES"
260 PRINT N;" NICKLES"
270 PRINT P;" PENNIES"
```

```
280 PRINT"PRESS M FOR MORE OR Q TO QUIT"
290 K$=INKEY$
300 IF K$="" THEN 290
310 IF K$="M" THEN 10
320 IF K$="Q" THEN END
330 GOTO 280
```

Income Property Cash Flow Analysis

Here's a handy program to put your computer to work on your real estate investments. Potential gross income, effective gross income, net operating income, and gross spendable cash are the before-tax cash flows of interest.

In computing these cash flows, one first finds the potential gross income by multiplying rent per unit you own times the number of units you own and that times the number of rental payment periods per year. The result will be the rental income you could expect if the property were fully occupied.

Next, you must deduct an allowance for vacancies and rental losses which you will have. This usually is a percentage and the result will be your rent collections. These rent collections would be the same as your effective gross income if you have no other income.

If you have other income, such as receipts from concessions like laundry equipment and other money produced by sources other than rental office space, add it in. The result will be effective gross income.

Now deduct your operating expenses which are those expenditures you must make to keep the property capable of producing the gross income. The result will be the net operating income.

Finally, deduct your annual debt service (interest) on the mortgage and you will find the gross spendable cash.

Program Listing

```
10 CLS:CLEAR
20 INPUT"NO. UNITS FOR RENT";U
30 INPUT"MONTHLY RENT PER UNIT $";R
40 G=12*R*U
```

```
50 INPUT"VACANCY RATE %";V
60 L=G*(.01*V)
70 INPUT"OTHER INCOME $";OI
80 EG=G+OI-L
90 INPUT"ANNUAL OPERATING COST $";OC
100 NI=EG-OC
110 INPUT"MORTGAGE ANNUAL DEBT SERVICE
    $";DS
120 SC=NI-DS
130 CLS
140 PRINT"POTENTIAL GROSS INCOME $";G
150 PRINT"VACANCY LOSS               $";L
160 PRINT"OTHER INCOME               $";OI
170 PRINT"EFFECTIVE GROSS INCOME $";EG
180 PRINT"NET OPERATING INCOME    $";NI
190 PRINT"MORTGAGE DEBT SERVICE  $";DS
200 PRINT "GROSS SPENDABLE CASH    $";SC
300 IF INKEY$="" THEN 300
310 GOTO 10
```

Daily Codes

Businesses everywhere are concerned about security. Banks, credit managers, warehousemen, shipping clerks, office managers, retail storekeepers, all need private daily codes for internal use to prevent unauthorized admission to private files, storage areas, financial records.

Now you can use your computer to generate a weekly set of codes for each day. If you feel insecure about a week's list in use, the computer will give you a new set of code numbers in a flash.

The computer generates a table of randomly-selected codes for seven days at a time.

Program Listing

```
 10 GOSUB 300
100 PRINT "SUNDAY:      ";C
110 GOSUB 300
120 PRINT "MONDAY:      ";C
130 GOSUB 300
140 PRINT "TUESDAY:     ";C
```

```
150 GOSUB 300
160 PRINT "WEDNESDAY:  ";C
170 GOSUB 300
180 PRINT "THURSDAY:   ";C
190 GOSUB 300
200 PRINT "FRIDAY:     ";C
210 GOSUB 300
220 PRINT "SATURDAY:   ";C
230 STOP
300 LET C=INT(10000*RND)
310 IF C<1000 THEN GOTO 300
320 RETURN
```

Invoice Computer

There's a lot of repetitious math work to be done before you mail invoices to your customers. This software has the computer collect a few pertinent bits of data from you and then present all the various totals you need to plug into an invoice.

It gives you a total retail price for all goods sold on the invoice, total sales tax if applicable, shipping charges and the grand total amount due you from your customer.

Program Listing

```
 10 PRINT "QUANTITY SOLD: ";
 20 INPUT Q
 30 PRINT Q
 40 PRINT "UNIT PRICE: $";
 50 INPUT P
 60 PRINT P
 70 PRINT "SALES TAX RATE PERCENT: ";
 80 INPUT S
 90 PRINT S
100 PRINT "SHIPPING CHARGES: $";
110 INPUT H
120 PRINT H
130 LET S=S*.01
140 LET C=Q*P
150 LET T=C*S
```

```
160 LET F=C+T+H
170 LET A=INT(100*C+.5)/100
180 LET B=INT(100*T+.5)/100
190 LET D=INT(100*F+.5)/100
200 CLS
210 PRINT "TOTAL PRICE = $";A
220 PRINT "SALES TAX = $";B
230 PRINT "SHIPPING CHARGES = $";H
240 PRINT
250 PRINT "INVOICE TOTAL = $";D
260 IF INKEY$="" THEN GOTO 260
270 CLS
280 GOTO 10
```

Hourly Wages

These useful lines compute total hours worked at regular pay and number of hours worked at time-and-a-half overtime. The computer then finds gross pay and rounds off to the nearest cent.

The program knows that overtime starts after 40 hours. It makes payroll bookkeeping quick and simple.

Program Listing

```
 10 LET T=Ø
 20 LET W=Ø
 30 PRINT "HOURLY PAY RATE = $";
 40 INPUT P
 50 PRINT P
 60 PRINT "NUMBER HOURS WORKED = ";
 70 INPUT H
 80 PRINT H
 90 IF H>40 THEN LET T=H-40
100 IF H>40 THEN GOTO 140
110 LET W=H*P
120 PRINT "GROSS WAGES = $";W
130 STOP
140 LET W=(40*P)+(T*P*1.5)
150 GOTO 120
```

Ad Campaign Profit

The ad salesman is standing in your office pressing for your answer. Do you want to advertise or not? Advertising costs plenty of money today. How can you make a quick decision about whether or not sales from advertising would be worth the cost?

In this program, the computer asks you for information about the list price of the item you would sell through advertising. It asks for the manufacturing cost of that item; the cost of the advertising campaign; and the number of units sold.

It computes your gross sales and deducts the cost of manufacturing and advertising to show an estimate of profits to be expected. If you key in a zero in response to the number-sold question, the machine will inquire as to the amount of profit you would like to make and then tell you how many units you would have to sell to make such a profit.

Program Listing

```
 10 PRINT "ITEM LIST PRICE: ";
 20 INPUT B
 30 PRINT "$";B
 40 PRINT "MFG COST: ";
 50 INPUT C
 60 PRINT "$";C
 70 PRINT "AD COST: ";
 80 INPUT D
 90 PRINT "$";D
100 PRINT "QUANTITY SOLD: ";
110 INPUT A
120 PRINT A
130 IF A=Ø THEN GOTO 300
200 LET E=A*B-A*C-D
210 PRINT "$";E;" PROFIT"
220 GOTO 400
300 PRINT "PROFIT WANTED: $";
310 INPUT F
320 PRINT F
```

```
330 LET A=(F+D)/(B-C)
340 PRINT "YOU MUST SELL ";A
350 PRINT "FOR $";F;" PROFIT"
400 PRINT
410 PRINT
420 PRINT "TO DO ANOTHER, PRESS ANY KEY"
430 IF INKEY$="" THEN GOTO 430
440 CLS
450 GOTO 10
```

Advertising Cost-per-Thousand

Suppose your local radio station time salesman told you he could deliver 51,000 listeners for each $133 ad run on his station. And your local newspaper space salesman said he could deliver 160,000 readers for each $330 ad run in his paper. Which would be the better quantity buy for you?

This program gives you the answers in black and white. The newspaper would cost you about $2.06 for each 1000 readers while the radio station would cost almost $2.61 per thousand listeners. Now all you need to decide is which audience you prefer.

By the way, the cost-per-thousand comparison applies to magazines, TV, or any medium.

Program Listing

```
 10 CLS
 20 CLEAR
 30 PRINT "COST OF AD ? ";
 40 INPUT A
 50 PRINT "$";A
 60 PRINT "CIRCULATION ? ";
 70 INPUT C
 80 PRINT C
 90 LET M=1000*(A/C)
100 PRINT
120 PRINT "$";M;" COST/THOUSAND"
130 FOR Q=1 TO 10
140 PRINT
150 NEXT Q
```

```
160 PRINT "TO DO MORE PRESS ENTER"
170 INPUT K$
180 GOTO 10
```

Advertising Cost-per-Unit Sold

Your favorite newspaper had the lowest cost-per-thousand so you ran an ad. The ad cost you $330. Lots of customers came by to check out your merchandise and you actually sold 77 pieces. What'd it cost you to sell each item?

With this quickie program you'll know it cost you $4.28 in ad money to sell each unit.

Program Listing

```
 10 CLS
 20 CLEAR
 30 PRINT "COST OF AD ? ";
 40 INPUT A
 50 PRINT "$";A
 60 PRINT "UNITS SOLD ? ";
 70 INPUT U
 80 PRINT U
 90 LET C=A/U
100 LET C=INT (100*C+0.5)/100
110 PRINT
120 PRINT "THE AD COST $";C;" PER UNIT
    SOLD"
130 FOR Q=1 TO 10
140 PRINT
150 NEXT Q
160 PRINT "TO DO MORE PRESS ENTER"
170 INPUT K$
180 GOTO 10
```

Media Money Massage

If you have used the *Ad Campaign Profit* program earlier in this book, you know how many bucks you can expect to make from advertising. But, suppose two salesmen are standing in your office. One from your local newspaper and the other from a local television station. Both want your advertising dollar and you can't decide which is the best buy. Let your computer decide!

This program compares the cost of advertising in two media and reports which is most favorable. First it computes cost-per-thousand. Then it highlights the least-expensive medium.

Program Listing

```
 10 PRINT "FIRST MEDIUM: ";
 20 INPUT N$
 30 PRINT N$
 40 PRINT "AD COST: $";
 50 INPUT A
 60 PRINT A
 70 PRINT "CIRCULATION: ";
 80 INPUT C
 90 PRINT C
100 LET M=1000*(A/C)
110 PRINT "SECOND MEDIUM: ";
120 INPUT P$
130 PRINT P$
140 PRINT "AD COST: $";
150 INPUT Q
160 PRINT Q
170 PRINT "CIRCULATION: ";
180 INPUT R
190 PRINT R
200 LET S=1000*(Q/R)
210 PRINT
220 PRINT
230 PRINT N$;" CPM: $";M
240 PRINT P$;" CPM: $";S
250 IF S>M THEN PRINT N$;" IS LOWER"
260 IF M>S THEN PRINT P$;" IS LOWER"
270 IF M=S THEN PRINT "NO DIFFERENCE"
300 PRINT
310 PRINT
320 PRINT "TO DO MORE, PRESS ANY KEY"
330 IF INKEY$="" THEN GOTO 330
340 CLS
350 GOTO 10
```

Salesman's Commission

Representatives, salesmen, account representatives, sales representatives. Here's the no-sweat way to compute commissions to be paid to your sales corps.

The computer will ask you for pertinent data and then display results including the salesman's name, the pay period, his commission percentage rate, gross sales, and commission payable.

Program Listing

```
 10 PRINT "SALESMAN COMMISSION"
 20 FOR L=1 TO 19
 30 PRINT "*";
 40 NEXT L
 50 PRINT
100 PRINT "PERIOD ENDING DATE: ";
110 INPUT D$
120 PRINT D$
200 PRINT "SALESMAN NAME: ";
210 INPUT N$
220 PRINT N$
300 PRINT "COMMISSION PERCENT: ";
310 INPUT P
320 PRINT P
330 LET K=P*.01
400 PRINT "GROSS SALES: ";
410 INPUT Q
420 PRINT "$";Q
430 LET T=K*Q
500 PRINT "COMMISSION: $";T
510 PRINT
520 PRINT
530 PRINT "FOR ANOTHER, PRESS ANY KEY"
600 IF INKEY$ ="" THEN GOTO 600
610 CLS
620 GOTO 10
```

Unit Price

Suppose you find 895 green Widgets and buy them

for $695. How much did each green Widget cost? Rounded off, $.77.

Unit price is total price divided by quantity. The quantity can be expressed in weight, total numbers, etc.

This program asks for the name of the item, quantity purchased and total price paid. It then displays quantity, name, total and unit price.

Program Listing

```
 10 LET U=Ø
 20 PRINT "ITEM NAME IS ";
 30 INPUT N$
 40 PRINT N$
 50 PRINT "QUANTITY OF ITEMS = ";
 60 INPUT Q
 70 PRINT Q
 80 PRINT"TOTAL PRICE PAID FOR ITEMS
    = $";
 90 INPUT P
100 PRINT P
110 LET U=P/Q
120 PRINT N$;" UNIT PRICE = $";U
200 PRINT
210 PRINT
220 PRINT "TO DO ANOTHER, PRESS ANY KEY"
230 IF INKEY$="" THEN GOTO 230
240 CLS
250 GOTO 10
```

Cash Receipts Comparer

Business been up? Or, dropping off? How have your cash receipts looked over the last six months?

This short, easy-to-key-in piece of software accepts data from you about each month's receipts and then displays that data in an easy-to-read graph. The graph shows exactly how one month's receipts compare with another.

Program Listing

```
10 CLEAR
```

```
 20 DIM R(6)
100 FOR M=1 TO 6
110 PRINT "DATA FOR MONTH ";M;" ?"
120 INPUT R(M)
130 IF R(M)>22 THEN GOTO 120
140 CLS
150 NEXT M
200 FOR M=1 TO 6
210 PRINT "MONTH ";M;
220 FOR L=Ø TO R(M)-1
230 PRINT CHR$ 128;
240 NEXT L
250 PRINT
260 PRINT
270 NEXT M
280 PRINT
290 PRINT TAB 10;"RECEIPTS"
300 IF INKEY$="" THEN GOTO 300
310 CLS
320 GOTO 10
```

Mark Up

Mr. Storekeeper, here's just what you have needed to compute mark ups. This program finds the retail price for which your percentage off would give the wholesale cost.

Program Listing

```
 10 LET D=Ø
 20 LET R=Ø
 30 PRINT "WHOLESALE COST = $";
 40 INPUT W
 50 PRINT W
 60 PRINT "MARK-UP PERCENTAGE = ";
 70 INPUT P
 80 PRINT P
 90 CLS
100 LET D=1-.01*P
110 LET R=W/D
120 PRINT "RETAIL PRICE = $";R
```

```
130 PRINT
140 PRINT
150 PRINT "TO DO MORE, PRESS ANY KEY"
160 IF INKEY$="" THEN GOTO 160
170 CLS
180 GOTO 10
```

Daily Receipts Adder

This program allows a businessman to quickly add up his day's receipts, from both wholesale and retail orders as desired.

Program Listing

```
  1 REM *****CONNECT A PRINTER
  2 REM *****TO THE COMPUTER
  3 REM *****BEFORE RUNNING
  4 REM *****OR DELETE LINES
  5 REM *****420, 440, 460,
  6 REM *****480, 500, 520,
  7 REM *****560  AND580.
 10 CLS
 15 CLEAR
 20 LET D=Ø
 21 LET U=Ø
 22 LET V=Ø
 23 LET F=Ø
 24 LET E=Ø
 25 LET T=Ø
 30 PRINT "WHOLESALE ? ";
 40 INPUT W$
 50 IF W$="" THEN GOTO 200
 60 LET T=T+1
 70 LET D=D+VAL W$
 80 PRINT W$
 90 LET W$=""
100 GOTO 30
200 CLS
210 PRINT "RETAIL ? ";
220 INPUT R$
230 IF R$="" THEN GOTO 400
```

```
240 LET V=V+1
250 LET E=E+VAL R$
260 PRINT R$
270 LET R$=""
280 GOTO 210
400 CLS
410 PRINT "WHOLESALE $";D
420 LPRINT "WHOLESALE $";D
430 PRINT T;" WHOLESALE ITEMS"
440 LPRINT T;" WHOLESALE ITEMS"
450 PRINT
460 LPRINT
470 PRINT "RETAIL $";E
480 LPRINT "RETAIL $";E
490 PRINT V;" RETAIL ITEMS"
500 LPRINT V;" RETAIL ITEMS"
510 PRINT
520 LPRINT
530 LET F=E+D
540 LET U=T+V
550 PRINT "TOTAL RECEIPTS $";F
560 LPRINT "TOTAL RECEIPTS $";F
570 PRINT U;" TOTAL ITEMS"
580 LPRINT U;" TOTAL ITEMS"
```

To Nearest 95 Cents

Many companies like to price their goods at a figure ending in 95 cents. For instance, a ten dollar item might be marked $9.95 or $10.95.

Here's a program which demonstrates how to make all prices come out to the nearest 95 cents.

Program Listing

```
10 LET P=Ø
20 PRINT "MANUFACTURING COST:"
25 INPUT C
30 PRINT "PRICING MULTIPLIER:"
35 INPUT M
40 LET P=INT (C*M)+0.95
50 CLS
```

```
60 PRINT "RETAIL PRICE: $";P
70 PRINT
80 GOTO 10
```

To the Nearest Penny

This program is useful when you have a dollar-and-cents figure with more than two decimal places. For example, $151.6972. You need to transform $151.6972 to the more common $151.70

Program Listing

```
 10 LET R=Ø
 20 PRINT "ENTER A NUMBER TO"
 30 PRINT "MORE THAN TWO DECIMAL PLACES"
 40 PRINT "ORIGINAL AMOUNT $ = "
 50 INPUT N
 60 LET R=INT(100*N+.5)/100
 70 CLS
 80 PRINT "TO THE NEAREST PENNY"
 90 PRINT "$";N;" IS $";R
100 PRINT
110 GOTO 10
```

Percentage Off

For example, how much is 40 percent off? This program can be used to interpret 40 percent off and compute the decimal value needed. Try 40 percent off $100. The computer will change 40 percent off into decimal value 0.60. If you multiply 0.60 times $100 you find $60 is 40 percent off $100.

Line 30 makes the important translation.

Program Listing

```
10 PRINT "PERCENTAGE OFF: ";
20 INPUT P
30 PRINT P
40 PRINT "DECIMAL: ";(1-0.01*P)
50 PRINT
60 GOTO 10
```

Dollars & Cents

If the result of your computation is a "money" answer, and you don't know whether to display it in dollars or cents, let the computer decide.

Program Listing

```
 10 LET T=Ø
 20 PRINT "QUANTITY = ";
 30 INPUT P
 40 PRINT P
 50 PRINT "TOTAL COST = $";
 60 INPUT C
 70 PRINT C
 80 LET T=C/P
 90 IF T<1 THEN GOTO 130
100 PRINT "EACH COST $";T
110 PRINT
120 GOTO 10
130 LET T=100*T
140 PRINT "EACH COST ";T;" CENTS"
150 PRINT
160 GOTO 10
```

Shipments

A bar graph displaying number of shipments per month can be a useful way to see the trend in the movement of inventory from your warehouse.

Program Listing

```
10 PRINT CHR$(147)
100 INPUT"JANUARY";JA
110 INPUT"FEBRUARY";FE
120 INPUT"MARCH";MA
130 INPUT"APRIL";AP
140 INPUT"MAY";MY
150 INPUT"JUNE";JU
160 INPUT"JULY";JL
170 INPUT"AUGUST";AU
180 INPUT"SEPTEMBER";SE
```

```
190 INPUT"OCTOBER";OC
200 INPUT"NOVEMBER";NO
210 INPUT"DECEMBER";DE
410 PRINT CHR$(147):REM CLEAR SCREEN
500 PRINT TAB(2);"MONTHLY SHIPMENTS"
510 PRINT TAB(3);"(RANGE:0 TO 17)"
520 PRINT"JAN";
530 Z=JA:GOSUB 900
540 PRINT"FEB";
550 Z=FE:GOSUB 900
560 PRINT"MAR";
570 Z=MA:GOSUB 900
580 PRINT"APR";
590 Z=AP:GOSUB 900
600 PRINT"MAY";
610 Z=MY:GOSUB 900
620 PRINT"JUN";
630 Z=JU:GOSUB 900
640 PRINT"JUL";
650 Z=JL:GOSUB 900
660 PRINT"AUG";
670 Z=AU:GOSUB 900
680 PRINT"SEP";
690 Z=SE:GOSUB 900
700 PRINT"OCT";
710 Z=OC:GOSUB 900
720 PRINT"NOV";
730 Z=NO:GOSUB 900
740 PRINT"DEC";
750 Z=DE:GOSUB 900
800 FOR L=1 TO 5:PRINT:NEXT L
810 INPUT"FOR MORE PRESS RETURN";K$
820 CLR:GOTO 10
900 FOR L=1 TO Z
910 PRINT CHR$(162);
920 NEXT L
930 PRINT
940 RETURN
```

Profit Estimator

How much cash flow will I generate if I sell 100

thingamabobs? A question faced everyday in the business office. Whether you sell large lots at wholesale, small quantities across the retail counter, or individual items via mail order, this program will give you a quick estimate of expected cash flow and potential profits.

Program Listing

```
10 PRINT "}":DIM Q$(1)
20 PRINT "PROFIT ESTIMATOR"
30 PRINT
40 PRINT "WHICH TYPE OF SALE:"
50 PRINT "WHOLESALE (W)"
60 PRINT "DIRECT MAIL (D)"
70 PRINT "MEDIA AD RESPONSE (M)"
80 PRINT
100 PRINT "}"
110 PRINT "W, D OR M ?"
120 INPUT Q$
130 IF Q$="W" THEN 1000
140 IF Q$="D" THEN 2000
150 IF Q$="M" THEN 3000
160 PRINT "OKAY, YOU SELECTED ";Q$
170 PRINT "HOWEVER, ";Q$;" IS NOT"
180 PRINT "A CHOICE.  TRY AGAIN."
200 PRINT
210 GOTO 100
1000 PRINT "}":CLR :DIM A$(1)
1010 PRINT "WHOLESALE"
1020 PRINT "PROFIT ESTIMATOR"
1030 PRINT
1040 PRINT "}"
1060 PRINT "PLEASE ANSWER THESE QUESTIONS"
1070 PRINT :PRINT "MANUFACTURING COST $"
1080 INPUT C
1090 PRINT "}":PRINT "QUANTITY MANUFACTURED"
1100 INPUT P
1110 PRINT "}":PRINT "LIST PRICE OF ITEM $"
1120 INPUT L
1130 PRINT "}":PRINT "TOTAL QUANTITY SOLD"
1140 INPUT S
1150 IF S<>0 THEN 1160
```

```
1155 GOTO 10
1160 PRINT "WHOLESALE DISCOUNT %"
1165 INPUT D
1170 UC=C/P
1180 UP=(L*((100-D)/100))-UC
1190 W=L*S*((100-D)/100)
1200 G=W-(S*UC)
1210 PRINT "}"
1220 PRINT
1230 PRINT "------"
1240 PRINT "UNIT COST IS $";UC
1250 PRINT "UNIT PROFIT IS $";UP
1260 PRINT "WHOLESALE GROSS $";W
1270 PRINT "WHOLESALE PROFIT $";G
1280 PRINT "------"
1290 PRINT
1300 PRINT "FOR MORE, PRESS M AND RETURN"
1310 PRINT
1320 INPUT A$
1330 IF A$="M" THEN 10
1340 PRINT "THANK YOU."
1350 END
2000 PRINT "}":CLR :DIM A$(1)
2010 PRINT "DIRECT MAIL"
2020 PRINT "PROFIT ESTIMATOR"
2030 PRINT
2050 PRINT "}"
2060 PRINT "PLEASE ANSWER THESE QUESTIONS"
2070 PRINT :PRINT "MANUFACTURING COST $"
2080 INPUT C
2090 PRINT "}":PRINT "QUANTITY MANUFACTURED"
2100 INPUT P
2110 PRINT "}":PRINT "LIST PRICE OF ITEM $"
2120 INPUT L
2130 PRINT "}":PRINT "TOTAL QUANTITY SOLD"
2140 INPUT S
2150 PRINT "}":PRINT "NUMBER FLYERS MAILED ?"
2160 INPUT K
2170 PRINT "}":PRINT "FLYER PRINTING COST $"
2180 INPUT R
2190 PRINT "}":PRINT "POSTAGE COST $"
2200 INPUT M
```

```
2210 UC=C/P
2220 J=100*S/K
2230 T=L*S-(R+M+UC*S)
2240 U=L*S
2250 PRINT "}"
2260 PRINT
2270 PRINT "--------"
2280 PRINT "DIRECT MAIL"
2290 PRINT "RETURN IS ";J;" PERCENT"
2300 PRINT "DIRECT MAIL GROSS $";U
2310 PRINT "DIRECT MAIL PROFIT $";T
2320 PRINT "--------"
2330 PRINT
2340 PRINT "FOR MORE, PRESS M AND RETURN"
2350 PRINT
2360 INPUT A$
2370 IF A$="M" THEN 10
2380 PRINT "THANK YOU"
2390 END
3000 PRINT "}":CLR :DIM A$(1)
3010 PRINT "RESPONSE TO ADVERTISEMENT"
3020 PRINT "PROFIT ESTIMATOR"
3030 PRINT
3050 PRINT "}"
3060 PRINT "PLEASE ANSWER THESE QUESTIONS"
3070 PRINT :PRINT "MANUFACTURING COST $"
3080 INPUT C
3090 PRINT "}":PRINT "QUANTITY MANUFACTURED"
3100 INPUT P
3110 PRINT "}":PRINT "LIST PRICE OF ITEM $"
3120 INPUT L
3130 PRINT "}":PRINT "AD COST PER INSERTION $"
3140 INPUT A
3150 PRINT "}":PRINT "NUMBER OF INSERTIONS ?"
3160 INPUT I
3170 PRINT "}"
3180 PRINT "}"
3190 PRINT "WHICH DO YOU WANT TO KNOW ?"
3200 PRINT
3210 PRINT "SALES QUANTITY NEEDED"
3220 PRINT "TO BREAK EVEN (Q)"
3230 PRINT
```

```
3240 PRINT "PROFIT FROM SELLING"
3250 PRINT "A SPECIFIC QUANTITY (P)"
3260 PRINT
3270 PRINT "P OR Q ?"
3280 INPUT A$
3290 IF A$="P" THEN 3460
3300 IF A$="Q" THEN 3330
3310 GOTO 3270
3320 PRINT
3330 PRINT
3340 B=INT((C+A)/L)+1
3350 PRINT "--------"
3360 PRINT "SELL ";B;" TO BREAK EVEN"
3370 PRINT "INCLUDING COVERING"
3380 PRINT "$";C;" MANUFACTURING COST"
3390 PRINT "AND $";A*I;" AD CAMPAIGN"
3400 PRINT "--------"
3410 PRINT
3420 PRINT "FOR MORE, PRESS M AND RETURN"
3430 INPUT A$
3440 IF A$="M" THEN 10
3450 PRINT "THANK YOU":END
3460 PRINT :PRINT "QUANTITY SOLD ?"
3470 INPUT S
3480 N=S*L
3490 UC=C/P
3500 E=S*L-S*UC-A*I
3510 PRINT
3520 PRINT "--------"
3530 PRINT "ORDERS GROSS IS $";N
3540 PRINT "DIRECT MAIL PROFIT IS $";E
3550 PRINT "--------"
3560 PRINT
3570 PRINT "FOR MORE, PRESS M AND RETURN"
3580 INPUT A$
3590 IF A$="M" THEN 10
3600 PRINT "THANK YOU"
3610 END
```

Sales Required For A Profit

This handy program gives a quick estimate of how

many units have to be sold, at a certain "profit" or cashflow amount per unit, to achieve a desired gross profit or cashflow.

Program Listing

```
10 PRINT "}":REM CLEAR SCREEN
20 DIM X$(1)
30 PRINT "INCOME WANTED = $"
40 INPUT I
50 PRINT "PROFIT/UNIT SOLD = $"
60 INPUT P
70 Y=I/P:M=Y/12:W=Y/52:D=W/6
100 PRINT :PRINT
110 PRINT "SELL ";Y;" PER YR"
120 PRINT "SELL ";M;" PER MO"
130 PRINT "SELL ";W;" PER WEEK"
140 PRINT "SELL ";D;" PER DAY"
200 PRINT :PRINT :PRINT
210 PRINT "TO DO MORE, PRESS RETURN"
220 INPUT X$
230 CLR :GOTO 10
```

Gross & Net Computer

In response to its inquiries on the display, tell the computer how much it costs to manufacture your thingamabob, what its list price is and at what discount you plan to sell the thingamabobs. As soon as you tell the computer how many thingamabobs you will sell, it will compute the total invoice amount you will charge your customer and your anticipated profits after manufacturing costs are deducted.

Program Listing

```
10 DIM T$(20),K$(1)
20 PRINT "}":REM CLEAR SCREEN
30 PRINT "ITEM:"
40 INPUT T$
50 PRINT "LIST PRICE $"
60 INPUT L
70 PRINT "MANUFACTURING COST $"
80 INPUT C
```

```
90 PRINT "WHOLESALE DISCOUNT %"
100 INPUT W
110 D=1-0.01*W
120 PRINT "QUANTITY SOLD"
130 INPUT S
140 I=L*S*D:P=I-S*C
200 PRINT "}":REM CLEAR SCREEN
210 PRINT "ITEM:",,T$
220 PRINT "LIST PRICE","$";L
230 PRINT "MFG COST",,"$";C
240 PRINT "SOLD",,S
250 PRINT "DISCOUNT",,W;"%"
260 PRINT
270 PRINT "INVOICE",,"$";I
280 PRINT "PROFIT",,"$";P
300 PRINT :PRINT :PRINT :PRINT
310 PRINT "FOR MORE, PRESS RETURN"
320 INPUT K$
330 CLR :GOTO 10
```

Yes/No Decision Maker

This is handy for the busy executive who doesn't have time for decisions.

Program Listing

```
10 PRINT CHR$(147):Z=RND(-TI)
20 IF (100*RND(1))>49 THEN PRINT"YES"
   :GOTO 40
30 PRINT"NO"
40 GET K$:IF K$="" THEN 40
50 GOTO 10
```

Executive Decision Maker

Stumped by a toughie? Got one too hot to handle alone? Need help with major decisions? When there is no other way to decide, punch up this quickie and get a definite YES or NO.

Program Listing

```
10 PRINT CHR$(147)
```

```
20 Q=RND(-TI)
30 R=INT(1000*RND(1))
40 PRINT:PRINT:PRINT
50 IF R>499 THEN PRINT TAB(8) "YES"
   :GOTO 100
60 PRINT TAB(8) "NO"
100 FOR L=1 TO 12:PRINT:NEXT L
110 PRINT" PRESS ANY KEY"
120 PRINT" TO MAKE ANOTHER"
130 PRINT" IMPORTANT DECISION"
140 GET K$
150 IF K$="" THEN 140
160 CLR
170 GOTO 10
```

Superior Decision Maker

In this superior edition, a choice of eight replies is possible.

Program Listing

```
10 DATA FIRE SOMEONE
20 DATA PASS THE BUCK
30 DATA YES
40 DATA MAYBE
50 DATA REORGANIZE
60 DATA SIT ON IT
70 DATA NO
80 DATA SEE YOUR ANALYST
90 Q=RND(-TI)
100 PRINT CHR$(147)
110 N=INT(9*RND(1))
120 IF N<1 THEN 110
130 FOR L=1 TO N
140 READ Z$
150 NEXT L
160 PRINT Z$
170 GET K$
180 IF K$="" THEN 170
190 RESTORE
200 GOTO 100
```

Selling Prices Of World Currencies

Your own world currency guide allows you to convert money from one currency to another quickly.

Program Listing

```
 10 CLS
100 DATA "ARGENTINA","PESO",.0001
110 DATA "AUSTRALIA","DOLLAR",.9815
120 DATA "AUSTRIA","SCHILLING",.0584
130 DATA "BAHAMAS","DOLLAR",1
140 DATA "BELGIUM","FRANC",.0215
150 DATA "BELIZE","DOLLAR",.5
160 DATA "BERMUDA","DOLLAR",1
170 DATA "BRAZIL","CRUZEIRO",.0053
180 DATA "CANADA","DOLLAR",.8114
190 DATA "CHILE","PESO",.0256
200 DATA "CHINA","YUAN",.5236
210 DATA "COLOMBIA","PESO",.0153
220 DATA "CYPRUS","POUND",2.1552
230 DATA "DENMARK","KRONE",.1178
240 DATA "ECUADOR","SUCRE",.0303
250 DATA "EGYPT","POUND",1.2195
260 DATA "FINLAND","MARKKA",.2129
270 DATA "FRANCE","FRANC",.1475
280 DATA "GERMANY","MARK",.4137
290 DATA "GREAT BRITAIN","POUND",1.776
300 DATA "GREECE","DRACHMA",.0146
310 DATA "HAITI","GOURDE",.2
320 DATA "HONG KONG","DOLLAR",.1682
330 DATA "HUNGARY","FORINT",.029
340 DATA "ICELAND","KRONA",.0994
350 DATA "INDIA","RUPEE",.1053
360 DATA "IRAQ","DINAR",3.3862
370 DATA "IRELAND","POUND",1.4155
380 DATA "ISRAEL","SHEKEL",.0377
390 DATA "ITALY","LIRA",.0008
400 DATA "JAPAN","YEN",.004
410 DATA "MEXICO","PESO",.0111
420 DATA "NETHERLANDS","GUILDER",.3781
```

```
430 DATA "NEW ZEALAND","DOLLAR",.7405
440 DATA "NIGERIA","NAIRA",1.4808
450 DATA "NORWAY","KRONE",.1523
460 DATA "PAKISTAN","RUPEE",.0809
470 DATA "PERU","SOL",.0014
480 DATA "POLAND","ZLOTY",.0125
490 DATA "PORTUGAL","ESCUDO",.0118
500 DATA "SAUDI ARABIA","RIYAL",.2907
510 DATA "SOUTH AFRICA","RAND",.8807
520 DATA "SPAIN","PESETA",.0091
530 DATA "SWEDEN","KRONA",.1653
540 DATA "SWITZERLAND","FRANC",.4902
550 DATA "THAILAND","BAHT",.0435
560 DATA "TURKEY","LIRA",.0066
570 DATA "USSR","RUBLE",1.3986
580 DATA "VENEZUELA","BOLIVAR",.2329
590 DATA "ZAMBIA","KWACHA",1.084
600 BEEP1,1
610 INPUT "COUNTRY: ";C$
700 FOR L=1 TO 50
710 READ CC$,M$,V
720 IF CC$=C$ THEN 800
730 CC$=""
740 NEXT L
750 RESTORE
760 GOTO 600
800 RESTORE
810 BEEP 3
820 WAIT Ø
830 PRINT M$;" = $X";V
900 IF INKEY$="" THEN 900
910 GOTO 600
```

Percent to Decimal

Here's another way to change percentages to decimals inside a program to simplify entry by permitting percents to be entered as simple numbers.

Program Listing

```
10 PRINT "}":REM CLEAR SCREEN
20 PRINT "PRICE $",,:INPUT P
```

```
30 PRINT "SALES TAX %",:INPUT R
40 T=0.01*R
50 S=T*P:B=P+S
60 PRINT "SALES TAX","$";S
70 PRINT "TOTAL BILL","$";B
80 PRINT :PRINT :PRINT :PRINT
90 CLR :GOTO 20
```

Volumes

Cones. Cubes. Cylinders. Prisms. Pyramids. Spheres. Name your object. This program computes the volume and displays it in cubic units.

Program Listing

```
10 GOSUB 900
20 PRINT:PRINT:PRINT
30 INPUT"OBJECT NAME";X$
50 PRINT
60 IF X$="CONE" THEN 100
65 IF X$="PYRAMID" THEN 100
70 IF X$="CUBE" THEN 200
75 IF X$="CYLINDER" THEN 300
80 IF X$="PRISM" THEN 400
85 IF X$="SPHERE" THEN 500
90 PRINT"TRY AGAIN"
95 GOTO 20
100 PRINT X$;" AREA";
110 INPUT A
120 PRINT X$;" HEIGHTH";
130 INPUT H
140 V=(A*H)/3
150 GOTO 600
200 PRINT X$;" LENGTH";
210 INPUT L
220 PRINT X$;" WIDTH";
230 INPUT W
240 PRINT X$;" HEIGHTH";
250 INPUT H
260 V=L*W*H
270 GOTO 600
```

```
300 PRINT X$;" RADIUS";
310 INPUT R
320 PRINT X$;" HEIGHTH";
330 INPUT H
340 V=3.141592654*2*R*H
350 GOTO 600
400 PRINT X$;" AREA";
410 INPUT A
420 PRINT X$;" HEIGHTH";
430 INPUT H
440 V=A*H
450 GOTO 600
500 PRINT X$;" RADIUS";
510 INPUT R
520 V=(3.141592654*4*(R↑3))/3
600 PRINT
610 PRINT X$;" VOLUME ";V
630 GOTO 20
900 PRINT CHR$(147);CHR$(28)
910 PRINT TAB(5);CHR$(111);
920 FOR L=1 TO 11:PRINT CHR$(163);:NEXT L
930 PRINT CHR$(112)
935 PRINT TAB(5);CHR$(165);
940 PRINT TAB(8);"VOLUMES";
950 PRINT TAB(17);CHR$(167)
955 PRINT TAB(5);CHR$(108);
957 FOR L=1 TO 11:PRINT CHR$(164);:NEXT L
960 PRINT TAB(17);CHR$(186)
970 PRINT CHR$(144)
980 RETURN
```

Areas

Circle. Ellipse. Parabola. Sphere. Square. Rectangle. Triangle. Name your shape. This program will compute its area. Surface area in the case of the sphere.

Program Listing

```
10 PRINT CHR$(147):REM CLEAR SCREEN
20 INPUT"SHAPE";S$
30 PRINT
```

```
40 IF S$="CIRCLE" THEN 200
50 IF S$="ELLIPSE" THEN 300
60 IF S$="PARABOLA" THEN 400
70 IF S$="SPHERE" THEN 500
80 IF S$="SQUARE" THEN 600
90 IF S$="RECTANGLE" THEN 600
100 IF S$="TRIANGLE" THEN 700
110 PRINT"NOT A RECOGNIZED SHAPE TRY AGAIN"
120 PRINT
130 GOTO 20
200 INPUT"RADIUS";R
210 A=3.141592654*(R↑2)
220 GOTO 800
300 INPUT"MAJOR AXIS";J
310 INPUT"MINOR AXIS";N
320 A=0.7854*J*N
330 GOTO 800
400 INPUT"BASE";B
410 INPUT"HEIGHTH";H
420 A=(2/3)*(B*H)
430 GOTO 800
500 INPUT"RADIUS";R
510 A=3.141592654*4*(R↑2)
520 GOTO 800
600 INPUT"LENGTH";L
610 IF S$="SQUARE" THEN A=L*L:GOTO 800
620 INPUT"WIDTH";W
630 A=L*W
640 GOTO 800
700 INPUT"BASE";B
710 INPUT"HEIGHTH";H
720 A=0.5*B*H
800 PRINT
810 PRINT"AREA ";A
820 PRINT
830 GOTO 20
```

Reciprocals

Key in any number. The computer will display its reciprocal. The actual conversion is done here at line 30.

Program Listing

```
10 PRINT CHR$(147):REM CLEAR SCREEN
15 PRINT"NUMBER TO BE CONVERTED"
20 INPUT"TO ITS RECIPROCAL";N
25 IF N=0 THEN PRINT:GOTO 15
30 R=1/N
40 PRINT:PRINT:PRINT
50 PRINT"RECIPROCAL OF";N
60 PRINT"IS";R
70 PRINT:PRINT:PRINT
80 INPUT"FOR MORE PRESS RETURN";K$
90 CLR:GOTO 10
```

Averages

Key in numbers in any order. A zero will end entry. The computer will tell you the average number of all numbers you entered.

Program Listing

```
10 PRINT CHR$(147):REM CLEAR SCREEN
20 INPUT"GIVE ME A NUMBER";Z
30 IF Z=0 THEN 70
40 N=N+1
50 T=T+Z
60 GOTO 20
70 A=T/N
100 PRINT:PRINT:PRINT
110 PRINT"THE AVERAGE IS";A
120 PRINT:PRINT:PRINT
130 INPUT"FOR MORE PRESS RETURN";K$
140 CLR:GOTO 10
```

Fractional feet

You are measuring a box and the computation comes out to 14.5 feet. How do you change 14.5 feet into 14 feet 6 inches? Here's how:

Program Listing

```
10 PRINT CHR$(147)
```

```
20 PRINT"TYPE FRACTIONAL FEET"
30 PRINT"(FEET TO A DECIMAL)"
40 INPUT F
45 W=INT(F)
50 B=F-W
60 D=12*B
62 IF (D-INT(D))<0.5 THEN I=INT(D):GOTO 80
70 I=INT(D)+1
80 PRINT
90 PRINT F;"FEET ="
100 PRINT W;"FEET";I;"INCHES"
200 FOR L=1 TO 10:PRINT:NEXT L
210 INPUT"PRESS RETURN FOR MORE";K$
220 CLR:GOTO 10
```

Standard Deviation

Here's a way to determine mean and standard deviation. In this particular program, you exit the entry cycle by entering the large number 999999999 (nine 9's) so you can't use 999999999 as one of your data points.

Program Listing

```
10 PRINT CHR$(147):REM CLEAR SCREEN
20 INPUT"DATA POINT:";X
30 IF X=999999999 THEN 60
40 T=T+X:S=S+X↑2:N=N+1
50 GOTO 20
60 A=T/N:V=S/N-A↑2:D=SQR(V)
70 PRINT:PRINT:PRINT
80 PRINT"DATA POINTS TOTAL";T
90 PRINT"MEAN";A
100 PRINT"VARIANCE";V
110 PRINT"STD DEVIATION";D
120 PRINT:PRINT:PRINT
130 INPUT"FOR MORE PRESS RETURN";K$
140 CLR:GOTO 10
```

Normal Distribution

This statistics program allows the computer to find normal distribution by Hastings' best approximation.

Program Listing

```
10 WAIT 120
20 PRINT "***NORMAL DISTRIBUTION***"
30 INPUT "X=";X
40 T=1/(1+(.2316419*X))
50 Q=(1/(√(2*π)))*(EXP (-(X∧2/2)))
60 A=.31938153
70 B=-.356563782
80 C=1.78147937
90 D=-1.821255978
100 E=1.330274429
110 PX=1-Q*((A*T)+(B*T∧2)+(C*T∧3)+(D*T∧4)
    +(E*T∧5))
120 PRINT PX
130 IF INKEY$ ="" THEN 130
140 CLEAR
150 GOTO 30
```

Spearman's Coefficient

The computer is great at statistics! Here it finds Spearman's coefficient of rank correlation.

Program Listing

```
10 WAIT 120
20 PRINT "****RANK CORRELATION****"
30 WAIT Ø
40 C=Ø
50 N=1
60 PRINT "A";N;"=";:INPUT A$
70 IF A$="X"THEN GOTO 150
80 A=VAL A$
90 CLS
100 PRINT "B";N;"=";:INPUT B
110 CLS
120 C=C+((A-B)∧2)
130 N=N+1
140 GOTO 60
150 WAIT 300
160 N=N-1
170 R=1-((6*C)/(N∧3-N))
```

```
180 PRINT "R=";R
190 GOTO 10
```

Aggregate Classification

The computer will find the aggregate classification and will do prorating. In this set of program lines, we treat the data as money or financial items. The program could just as well be used as an exam-score sorter or inventory dollar-value sorter or some other kind of sorter.

The result of the run is a neat list, broken down by code group classification. You can change the print wording if you like.

Program Listing

```
 10 WAIT 120
 20 PRINT "*AGGREGATE CLASSIFICATION*"
 30 CLEAR
 40 DIM C(10)
 50 INPUT "CODE: ";N$
 60 IF N$="X"THEN 200
 70 N=VAL N$
 80 INPUT "AMOUNT: $";D
 90 C(N)=C(N)+D
100 T=T+D
110 GOTO 50
200 GOSUB 300
210 LPRINT "CODE";TAB 8;"AMOUNT"
220 GOSUB 300
230 FOR N=1 TO 10
240 LPRINT N;TAB 8;"$";C(N)
250 NEXT N
260 GOSUB 300
270 LPRINT "TOTAL:";TAB 8;"$";T
280 GOSUB 300
290 GOTO 10
300 FOR L=1 TO 16
310 LPRINT "-";
320 NEXT L
330 LPRINT
340 RETURN
```

N-Month Moving Average

This statistical routine finds the n-month moving average.

You type in the data and the results will be displayed.

Program Listing

```
 10 CLEAR
 20 WAIT 120
 30 PRINT "*****MOVING AVERAGE*****"
 40 INPUT "NO. MONTHS: ";X
 50 WAIT Ø
 60 DIM A(X)
 70 FOR Y=1 TO X
 80 PRINT "MO.";Y;" DATA: ";
 90 INPUT A(Y)
100 CLS
110 W=W+A(Y)
120 NEXT Y
130 Z=Z+1
140 IF Z>X THEN LET Z=1
150 V=W/X
160 W=W-A(Z)
170 WAIT 120
180 PRINT "AVERAGE =";V
190 WAIT Ø
200 PRINT "MO.";Z+6;" DATA: ";
210 INPUT A(Z)
220 PRINT
230 W=W+A(Z)
240 GOTO 130
```

f-Distribution

Here the computer finds f-distribution in a simple easy-to-use statistical program. The result is Q(x).

Program Listing

```
10 WAIT Ø
20 PRINT "F-DISTRIBUTION"
30 IF INKEY$="" THEN 30
40 INPUT "X=";X
```

```
 50 INPUT "V1=";B
 60 INPUT "V2=";C
 70 G=C/(C+X*B):A=1:J=1:K=1
 80 F=C/2:IF ((B/2)-(INT (B/2)))=ØTHEN 110
 90 IF (F-INT F) =Ø THEN 170
100 Z=Ø:GOTO 270
110 IF (F-INT F)=Ø THEN 130
120 GOTO 140
130 IF B-C>=Ø THEN 170
140 X=Ø:F=Ø:E=C:H=1-G
150 IF (B-2)/2=K THEN 230
160 K=(B-2)/2:GOTO 200
170 X=1:F=Ø:E=B:H=G
180 IF (C-2)/2=K THEN 230
190 K=(C-2)/2
200 I=I+1:IF I=K THEN 230
210 F=F+2:J=J*E/F*H:A=A+J
220 E=E+2:GOTO 200
230 A=A+J*E/(F+2)*H
240 IF X=ØTHEN 260
250 H=1-G:Z=1-A*H∧(B/2):GOTO 270
260 Z=A*G∧(C/2)
270 PRINT "QX=";Z
280 IF INKEY$ =""THEN 280
290 CLEAR
300 GOTO 40
```

t-Distribution

This quick-typing program allows the computer to find t-distribution, I(x,v).

Program Listing

```
10 PAUSE "T-DISTRIBUTION"
20 IF INKEY$ ="" THEN 20
30 CLEAR
40 INPUT "X=";X
50 INPUT "V=";V
60 G=1:F=1:A=1
70 X=ATN (X/√V):C=COS X∧2
80 IF ((V/2)-INT(V/2))=ØTHEN 130
90 B=2*X/π:IF V=G THEN 180
```

```
100 G=V-1:D=3
110 E=E+2:IF E=G THEN 190
120 F=F*E/D*C:A=A+F:D=D+2:GOTO 110
130 G=V:D=1
140 E=E+2:IF E=G THEN 170
150 F=F*D/E*C
160 A=A+F:D=D+2:GOTO 140
170 Z=SIN X*A:GOTO 200
180 Z=B:GOTO 200
190 Z=2/π*COS X* SIN X*A+B
200 PAUSE "I=";Z
210 IF INKEY$ ="" THEN 210
220 GOTO 30
```

2x2 Contingency Table

This statistical table finds $X_\emptyset^2$ and Yeat's correction, X_s^2.

The software considers A and B are dependent if $X_\emptyset^2$ is greater than 3.84 (risk 5 percent).

Here's the 2-by-2 table set up:

	B_1	B_2	Total
A_1	a	b	a + b = g
A_2	c	d	c + d = h
Total	a + c = e	b + d = f	a + b + c + d = n

Program Listing

```
10 WAIT Ø
20 PRINT "2x2 CONTINGENCY TABLE"
30 IF INKEY$ ="" THEN 30
40 INPUT "A=";A:LPRINT "A=";A
50 INPUT "B=";B:LPRINT "B=";B
60 INPUT "C=";C:LPRINT "C=";C
70 INPUT "D=";D:LPRINT "D=";D
80 E=A+C
90 F=B+D
100 G=A+B
```

```
110 H=C+D
120 N=E+F
130 XO=(A*D-B*C)^2*N/(E*F*G*H)
140 XS=N*(ABS (A*D-B*C)-N/2)^2/(E*F*G*H)
150 PAUSE "XO=";XO:LPRINT "XO=";XO
160 PAUSE "XS=";XS:LPRINT "XS=";XS
170 IF INKEY$ =""THEN 170
180 CLEAR
190 GOTO 40
```

Convert Any Base To Any Base

You may move freely from number system to number system with this base-conversion software. The computer will convert any base, 2 to 9, to base 10. Or it will convert base 10 to any base, 2 to 9.

Program Listing

```
 10 CLEAR :WAIT Ø
 20 PRINT "1:(DEC TO N) 2:(N TO DEC)"
 30 K$=INKEY$
 40 IF K$=""THEN 30
 50 IF K$="1"THEN 100
 60 IF K$="2"THEN 200
 70 GOTO 30
100 INPUT "BASE WANTED",N
110 INPUT "NUMBER TO CONVERT",C
120 CC=C
130 A=N
140 Z=N
150 B=10
160 GOTO 300
200 INPUT "PRESENT BASE",N
210 INPUT "NUMBER TO CONVERT",C
220 CC=C
230 B=N
240 A=10
250 Z=Ø
300 E=INT (C/A)
310 IF E=ØTHEN 340
320 D=D+(C-E*A)*B^M
330 C=E:M=M+1:GOTO 300
```

```
340 D=D+C*B^M
350 IF Z=ØTHEN 500
400 PRINT "BASE";A;":";D
410 LPRINT "NUMBER";CC
420 LPRINT "IN BASE 10"
430 LPRINT "IS ";D
440 LPRINT "IN BASE";A
450 LF 3
460 IF INKEY$ =""THEN 460
470 GOTO 10
500 PRINT "BASE 10:";D
510 LPRINT "NUMBER ";CC
520 LPRINT "IN BASE ";B
530 LPRINT "IS ";D
540 LPRINT "IN BASE 10"
550 LF 3
560 IF INKEY$ =""THEN 560
570 GOTO 10
```

Binary/Decimal Decimal/Binary Converter

This is a simplified, shortened version of the any-base conversion program. Use this where you only need to go from base-2 to base-10 or base-10 to base-2. This set of program lines is easier to type into your computer.

Program Listing

```
 10 CLEAR :WAIT Ø:N=2
 20 PRINT "1:(D TO B) 2:(B TO D)"
 30 K$=INKEY$
 40 IF K$=""THEN 30
 50 IF K$="1"THEN 100
 60 IF K$="2"THEN 200
 70 GOTO 30
100 INPUT "NUMBER TO CONVERT",C
110 CC=C
120 A=N
130 Z=N
140 B=10
150 GOTO 300
```

```
200 INPUT "NUMBER TO CONVERT",C
210 CC=C
220 B=N
230 A=10
240 Z=Ø
300 E=INT (C/A)
310 IF E=ØTHEN 340
320 D=D+(C-E*A)*B^M
330 C=E:M=M+1:GOTO 300
340 D=D+C*B^M
350 IF Z=ØTHEN 500
400 PRINT CC;":";D
410 IF INKEY$ =""THEN 410
420 GOTO 10
500 PRINT CC;":";D
510 IF INKEY$ =""THEN 510
520 GOTO 10
```

Slope and Distance

This program computes the slope of a line between two points on a graph and the distance between those two points. The letter X designates the horizontal position on the graph and Y the vertical position.

Program Listing

```
10 "S" CLEAR
20 BEEP 1:INPUT"X1= ";A
30 BEEP 1:INPUT"Y1= ";B
40 BEEP 1:INPUT"X2= ";C
```

Metric Converter

Keep this math conversion program loaded in your Computer and you'll always have a handy way to quickly change feet, inches or yards into millimeters, centimeters or meters. Or vice versa.

Program Listing

```
10 "=" CLEAR
```

```
 20 PAUSE"METRIC CONVERSION"
 30 INPUT"TO METRIC (Y OR N) ?",A$
 40 IF A$="N" THEN "METERS"
 50 INPUT"IN, FT OR YDS ?",B$
 60 IF B$="IN" THEN "INCHES"
 70 IF B$="FT" THEN "FEET"
 80 IF B$="YDS" THEN "YARDS"
 90 GOTO 30
100 "INCHES" INPUT"INCHES = ";I
110 M=I/39.37:C=100M:N=1000M
120 PRINT I;"IN = ";N;"MM"
130 PRINT I;"IN = ";C;"CM"
140 PRINT I;"IN = ";M;"MTRS"
150 GOTO 30
200 "FEET" INPUT"FEET = ";F
210 I=12F:M=I/39.37:C=100M:N=1000M
220 PRINT F;"FT = ";N;"MM"
230 PRINT F;"FT = ";C;"CM"
240 PRINT F;"FT = ";M;"MTRS"
250 GOTO 30
300 "YARDS" INPUT"YARDS = ";Y
310 I=36Y:M=I/39.37:C=100M:N=1000M
320 PRINT Y;"YDS = ";N;"MM"
330 PRINT Y;"YDS = ";C;"CM"
340 PRINT Y;"YDS = ";M;"MTRS"
350 GOTO 30
400 "METERS"
410 INPUT"CM, MM OR MTRS ?",D$
420 IF D$="CM" THEN "CM"
430 IF D$="MM" THEN "MM"
440 IF D$="MTRS" THEN "MTRS"
450 GOTO 30
500 "CM" INPUT"CENTIMETERS = ";C
510 I=.3937C:F=I/12:Y=I/36
520 PRINT C;"CM = ";I;"IN"
530 PRINT C;"CM = ";F;"FT"
540 PRINT C;"CM = ";Y;"YDS"
550 GOTO 30
600 "MM" INPUT"MILLIMETERS = ";N
610 I=.03937N:F=I/12:Y=I/36
620 PRINT N;"MM = ";I;"IN"
630 PRINT N;"MM = ";F;"FT"
```

```
640 PRINT N;"MM = ";Y;"YDS"
650 GOTO 30
700 "MTRS" INPUT"METERS = ";M
710 I=39.37M:F=I/12:Y=I/36
720 PRINT M;"MTRS = ";I;"IN"
730 PRINT M;"MTRS = ";F;"FT"
740 PRINT M;"MTRS = ";Y;"YDS"
750 GOTO 30
```

Pythagorean Theorem

The theorem lets you find the length of any side of a right triangle if you know the length of the other two sides. The two shorter sides of the triangle are labeled A and B. The longer side, the hypotenuse, is C. The length of C is always longer than A or B.

Program Listing

```
 10 "H" CLEAR
 20 BEEP 1:INPUT"SIDE A LENGTH = ";A
 30 BEEP 1:INPUT"SIDE B LENGTH = ";B
 40 IF A THEN 60
 50 GOTO 70
 60 IF B THEN 150
 70 BEEP 1:INPUT"HYPOTENUSE (C) = ";C
 90 IF A THEN 120
100 A=√(C∧2-B∧2)
110 GOTO 170
120 IF B THEN 150
130 B=√(C∧2-A∧2)
140 GOTO 190
150 C=√(A∧2+B∧2)
160 GOTO 210
170 BEEP 2:PRINT"SIDE A = ";A
180 GOTO 10
190 BEEP 2:PRINT"SIDE B = ";B
200 GOTO 10
210 BEEP 2:PRINT"HYPOTENUSE = ";C
220 GOTO 10
```

Rounding Off Numbers

You often don't need a number answer from the computer with a fractional part displayed as decimal. Rounded off to the nearest whole number is fine. This program, which can stand alone or be worked into a larger program as a subroutine, rounds a decimal to the nearest whole number.

There are two views on how to round off. One holds that "if the number is more than five, you round up." Which means that exactly .5 rounds down. Another view is that "any number less than five rounds down," in which case exactly .5 rounds up!

The first set of line listings below is for the fellow with the "more than five rounds up" philosophy.

Program Listing

```
 10 "A" CLEAR
 20 BEEP 1
    :INPUT" NUMBER TO BE ROUNDED",N
 30 IF N>INT N THEN 50
 40 R=N:GOTO 100
 50 D=N-INT N
 60 IF D>.5 THEN 90
 70 R =INT N
 80 GOTO 100
 90 R=INT N +1
100 BEEP 1:PAUSE N;" ROUNDS TO..."
110 PRINT R
120 GOTO 10
```

The second set of program lines rounds off on the "less than five rounds down" theory.

Program Listing

```
 10 "B" CLEAR
 20 BEEP 1
    :INPUT" NUMBER TO BE ROUNDED",N
 30 IF N>INT N THEN 50
 40 R=N:GOTO 100
```

```
50 D=N-INT N
60 IF D<.5 THEN 90
70 R=INT N + 1
80 GOTO 100
90 R=INT N
100 BEEP 1:PAUSE N;" ROUNDS TO..."
110 PRINT R
120 GOTO 10
```

Fractional Portion of a Number

Most computers make it easy to obtain the integer value of a number. It's a bit harder to get rid of the integer and keep only the decimal value, to the right of the decimal point in the original number. This program gets rid of the integer portion of the number and displays the decimal part. It also would make a good subroutine in a larger program.

Program Listing

```
10 "D" CLEAR
20 BEEP 1:INPUT"ORIGINAL NUMBER =",N
30 F=N - INT N
40 BEEP 2:PRINT F
50 GOTO 20
```

Median and Mean

Frequently it's important to know some facts about a group of numbers. It's convenient to have a list of the highest number among several; the lowest number; the full span of the range of numbers; the total of all numbers; the average number and the median number.

This program lets you enter a set of numbers into the computer. You key in the letter X after your last entry and the computer crunches the numbers down into median, mean, total, range, low and high.

Program Listing

```
10 "M" CLEAR
```

```
20 X=999
30 FOR E=1 TO 999
40 INPUT "NUMBER = ";G
50 IF G=X THEN 120
60 N=N+1
70 IF N=1 LET L=G:H=G
80 IF G<L LET L=G
90 IF G>H LET H=G
100 S=S+G
110 NEXT E
120 P=S/N:M=L+((H-L)/2)
140 PRINT "THERE WERE ";N;" NUMBERS"
150 PRINT "NUMBERS RANGED"
160 PRINT "FROM ";L;" TO ";H
170 PRINT "NUMBERS TOTALED ";S
180 PRINT "MEDIAN IS ";M
190 PRINT "AVERAGE (MEAN) IS ";P
200 GOTO 10
```

Circle Circumference

Know the diameter of a circle? The radius? This program will take your information and tell you how far it is around the perimeter of the circle.

We store the radius in memory location R. After computation, the circumference of the circle is stored in C. If you know the diameter, divide it by two to get the radius. Enter that radius in the computer when it asks for it.

Program Listing

```
10 "C" CLEAR
20 INPUT "RADIUS = ";R
30 C=2πR
40 PRINT "CIRCUMFERENCE = ";C
50 GOTO 10
```

Delta Y Conversion

Electrical engineers, technicians, experimenters, now you can use your computer to convert Δ—>Y and Y—>Δquickly.

Figure 1 is the schematic diagram for Δ—>Y conversion and figure 2 is for Y—> Δ conversion. When you run the program, the computer will clearly ask which you want.

Depending upon your selection of conversion direction, the computer then will ask for values for R_1 and R_2 and R_3 or it will ask for R_4 and R_5 and R_6.

For a sample run, try these values in a RUN:

Input

R_1	12 ohms
R_2	47 ohms
R_3	82 ohms

Output

R_4	4 ohms
R_5	27.33333333 ohms
R_6	6.978723404 ohms

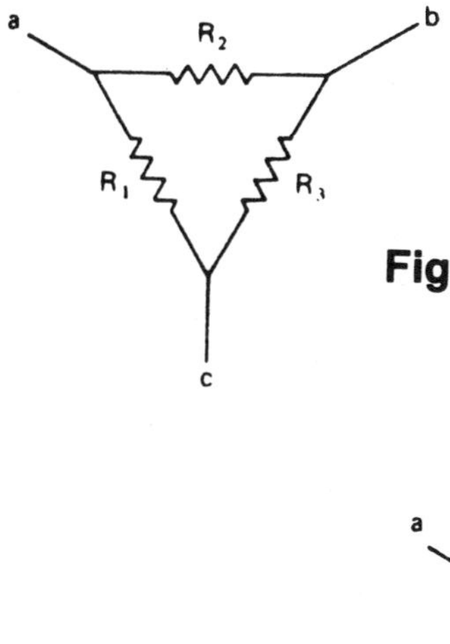

Figure 1

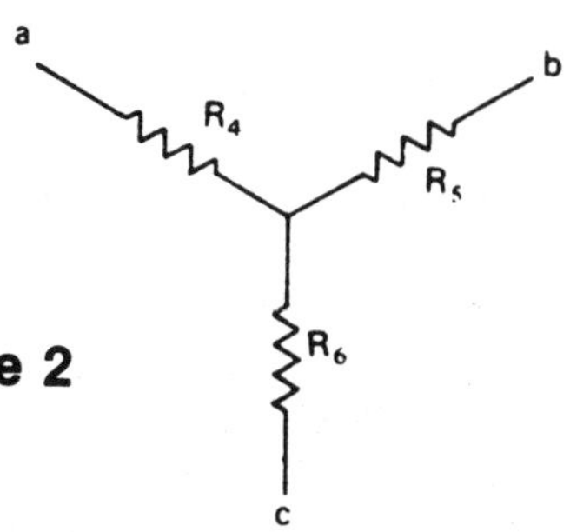

Figure 2

Program Listing

```
 10 WAIT Ø
 20 GPRINT 64;96;80;72;68;66;65;66;68;
    72;80;96;64;
 30 GPRINT 8;28;42;8;8;8;8;8;8;8;8;8;42;
    28;8;
 40 WAIT 120
 50 PRINT "Y"
 60 WAIT Ø
 70 PRINT "PICK: (1)";
 80 GPRINT 64;96;80;72;68;66;65;66;68;72;
    80;96;64;
 90 GPRINT 8;8;8;8;34;28;8;
100 PRINT "Y OR (2)Y";
110 GPRINT 8;8;8;8;34;28;8;
120 GPRINT 64;96;80;72;68;66;65;66;68;
    72;80;96;64
130 K$=INKEY$
140 IF K$=""THEN 130
150 IF K$="1"THEN 200
160 IF K$="2"THEN 400
170 GOTO 130
200 CLS
210 INPUT "R1=";A
220 INPUT "R2=";B
230 INPUT "R3=";C
240 D=A+B+C
250 WAIT 120
260 PRINT "R4=";(A*B)/D
270 PRINT "R5=";(B*C)/D
280 PRINT "R6=";(A*C)/D
290 CLEAR
300 GOTO 60
400 CLS
410 INPUT "R4=";E
420 INPUT "R5=";F
430 INPUT "R6=";G
440 H=(E*F)+(F*G)+(G*E)
450 WAIT 120
460 PRINT "R1=";H/F
470 PRINT "R2=";H/G
```

```
480 PRINT "R3=";H/E
490 CLEAR
500 GOTO 60
```

Which is largest?

Suppose you have a group of numbers and you would like to know which is the largest within the group. Here's a software routine to locate the largest number.

Program Listing

```
 10 "A" CLEAR
 20 FOR Z=1 TO 10
 30 BEEP 1:INPUT"NUMBER = ";A(Z)
 40 IF A(Z)=ØTHEN 70
 50 N=N+1
 60 NEXT Z
 70 Y=A
 80 FOR X=2 TO N
 90 IF A(X) <= A THEN 110
100 Y=A(X)
110 NEXT X
120 BEEP 1:PRINT" LARGEST # = ";Y
130 GOTO 10
```

Highest and lowest

Here's how to find the highest and lowest numbers within a group of numbers. Lines 130, 140 and 150 accomplish the task.

In 130, if the number is the first of a series, then it is set to both highest (H) and lowest (L). At 140, any number lower than L gets to be the new lowest number. at 150, any higher than H gets to be highest.

Program Listing

```
10 "G" CLEAR
20 PAUSE"ENTER SCORES"
30 X=999
40 FOR E=1 TO 999
```

```
50 INPUT"SCORE = ";G
60 IF G=X THEN 180
70 N=N+1
80 IF G<60 LET F=F+1:GOTO 130
90 IF G<70 LET D=D+1:GOTO 130
100 IF G<80 LET C=C+1:GOTO 130
110 IF G<90 LET B=B+1:GOTO 130
120 A=A+1
130 IF N=1 LET L=G:H=G
140 IF G<L LET L=G
150 IF G>H LET H=G
160 S=S+G
170 NEXT E
180 P=S/N:M=L+((H-L)/2)
190 PRINT"SCORES RANGE ";L;" TO ";H
200 PRINT"MEDIAN SCORE =";M
210 PRINT"AVERAGE (MEAN) =";P
220 PAUSE"TOTALS OF EACH GRADE"
230 PRINT A;" A"
240 PRINT B;" B"
250 PRINT C;" C"
260 PRINT D;" D"
270 PRINT F;" F"
280 PRINT"TOTAL ";N;" SCORES"
290 GOTO 10
```

Mid-range number

How to know the middle of a range of numbers? Line 180, above, accomplished the job.

Every 10th Answer

This program generates a random number in the range of zero to 999. However, it has a difference. It only shows you every tenth number it generates.

Line 20 generates the numbers. Line 40 selects the tenth number from each set.

Program Listing

```
10 PRINT "}":REM CLEAR SCREEN
20 T=INT(1000*(RND(1)))
30 V=V+1
40 IF 0.1*V=INT(0.1*V) THEN PRINT V,T
50 GOTO 20
```

Random Numbers: Zero To Nine

Although you see four program lines below, what we really have here is a very convenient single-line program for you to insert in a larger game or educational-testing program.

Line 20 is the winner here. It prints a random number from zero to nine every time. For your use here, we print that number on the screen. You could just as easily have the computer store that random number in a memory location for later recall and use.

We have added lines 10, 30 and 40 to make your **computer** show a whole series of random numbers from zero to nine. Remember, line 20 is the important single-line program element here.

If you would like random numbers in the range from zero to 99, make it 100* in line 20. For zero to 999, use 1000* in line 20.

Program Listing

```
10 PRINT "}":REM SCREEN CLEAR
20 PRINT INT(10*(RND(1)))
30 FOR L=1 TO 200:NEXT L
40 GOTO 20
```

Random Numbers: Distribution

Ever wonder how "random" are the numbers

generated by the random-number generator in your computer when you use the RND instruction? Try this program.

It generates 100 random numbers in a range from zero to nine and counts how many there are of each number between zero and nine.

By the way, while it is doing that it will display the message "counting" so you can tell it is working.

At the end of its run, the computer prints a neat chart, on the video display, of results.

Program Listing

```
10 PRINT "}":REM SCREEN CLEAR
20 FOR L=1 TO 100
30 N=INT(10*(RND(1)))
40 IF N=0 THEN A=A+1
50 IF N=1 THEN B=B+1
60 IF N=2 THEN C=C+1
70 IF N=3 THEN D=D+1
80 IF N=4 THEN E=E+1
90 IF N=5 THEN F=F+1
100 IF N=6 THEN G=G+1
110 IF N=7 THEN H=H+1
120 IF N=8 THEN I=I+1
130 IF N=9 THEN J=J+1
140 PRINT "COUNTING"
150 NEXT L
160 PRINT "}":REM CLEAR SCREEN
170 PRINT "}":REM BUZZER
200 PRINT "0",A
210 PRINT "1",B
220 PRINT "2",C
230 PRINT "3",D
240 PRINT "4",E
250 PRINT "5",F
260 PRINT "6",G
270 PRINT "7",H
280 PRINT "8",I
290 PRINT "9",J
300 END
```

Random Numbers: Averages

This program generates 100 random numbers and totals them. Then it finds the average of all 100 numbers.

In fact, the average number itself is a useful new random number.

To make the program run again, press the RETURN key on the computer's keyboard.

Program Listing

```
10 PRINT "}":REM CLEAR SCREEN
20 FOR L=0 TO 99
30 N=INT(10*(RND(1)))
40 NT=NT+N
50 PRINT "AVERAGING"
60 NEXT L
70 PRINT "}":REM SCREEN CLEAR
80 AV=NT/100
90 PRINT "TOTAL OF 100 RANDOM NUMBERS"
100 PRINT "BETWEEN ZERO AND NINE IS ";NT
110 PRINT "AVERAGE IS ";AV
200 DIM K$(1)
210 PRINT "FOR MORE, PRESS RETURN"
220 INPUT K$
230 CLR :GOTO 10
```

Random Numbers: Sorting High/Low

It's important to be able to sort a group of numbers to see what the highest and lowest values are. This program does that.

The random number generator is in line 30. It gives numbers in a range of zero to 999. Line 50 determines the lowest number in the set and line 60 finds the highest number.

Program Listing

```
10 PRINT "}":REM SCREEN CLEAR
20 FOR L=0 TO 99
30 N=INT(1000*(RND(1)))
40 IF L=0 THEN LN=N:HN=N
50 IF N<LN THEN LN=N
60 IF N>HN THEN HN=N
70 PRINT "SORTING"
80 NEXT L
90 PRINT CHR$(253):REM BUZZER
100 PRINT "}":REM CLEAR SCREEN
110 PRINT "LOW NUMBER IS ",LN
120 PRINT "HIGH NUMBER IS ",HN
200 END
```

Random Number Quality Checker

Ever wonder just how unintentional, haphazard, or unrelated your random numbers are? This program reinforces your confidence in the pseudorandom number generator in the computer.

It causes the machine to generate 100 numbers between zero and 100 and reports how many are above 49 and how many are below 50.

Just for fun, we've thrown in an executive decision maker. That is, the board of directors voted 47 yes, 53 no. Can you imagine it?

Program Listing

```
10 PRINT "}":REM CLEAR SCREEN
20 CLR
30 FOR L=1 TO 100
40 X=INT(100*(RND(1)))
50 IF X<50 THEN Y=Y+1
60 IF X>49 THEN N=N+1
70 NEXT L
```

```
80 PRINT "YES:",Y
90 PRINT "NO:",N
100 PRINT
110 GOTO 20
```

Sample Run

```
YES:          48
NO:           52

YES:          58
NO:           42

YES:          50
NO:           50

YES:          54
NO:           46
```

Sneaky seeds

Random numbers are very important in many computer programs. Most of all, in games. One of the few shortcomings of several computers is the lack of a convenient RND command to generate random numbers. In lieu of this easy method, you have to use a brief math exercise to generate numbers. This way you can generate pseudorandom numbers.

Why pseudorandom? Because though they often appear not to repeat themselves, eventually a string of numbers from any of these generators will repeat. The longer the string gets before the series of numbers starts over, the better the generator.

Sometimes, you need any old random number. In that case, the easiest to obtain is a decimal between zero and one. At other times, you'll need random numbers between one and six (for dice games); between zero and nine (for games where moves depend upon spinning for a number between zero and nine); between zero and 99 (where two-digit numbers are needed); etc.

Any of these combinations can be obtained by the computer.

The *seed* number in a generator is the number you give it, before it generates, to set a starting point for its internal math. Games aren't as much fun if you have the computer ask: GIVE ME A SEED NUMBER.

You need something more attuned to the game at hand. Or to the player. Often, one of the best ways to be sneaky in getting a seed number is to have the computer converse with the player. For instance, the computer might ask, HOW OLD ARE YOU? This should generate a seed number from the player, somewhere between 1 and 99.

Other good conversational gambits include WHAT GRADE ARE YOU IN? for young players; HOW MANY PLAYERS? for a complex game; HOW MANY ASSISTANTS DO YOU NEED? for a detective game; HOW MANY MEN ON DECK? for a battleship game; or HOW MUCH GOLD IS BURIED? for a treasure game.

Players will enjoy the game more if they feel as if they are talking with the computer. Be sure they don't use the same seed over or the string of random numbers will be the same.

By the way, you could have the machine think up the first number but, since it has no RND function, that first seed would always be the same so the string of numbers would always be the same.

Program Listing

```
10 CL.:PA."YOU ARE SEARCHING"
   :PA."FOR BURIED TREASURE":PA.""
20 PA."HOW MUCH GOLD":B.1
   :I."IS BURIED?  $";A
30 R=.01A
40 R=((π+R)^5)-INT((π+R)^5):T=10*R
   :X=INTT
```

```
 50 IF X>6THEN40
 60 IF X<1THEN40
 65 IF Q=1THEN200
 70 PA."THE MAP SAYS"
    :PA." X MARKS THE SPOT"
 80 GOTO 950
200 PA."WHERE IS IT?"
220 B.1:I."IN THE GARDEN ?",D$
230 IFD$="YES"THEN400
240 B.1:I."SUNK IN THE POND ?",F$
250 IF F$="YES"THEN500
260 B.1:I."BESIDE THE TREE ?',H$
270 IF H$="YES"THEN600
280 B.1:I."BENEATH THE BOULDER ?",I$
290 IF I$="YES"THEN700
300 B.1:I."INSIDE THE CAVE ?",J$
310 IF J$="YES"THEN800
320 B.1:I."UNDER THE SHED ?",K$
330 IF K$="YES"THEN900
340 IF K$="NO"THEN950
400 IF X=1 THEN430
410 PA."WRONG !":W=W+1:PA."TRY AGAIN."
    :GOTO240
430 PA."WOW !":P=P+1
    :PA."ON THE FIRST TRY" :GOTO980
500 IF X=2THEN 530
510 PA."NO. TRY AGAIN":W=W+1:GO TO260
530 PA."WOW !":P=P+1:PA."THAT WAS QUICK"
```

```
    :GOTO980
600 IF X=3THEN630
610 PA."SORRY. WRONG":W=W+1
    :PA."TRY ELSEWHERE":GOTO280
630 PA."FANTASTIC !":P=P+1:GOTO980
700 IF X=4 THEN730
710 PA."WRONG. NOT THERE":W=W+1:GOTO300
730 PA." GREAT !":P=P+1:GOTO980
800 IF X=5 THEN830
810 PA."NOT THERE":W=W+1:GOTO320
830 P=P+1:PA."AT LAST...":GOTO980
900 IF X=6THEN930
910 PA."NOT UNDER THERE":W=W+1
    :PA."BETTER THINK HARD":GOTO200
930 PA."FINALLY...":P=P+1:GOTO980
950 PA."IT HAS TO BE"
970 PA."IN THE GARDEN"
971 PA."SUNK IN THE POND"
972 PA."BESIDE THE TREE"
973 PA."BENEATH THE BOULDER"
974 PA."INSIDE THE CAVE"
975 PA."OR UNDER THE SHED."
976 GOTO 200
980 PA."YOU FOUND"
    :PA."THE TREASURE CHEST"
    :PA." WITH $";A
981 PA."":B.1:I."WANT TO PLAY AGAIN ?",L$
982 IF L$="YES"THEN985
```

```
983 IF L$="NO"THEN991
984 PA."YES OR NO":GOTO981
985 Q=1:PA."HOW MUCH GOLD":B.1
    :I."IS BURIED? $";A
986 GOTO30
991 Z=P+W:M=(P/Z)*1000:M=INTM:PA."OKAY"
    :P."YOUR SCORE IS ";M
999 END
```

Computer Books From ARCsoft Publishers

For the IBM PCjr Computer:

IBM PCjr Games Programs
George Bridges | $7.95 | ISBN 0-86668-036-5

40 IBM PCjr Programs for Home, School & Office
George Bridges | $7.95 | ISBN 0-86668-037-3

101 Programming Tips & Tricks for IBM PCjr
George Bridges | $8.95 | ISBN 0-86668-038-1

For the IBM Personal Computer:

Quick 'n Fun GAMES for the IBM Personal Computer
Michael Fox | $8.95 | ISBN 0-86668-044-6

Practical IBM Personal Computer Programs for Beginners
Michael Fox | $8.95 | ISBN 0-86668-045-4

99 Programming Tips & Tricks for the IBM Personal Computer
Michael Fox | $8.95 | ISBN 0-86668-046-2

IBM Personal Computer Program Writing Workbook
George Bridges | $4.95 | ISBN 0-86668-818-8

For the APPLE Computers:

Easy APPLE Computer Programs
Fred White | $8.95 | ISBN 0-86668-047-0

APPLE Computer Programs for Beginners
Fred White | $8.95 | ISBN 0-86668-035-7

101 APPLE Computer Programming Tips & Tricks
Fred White | $8.95 | ISBN 0-86668-015-2

33 New APPLE Computer Programs for Home, School & Office
Fred White | $8.95 | ISBN 0-86668-016-0

APPLE Computer Program Writing Workbook
Fred White | $4.95 | ISBN 0-86668-813-7

Universal for use with any computer system:

222 BASIC Computer Programs for Home, School & Office
Don Roberts | $9.95 | ISBN 0-86668-039-X

Universal BASIC Computer Program Writing Workbook
Don Roberts | $4.95 | ISBN 0-86668-819-6

For the Commodore Computers:

Commodore 64 Computer Programs for Beginners
Howard Adler | $8.95 | ISBN 0-86668-033-0

101 Programming Tips & Tricks for the VIC-20 and Commodore 64
Howard Adler | $8.95 | ISBN 0-86668-030-6

34 VIC-20 Computer Programs for Home, School & Office
Howard Adler | $8.95 | ISBN 0-86668-029-2

VIC-20 Computer Program Writing Workbook
Howard Adler | $4.95 | ISBN 0-86668-811-0

For the ATARI Computers:

101 ATARI Computer Programming Tips & Tricks
Alan North | $8.95 | ISBN 0-86668-022-5

31 New ATARI Computer Programs for Home, School & Office
Alan North | $8.95 | ISBN 0-86668-018-7

ATARI Computer Program Writing Workbook
Alan North | $4.95 | ISBN 0-86668-814-5

For the TRS-80 Model 100 and other portable computers:

44 Programs for the TRS-80 Model 100 Portable Computer
Jim Cole | $8.95 | ISBN 0-86668-034-9

For the TRS-80 Color Computer and TDP-100 Computers:

Color Computer Graphics
Ron Clark $9.95 ISBN 0-86668-012-8

101 Color Computer Programming Tips & Tricks
Ron Clark $7.95 ISBN 0-86668-007-1

55 Color Computer Programs for Home, School & Office
Ron Clark $9.95 ISBN 0-86668-005-5

55 MORE Color Computer Programs for Home, School & Office
Ron Clark $9.95 ISBN 0-86668-008-X

The Color Computer Songbook
Ron Clark $7.95 ISBN 0-86668-011-X

TRS-80 Color Computer Program Writing Workbook
Ron Clark $4.95 ISBN 0-86668-816-1

For the TRS-80, Sharp and Casio Pocket Computers:

Practical PC-2/PC-1500 Pocket Computer Programs
Jim Cole $7.95 ISBN 0-86668-028-4

Pocket Computer Programming Made Easy
Jim Cole $8.95 ISBN 0-86668-009-8

99 Tips & Tricks for the New Pocket Computers
Jim Cole $7.95 ISBN 0-86668-019-5

101 Pocket Computer Programming Tips & Tricks
Jim Cole $7.95 ISBN 0-86668-004-7

Murder In The Mansion and Other Computer Adventures — 2nd Edition
Jim Cole $6.95 ISBN 0-86668-501-4

50 Programs in BASIC for Home, School & Office — 2nd Edition
Jim Cole $9.95 ISBN 0-86668-502-2

50 MORE Programs in BASIC for Home, School & Office
Jim Cole $9.95 ISBN 0-86668-003-9

Pocket Computer Program Writing Workbook
Jim Cole $4.95 ISBN 0-86668-817-X

35 Practical Programs for the CASIO Pocket Computer
Jim Cole $8.95 ISBN 0-86668-014-4

For the TRS-80 Model IV Computers:

45 Programs for the TRS-80 Model 4 Computer
Mark Lewis $8.95 ISBN 0-86668-040-3

For the Texas Instruments TI-99/4A Home Computer:

Texas Instruments Home Computer Games Programs
Len Turner $8.95 ISBN 0-86668-032-2

Texas Instruments Home Computer Graphics Programs
Len Turner $9.95 ISBN 0-86668-031-4

101 Programming Tips & Tricks for the Texas Instruments TI-99/4A
Len Turner $8.95 ISBN 0-86668-025-X

36 Texas Instruments TI-99/4A Programs for Home, School & Office
Len Turner $8.95 ISBN 0-86668-024-1

Texas Instruments Computer Program Writing Workbook
Len Turner $4.95 ISBN 0-86668-812-9

For the TIMEX/Sinclair 1000, Sinclair ZX-81 and MicroAce:

Practical TIMEX/Sinclair Computer Programs for Beginners
Edward Page $7.95 ISBN 0-86668-027-6

101 TIMEX 1000/Sinclair ZX-81 Programming Tips & Tricks
Edward Page $7.95 ISBN 0-86668-020-9

TIMEX/Sinclair Computer Games Programs
Edward Page $7.95 ISBN 0-86668-026-8

37 TIMEX 1000/Sinclair ZX-81 Programs for Home, School & Office
Edward Page $8.95 ISBN 0-86668-021-7

Other books from ARCsoft Publishers

SPACE TODAY CHRONICLES

THE ONGOING STORY OF WHAT'S HAPPENING IN SPACE TODAY FROM THE EDITORS OF SPACE TODAY MAGAZINE *by Anthony R. Curtis, editor of SPACE TODAY monthly newsmagazine.*

200-page book filled with all the exciting recent news from Space. Easy-to-read newsbook about shuttles, Space Stations, planet explorers, Solar System, Milky Way, Deep Space, supernova, quasars, Russia, Japan, China, India, Europe in Space. Manned flights, unusual satellites, amateur radio satellites. Everything to satisfy the deep hunger to know what's going on Out There. Must-read sourcebook for any Space-minded enthusiast, student, teacher, hobbyist, astronomer, scientist, anyone wanting to keep up to date. For all ages. ISBN 0-86668-064-0. $14.95

SPACE SATELLITE HANDBOOK

ALL SATELLITES EVER IN ORBIT *edited by Anthony R. Curtis, editor of SPACE TODAY monthly newsmagazine.*

Giant annual encyclopedia, 320 pages listing 17,304 payloads, platforms, rockets, debris ever in orbit from all countries; 6,237 objects from spacefaring nations in orbit; 11,067 no longer in orbit are listed. Authoritative guidebook with maps, charts, special explanations. ISBN 0-86668-063-2. $19.95

AIDS: BLUNT TALK ON HOW TO AVOID IT

by Randolph Norman. Plain talk, down-to-earth language, easy to read handbook debunks halftruths, misinformation about Acquired Immune Deficiency Syndrome: AIDS. Excellent for all ages, both sexes. Quickly-understood. 32 pgs. ISBN 0-86668-057-8. $5.95

QUICK-N-EASY ELECTRONICS PROJECTS

by Bob Greene. 40 one-night projects for hobbyists, experimenters, students, use easy-to-find parts. ISBN 0-86668-049-7. $7.95

EASY-TO-BUILD ELECTRONICS PROJECTS

by Bob Greene. 40 different projects. ISBN 0-86668-050-0. $7.95